A GUIDE TO C++ PROGRAMMING

GW00566672

A

GUIDE

TO

C++ PROGRAMMING

Paul Kelly, MSc

Gill & Macmillan Ltd
Hume Avenue
Park West
Dublin 12
with associated companies throughout the world
www.gillmacmillan.ie

0 7171 3172 6

The paper used in this book is made from the wood pulp of managed forests. For every tree felled, at least one tree is planted, thereby renewing natural resources.

Acknowledgments

To Robert, Philip, James and Brian for their many corrections and suggestions

Dedication

To my wife and family

CONTENTS

Chapter Five: Arrays and Structures

Typographic conventions used in this book.

```
Program examples and screen output are printed in this typeface.
```

Program examples are annotated in this typeface.

Keyboard input to a program is printed in this typeface.

```
Reference to part of a C++ statement, a variable, a value in a
program or a C++ keyword is in this typeface.
```

italic type is used for emphasis and when a new term is introduced.

The line numbers to the left of the program examples are for reference purposes only and are not part of the C++ language.

CHAPTER ONE

Introduction

1.1 What is a computer program?

Computers are involved in a wide variety of tasks that we do in our everyday lives. Some of these tasks such as using a word processor or checking e-mail obviously use a computer. Less direct examples occur when we use an ATM at a bank, pay at a supermarket checkout or use a phone.

A computer performs all of these tasks by following a predefined set of instructions. This set of instructions is called a *computer program.*

A computer program to a computer is like a recipe to a chef; it specifies the steps needed to perform a certain task. But unfortunately, unlike a recipe, you can't give your instructions to a computer in plain English. For instructions to be 'intelligible' to a computer, they need to be expressed in a language 'understood' by the computer. The only language 'understood' by a computer is its own machine language, which consists of a series of binary ones and zeroes. Machine language is very difficult to use directly and so instructions to a computer are given in a special language called a *programming language.* The programming language is neither English nor machine language, but is somewhere in between. In fact, as you will see, it is more like English than machine language.

Machine languages are known as low-level languages and programming languages are known as high-level languages.

Writing instructions in a high level language is much easier than writing them in low-level machine language, but is still not as easy as writing them in English.

For the computer to carry out the program instructions written in a high level language, they have to be translated from the high level language to the machine language of the computer. A *compiler* does this translation.

1.2 Developing a computer program

The first step in developing a computer program is to define and understand the problem to be solved. If you cannot understand the problem then you will certainly not be able to tell a computer how to solve the problem. This is called the analysis phase and basically answers the question "what is to be done?", ignoring for the time being the question of how the problem is to be solved.

Once it is known what has to be done, the question "how is it to be done?" arises. This is called the design phase and it is in this phase that a solution to the problem is developed. The design phase may reveal problems not previously considered in the analysis phase. So rather than being independent phases, the design and analysis phases are closely related and interact with each other.

The analysis and design phases are important to developing a successful solution to a problem. Neglect at either of these phases will result in a 'solution' that will not solve the original problem and may even contribute to making it worse.

Analysis and design are subjects in their own right and are not covered in this book. This book concentrates on the next phase – writing, compiling and testing C++ programs.

There are many different compilers on the market, with updated versions being released regularly. Up to date instructions for writing, compiling and running C++ programs with some of the popular compilers can be found on the web site for this book at

www.gillmacmillan.ie/guide2cpp

1.2.1 Program development cycle
Despite the differences between compilers, the following is a general description of the steps involved in the development of a C++ program.

Step 1: Design the program.
A computer system consists of one or more programs. Each program has to be individually designed to implement the overall solution developed at the analysis and design phases.
After each program is designed, it is important to check its logic before starting to write the program.

Step 2: Write the program.
Firstly, the C++ program instructions are typed into a file using a *text editor*. The file containing the C++ statements is called the *source file* and is usually stored on disk. The program instructions are also called the *source code* or the *program code*.

Step 3: Compile the program.
Next the C++ program is passed through a compiler, which translates the C++ program instructions to machine instructions. The compiler reads the source file, translates the C++ statements into machine or *object code*, and stores the object code in an *object file*.
Some errors are likely to occur in this step. An error in the source code is indicated by the compiler and is referred to as a *compile-time error*. The simplest kind of compile-time error is a *syntax error*. This type of error is relatively easy to correct, as the compiler will indicate where in the source code the error has occurred. Typical syntax errors involve missing punctuation and misspellings. All compile-time errors must be corrected before the compilation process can be completed.
The compiler may sometimes issue a warning message during compilation. A warning message is not as serious as a syntax error and will not prevent the program from being compiled. However, warnings are the compiler's way of drawing attention to what it 'thinks' may be a problem and should be investigated.

Step 4: Link the program.
The final step before running the program is to *link* the program using the *linker*. Linking involves combining the object file of the program with other object files from the C++ run-time library to form an *executable file*.

Step 5: Test the program.
When the program is run you may find that it is not working as expected. The fact that a program does not have any compile-time errors does not guarantee that the program will work as required. For example, the programmer may mistakenly have given an instruction to divide a number by zero. This type of error is called a *run-time error* and causes the program to stop before it has completed its task.
The program may complete its task but produce incorrect results or display them at the wrong position on the screen.

These kinds of errors are known as *logic errors* or more commonly as *bugs*. Bugs are much harder to find and fix than compile-time errors. Some bugs appear only under certain conditions, for example when a program is run with a particular set of data.

The process of locating and correcting program errors is called *debugging*.

Step 6: Debug the program

Once a bug has been identified, the next step is to find where in the source code the problem lies. Many compilers have tools that can be used to help locate bugs.

Correcting bugs involves going back to step 2, but hopefully not any further. Going back to step 1 or even back to the analysis and design phases would be like asking an architect to redesign parts of the house while it is being built! In general, try to catch errors as early as possible.

1.3 Learning C++

You'll learn more from designing, writing, running, and correcting programs than you ever will by simply reading a book. A successful approach to learning to program in C++ depends on large amounts of practice.

To help you practise, there are exercises at the end of each chapter. Do as many of the exercises as possible and get some feedback on your solutions from people who know C++. There are solutions to selected exercises at the web site for this book.

1.4 Web site for this book

The web site for this book is at www.gillmacmillan/guide2cpp. The source code for all the sample programs used in this book as well as answers to selected exercises are available here. In addition, details of various compilers are also available at the web site.

1.5 Brief history of C++

C++ is a direct descendent of the C programming language, which was originally developed in 1972 at Bell Laboratories, New Jersey, USA. C evolved from a language called B, which in turn evolved from a language called BCPL (Basic Combined Programming Language).

C++ was developed by Bjarne Strostrup at AT&T Bell Laboratories from 1979 to 1983. The initial version of the language was called "C with Classes" and was used internally in AT&T in 1983. Later that year, the name was changed to "C++". The first commercial version of C++ was marketed in 1985, and since then, C++ has evolved to the latest ANSI/ISO (American National Standards Institute/International Organization for Standardization) C++ standard.

1.6 ANSI/ISO C++ standard

The ANSI/ISO C++ standard can be referenced in "Information Technology – Programming languages – C++ ". This document can be purchased from ANSI's web site at www.ansi.org. The document number is ISO/IEC 14882:1998. Older draft versions of this document are available free from various web sites. See the web site for this book for details.

The example programs used in this book conform to the ANSI/ISO C++ standard. Not all compilers conform to this standard, so some compilers may not correctly compile the example programs. Some of the sample programs may have to be modified for use with these other compilers. See the web site for details.

CHAPTER TWO

Beginning to Program in C++

As in other programming languages, data can be of two types: *constants* and *variables*.

2.1 Constants

As the name suggests, a constant does not change its value in a program.
Some examples of constants:

Type of constant	Examples	Remarks
Integer	`8, 100, -3`	Whole numbers, both positive and negative.
Floating-point	`0.34, -12.34, 8.0`	Numbers with decimal parts.
Character	`'x', 'X', '*', '9'`	A single character enclosed in single quotation marks.
String	`"abc", "A100", "9"`	One or more characters enclosed in double quotation marks.

2.2 Variables

Unlike a constant, a variable can vary its values in a program, and a variable must be defined before it can be used. A variable is defined by giving it a data type and a name.

Program example P2A

```
1   void main()
2   {
3       int v1 ;
4       float v2 ;
5       char v3 ;
6       v1 = 65 ;
7       v2 = -18.23 ;
8       v3 = 'A';
9   }
```

← *Lines 3, 4 and 5 define three variables.*

← *Lines 6, 7 and 8 assign a value to each variable.*

The line numbers on the left are for reference purposes only and are not part of the program.

C++ programs start with the line

```
void main()
```

This marks the point where a C++ program starts to execute and must appear once only in a C++ program.

The program statements are contained within the braces { and } on lines 2 and 9. Each statement ends with a semicolon. The spaces before the semicolon and on each side of the equals sign are not essential and are used here only to improve the readability of the program.

4

Lines 3, 4 and 5 of this program define three variables: v1, v2, and v3. A variable can be given any name, called an *identifier* in C++, provided it is within the following rules:

- An identifier can only be constructed using letters, numerals or underscores (_).
- An identifier must start with a letter or an underscore.
- An identifier cannot be a C++ *keyword*. A keyword is a word that has a special meaning. (See appendix A for a list of keywords.)
- An identifier can contain any number of characters, but only the first thirty-one characters are significant to the C++ compiler.

Lines 3 to 5 of program P2A define v1 as an integer variable, v2 as a floating-point variable, and v3 as a character variable. Note that identifiers are *case-sensitive*, i.e. the variable V1 is different from the variable v1.

A variable is like a box in the memory of the computer. The box has a name and contains a value. Each box has a name given to it by you, the programmer. The box keeps its value until it is changed by replacing it with some other value.

Lines 6 to 8 of the program assign values to the variables. The value assigned to each variable is stored in the computer's memory.

2.3 Simple output to the screen

Now that values are assigned to the variables, how are the values displayed on the screen? This can be done with cout (pronounced c-out), as demonstrated in the next program.

Program Example P2B

```
1    #include <iostream>
2    using namespace std ;
3    void main()
4    {
5      int v1 ;
6      float v2 ;
7      char v3 ;
8      v1 = 65 ;
9      v2 = -18.23 ;
10     v3 = 'a' ;
11     cout <<  "Program Example P2B" << endl ;
12     cout <<  "v1 has the value " << v1 << endl ;
13     cout <<  "v2 has the value " << v2 << endl ;
14     cout <<  "v3 has the value " << v3 << endl ;
15     cout <<  "End of program" << endl ;
16   }
```

Display the values of the variables on the screen.

When you compile and run this program you will get the following on your screen:

```
Program Example P2B
v1 has the value 65
v2 has the value -18.23
v3 has the value a
End of program
```

Line 1 is an example of a *preprocessor directive* and is pronounced "hash include io stream". This line, along with line 2, will be in every program that involves output to the screen or input from the keyboard.

The #include preprocessor directive causes the file in the angle brackets, called a header file, to be made available to the program. The header file iostream contains some C++ statements to make it easy to perform input and output from a C++ program. (Preprocessor directives are covered in Appendix G.)

C++ refers to your computer as a console. To display data to the screen, C++ sends the data to cout (console output). cout is called an output stream object.

In C++, letters or numbers enclosed in double quotation marks is called a string of characters or a character string.

In line 11 the insertion operator << is used to insert a string of characters into the output stream object cout. endl (end line, pronounced end-ell) is used to go the start of the next line on the screen.

Line 12 has a string of characters enclosed in double quotation marks followed by << and a variable name. The variable name is not in quotation marks.

This statement displays the string of characters followed by the value of the variable v1.

The variable v1 has the value 65, so the output from line 12 is:

```
v1 has the value 65
```

The spaces on either side of << on line 12 are for readability only.

The insertion operator << may be used any number of times with cout. For example, you can combine lines 14 and 15 as:

```
cout<<"v3 has the value "<<v3<<endl<<"End of program"<<endl;
```

If the line gets too long it can split up between two or more lines:

```
cout<<"v3 has the value "<<v3<<endl
    <<"End of program"<<endl;
```

2.4 Comments

Comments are added to a C++ program to make it more readable for the programmer, but they are completely ignored by the compiler. In C++, comments start with the characters //. Some comments can be added to the last program.

```
1   // Program example P2C
2   // Program to introduce variables in C++.
3   #include <iostream>
4   using namespace std ;
```

```
5
6   void main()
7   {
8     int v1 ;      // v1 is an integer variable.
9     float v2 ;    // v2 is a floating-point variable.
10    char v3 ;     // v3 is a character variable.
11
12    // Now assign some values to the variables.
13    v1 = 65 ;
14    v2 = -18.23 ;
15    v3 = 'a' ;
16
17    // Finally display the variable values on the screen.
18    cout << "Program Example P2C" << endl ;
19    cout << "v1 has the value " << v1 << endl ;
20    cout << "v2 has the value " << v2 << endl ;
21    cout << "v3 has the value " << v3 << endl ;
22    cout << "End of program" << endl ;
23  }
```

Comments can be placed anywhere in a C++ program and start after // and end at the end of the line. C++ comments cannot span more than one line.

You may also use the older C-style comments in a C++ program. Comments in the C programming language begin with the characters /* and end with the characters */. Unlike C++ comments, C-style comments can span more than one line.

Typically, comments are placed at the start of the program to describe the purpose of the program, the author, date written and any other relevant information, such as the version number. For example:

```
//    Program name   : P2A.
//                     Introduction to variables.
//    Written by     : Paul Kelly.
//    Date           : 29/6/2000.
//    Version number : 1.0
```

You can also write these comments in the C-style:

```
/*    Program name   : P2A.
                       Introduction to variables.
      Written by     : Paul Kelly.
      Date           : 29/6/2000.
      Version number : 1.0                              */
```

Comments are also used to describe in plain language the function of a particular section of a program. Get into the habit of using comments; the more complicated the program becomes the more valuable they are to the programmer. However, writing bad comments can lead to confusion and are worse than no comments at all. A comment must be easier to understand than the code that it is trying to explain!

The blank lines at 5, 11 at 16 are used to separate different sections of the program. A blank line can be placed anywhere in the program and like comments are ignored by the compiler.

2.5 Data types

In previous programs, you have seen how to declare a variable and associate it with a particular data type (char, int or float). The C++ language has a variety of other data types besides the three basic types of char, int and float. Different data types require different amounts of memory and therefore vary in the range of values they can store.

Details of the various C++ data types are given in appendix D.

2.5.1 Integer data types

To define a variable v1 as a long integer:

```
long int v1 ;
```

The keyword int is optional here, so v1 can also be defined as:

```
long v1 ;
```

2.5.2 Boolean data types

The Boolean data type bool can store only one of two values: true or false. Normally true is numerically 1 and false is numerically 0.

The following defines a Boolean variable b:

```
bool b ;
```

2.5.3 Floating-point data types

The double data type allows you to increase the range and precision (or accuracy) of a floating-point number.

To define a variable v2 as a double data type:

```
double v2 ;
```

2.6 Data type sizes

The next program uses the sizeof operator to display the number of bytes of memory required by some common data types.

```
1  // Program example P2D
2  // Program to display the memory required by C++ data types.
3  #include <iostream>
4  using namespace std ;
5
6  void main()
7  {
8     cout << " Data type         Number of bytes" << endl ;
9     cout << " ---------         ---------------" << endl ;
10    cout << "   char            " << sizeof( char )   << endl ;
11    cout << "   int             " << sizeof( int )    << endl ;
12    cout << "   long int        " << sizeof( long )   << endl ;
13    cout << "   bool            " << sizeof( bool )   << endl ;
14    cout << "   float           " << sizeof( float )  << endl ;
15    cout << "   double          " << sizeof( double ) << endl ;
16 }
```

The output from this program is:

```
Data type          Number of bytes

---------          ---------------
  char                  1
  int                   4
  long int              4
  bool                  1
  float                 4
  double                8
```

2.7 Operators

2.7.1 The assignment operator

The assignment operator (=) is used to assign values to variables. For example, the statement

```
v = 1 ;
```

assigns the value 1 to the variable v.

Further examples are:

```
total = 0 ;
value = 100.12 ;
reply = 'y' ;
v1 = v2 = v3 = 123 ;
```

In the last example, the value 123 is assigned to the three variables v1, v2, and v3.

2.7.2 Arithmetic operators

There are five arithmetic operators in C ++:

Operator	Used for
+	addition
-	subtraction
*	multiplication
/	division
%	modulus (this gives the remainder after division)

The next program demonstrates the use of the arithmetic operators.

```
1   // Program example P2E
2   // Demonstration of the arithmetic operators.
3   #include <iostream>
4   using namespace std ;
5
6   void main()
7   {
8      // Define the variables used in the program.
9      int var1, var2 ;
```

```
10
11     // Place values into the variables and display
12     // the values in the variables.
13     var1 = 0 ;
14     var2 = 10 ;
15     cout << "var1 starts at " << var1 << endl
16           << "var2 starts at " << var2 << endl ;
17
18     // Do some arithmetic with the variables and display
19     // the values in the variables.
20
21     var2 = var1 + 18 ;
22     cout << "var2 is now " << var2 << endl ;
23
24     var1 = var2 * 3 ;
25     cout << "var1 is now " << var1 << endl ;
26
27     var1 = var2 / 3 ;
28     cout << "var1 is now " << var1 << endl ;
29
30     var2 = var1 - 1 ;
31     cout << "var2 is now " << var2 << endl ;
32
33     var1 = var2 % 3 ;
34     cout << "var1 is now " << var1 << endl ;
35
36     var1 = var1 + 1;
37     cout << "var1 is finally " << var1 << endl ;
38
39     var2 = var2  * 5 ;
40     cout <<  "and var2 is finally " << var2 << endl ;
41 }
```

When you run this program the following will be displayed on your screen:

```
var1 starts at 0
var2 starts at 10
var2 is now 18
var1 is now 54
var1 is now 6
var2 is now 5
var1 is now 2
var1 is finally 3
and var2 is finally 25
```

2.7.3 Increment and decrement operators
It is very common in programming to add or subtract 1 from a variable; so common, in fact, that
C++ provides operators specifically to do these tasks.
In line 36 of program P2E, 1 is added to var1 by the statement

```
  var1 = var1 + 1 ;
```

This statement can be replaced by the statement

```
  var1++ ;
```

The increment operator ++ adds 1 to the value of a variable.

The statement

```
var1 = var1 - 1 ;
```

subtracts 1 from the variable var1. An equivalent statement is

```
var1 -- ;
```

The next program demonstrates the increment and decrement operators.

```
1   // Program example P2F
2   // Demonstration of the increment and decrement operators.
3   #include <iostream>
4   using namespace std ;
5
6   void main()
7   {
8    // Define variables and initialise them.
9      int var1 = 1, var2 = 2 ;
10
11     cout << "Initial values: " ;
12     cout << "var1 is " << var1
13         << " and var2 is " << var2 << endl ;
14
15     var1++ ;   // Add 1 to var1.
16     var2-- ;   // Subtract 1 from var2.
17
18     cout << "Final values: " ;
19     cout << "var1 is " << var1
20         << " and var2 is " << var2 << endl ;
21 }
```

The output from this program is:

```
Initial values: var1 is 1 and var2 is 2
Final values: var1 is 2 and var2 is 1
```

Line 9 of this program defines the variables var1 and var2 as integers and initialises them to 1 and 2, respectively.
Line 15 adds 1 to var1, and line 16 subtracts 1 from var2.
Lines 19 and 20 display the final value of var1 and var2.

The increment operator ++ has two forms, *prefix* and *postfix*, which are demonstrated in the next program.

```
1   // Program example P2G
2   // Demonstration of the prefix and postfix ++ operators.
3   #include <iostream>
4   using namespace std ;
5
6   void main()
```

```
7  {
8     int var1, var2, var3, var4 ;
9
10    var1 = var2 = 1 ;
11
12    var3 = var1++ ;   // var3 is 1, var1 is 2.
13    var4 = ++var2 ;   // var4 is 2, var2 is 2.
14
15    cout << "var1 is " << var1
16           << ", var2 is " << var2 << endl ;
17    cout << "var3 is " << var3
18           << ", var4 is " << var4 << endl ;
19 }
```

The output from this program is:

```
var1 is 2, var2 is 2
var3 is 1, var4 is 2
```

The program starts by initialising both variables var1 and var2 to 1.

In line 12 the variable var3 is assigned the value of var1 (=1), and then var1 is incremented to 2. This is an example of a *postfix* operation.
In contrast, line 13 shows an example of a *prefix* operation. In line 13, var2 is incremented first, and then the new value (2) is assigned to var4.

If the ++ is before a variable, the variable is incremented before it is used. If the ++ is after the variable, the variable is used and then incremented. The difference between prefix and postfix is only relevant where an assignment is involved. So in line 15 of program P2F on page 11 either var1++ or ++var1 could be used.

The decrement operator -- also has prefix and postfix forms. If the -- is before a variable, the variable is decremented before it is used. If -- is after the variable, the variable is used and then decremented. Again this is only relevant if an assignment is involved. In line 16 of program P2F either var2-- or --var2 could be used.

2.7.4 Combined operators
A statement such as

```
   var = var + 3 ;
```

may also be written as

```
   var += 3 ;
```

The += operator adds the value on its right to the variable on its left.

There are five combined operators: +=, -=, *=, /=, and %=, corresponding to the five arithmetic operators +, -, *, /, and %.
Here are some examples of their use:

Operator	Examples	Equivalent
+=	count += 11 ; a += b ;	count = count + 11 ; a = a + b ;
-=	count -= 20 ; a -= b ;	count = count - 20 ; a = a - b ;
*=	rabbits *= 2 ; a *= b ;	rabbits = rabbits * 2 ; a = a * b ;
/=	money /= 2 ; a /= b ;	money = money / 2 ; a = a / b;
%=	pence %= 100 ; a %= b ;	pence = pence % 100 ; a = a % b ;

2.8 Operator precedence

Consider the following statement:

```
var = 2 + 7 * 8 ;
```

Does this mean
>   (a) that 2 is added to 7, giving 9, which is multiplied by 8, giving var a value of 72,

or
>   (b) that 7 is multiplied by 8, giving 56, which is added to 2, giving var a value of 58?

Clearly the order of evaluation is important. With (a) you get 72 and with (b) you get 58.

C++ has rules to remove any ambiguity present in a statement such as the one above. *Operator precedence* provides these rules.

Operator	Precedence	Meaning	Associativity
-	Highest	Unary minus	Right to left
* / %	Lower	Multiplication, division, and modulus	Left to right
+ -	Lowest	Addition and subtraction	Left to right

From this table, multiplication and division have a higher priority than addition and subtraction, so these operators get evaluated first. Thus the statement

```
var = 2 + 7 * 8 ;
```

evaluates to

```
var = 2 + 56 = 58.
```

You can use parentheses to change the order of evaluation. Thus the statement

```
var = ( 2 + 7 ) * 8 ;
```

evaluates to

```
var = 9 * 8 = 72
```

because any expressions contained within parentheses get evaluated first.

Expressions containing operators of the same precedence are evaluated according to their *associativity*, as shown in the above table. Associativity gives the order in which operators of the same precedence are evaluated. For example, in the statement

```
var = 1 + 6 * 9 % 5 / 2 ;
```

the *, / and % have equal precedence, so which is done first? The *, / and % associate left to right, so the order is:

```
1 + 6 * 9 % 5 / 2 = 1 + 54 % 5 / 2  = 1 + 4 / 2  = 1 + 2 = 3.
```

Precedence and associativity can be a source of errors. Use parentheses to group the variables, constants and operators in a clear and unambiguous way. Expressions within parentheses are evaluated first; therefore, using parentheses will remove any confusion about which operations are done first. For example, the last statement could be written much more clearly as:

```
var = 1 + ( ( 6 * 9 ) % 5 ) / 2 ;
```

and the result will be the same.

The unary minus operator, like the binary minus operator, is represented as -.
In the expression

```
var = -3*2-1 ;
```

the first - is a unary minus and the second - is a binary minus. The unary minus appears before an operand and the binary minus appears between two operands. Because the unary minus has highest priority, the above expression is equivalent to

```
var = ((-3)*2)-1 ;
```

and not

```
var = -(3*2-1) ;
```

In the first case var is assigned a value of –7, while in the second case –5 is assigned to var.

2.9 Type conversions and casts

Consider the following program, which divides an integer variable `var1` by a floating-point variable `var2`, placing the result in a floating-point variable `var3`.

```
1   // Program example P2H
2   // Demonstration of a mixed data type expression.
3   #include <iostream>
4   using namespace std ;
5
6   void main()
7   {
8      int var1 = 10 ;
9      float var2 = 2.5 ;
10     float var3 ;
11     int var4 ;
12     float var5 ;
13
14     var3 = var1 / var2 ;  // Mixed expression assigned to a
15                           // float.
16     var4 = var1 / var2 ;  // Mixed expression assigned to an
17                           // int.
18     var5 = var1 / 4 ;     // Non-mixed expression assigned to a
19                           // float.
20     cout << "var3 = "  << var3
21          << " var4 = " << var4
22          << " var5 = " << var5 << endl ;
23 }
```

The output from this program is:

```
var3 = 4 var4 = 4 var5 = 2
```

Line 14 is an example of a *mixed expression*, where the variable `var1` of type `int` is divided by the variable `var2` of type `float`. The value of the variable `var1` is automatically converted to a `float` before being divided by the value of `var2`. The result of the division is a value of type `float`, which is then assigned to the `float` variable `var3`. (Note that only a copy of the value of `var1` is converted to a `float`. The variable `var1` is still of type `int`.)

In line 16, the result of the division is assigned to an `int` type variable `var4`, resulting in a loss of the fractional part of the number.

In line 18, the division involves two integers, so there is no need for any type conversions. The result of the division is the integer value 2, which is converted to a `float` and assigned to `var5`.

When doing calculations involving mixed data types, C++ ranks the data types in this order:

$$\text{char} < \text{short} < \text{int} \le \text{long} < \text{float} < \text{double}$$

and a signed data type is less than the corresponding unsigned data type (for example, a signed `long` < unsigned `long`).

For calculations involving mixed data types, C++ automatically converts the value in the lower data type to a higher type. This is called a *promotion* or *widening* of the data. Promotion will cause no loss of data, because the higher data types occupy more memory than the lower types and can therefore hold the data precisely. On the other hand, when data is assigned to a variable of a lower type, *demotion* or *narrowing* occurs. Demotion may result in a loss of data, because the lower data type may not have enough bytes of memory to store the higher data type.

In addition to automatic conversion, C++ allows you to perform manual conversion with a *static cast*. The general format of a static cast is:

```
static_cast<type>( expression )
```

Using a static cast is equivalent to assigning the expression to a variable of the specified type and using that variable in place of the expression. For example, if you change line 18 of P2H to

```
var5 = static_cast<float>( var1 ) / 4 ;
```

the value of var1 is cast from an integer to a double floating-point value. The expression is now mixed, and the integer value 4 will be promoted to a double. The result of the division is now 2.5, which is assigned to var5. Without the static cast, var5 would have a value of 2.0.

The same result is achieved by rewriting line 18 as:

```
var5 = var1 / 4.0 ;
```

Here 4.0 is a floating-point constant. The expression var1/4.0 is now mixed, and the value of var1 is therefore promoted to a floating-point value automatically.

As a further example of static casting, consider two double variables defined as

```
double num1 = 1.9, num2 = 2.9 ;
```

To display the total of the integer parts these numbers, the following statement can be used:

```
cout <<  static_cast<int>( num1 ) + static_cast<int>( num2 ) ;
```

The values in num1 and num2 are cast to integers, losing their fractional parts and resulting in the total of 3 being displayed.

Note: `(float)(expression)` and `float(expression)` are older equivalents of `static_cast<float>(expression)`. These may still be used, but the newer `static_cast` is recommended.

Programming pitfalls

1. Do not type a semicolon after either

   ```
   #include <iostream>
   ```
   or
   ```
   void main()
   ```

2. End each C++ statement with a semicolon.

3. A semicolon is not always at the end of a line. For example,

   ```
   int xy    // x and y coordinates of a point ;
   ```

   This will cause a compiler error, because the semicolon is part of the comment.

4. A typing error may result in a statement that does nothing but that is valid nonetheless.
   For example,

   ```
   a + b ;    // Valid, but the result is not stored.
   ```

   This was probably meant to be:

   ```
   a += b ;   // Adds b to a.
   ```

   or:

   ```
   a = b ;    // Assigns b to a.
   ```

5. You must initialise a variable before using it in an arithmetic expression.

   ```
   int counter ;   // What value is in counter?
   counter++ ;
   ```

   This code adds 1 to the value in the storage location occupied by `counter`. We have no idea what this value is, as the program did not assign `counter` a value. The problem is fixed by initialising `counter` to some value.
   For example:

   ```
   int counter = 0 ;
   ```

6. Be aware of the operator precedence rules. If you are unsure, use parentheses. If you are using parentheses in an expression, count the number of opening and closing parentheses. They should be equal.

7. Each variable has an associated data type (`int`, `float`, etc.). Be careful not to go outside the range of valid values for a variable. For example, a `short int` cannot hold values bigger than 32,767 or smaller than –32,768. See appendix D.

8. You may not always get what you expect when doing arithmetic in C++.
    For example:

    ```
    int a = 100 ;
    int b = 8 ;
    float f ;

    f = a / b ;
    ```

    The variable f will contain 12, and not the 12.5 you would expect. As a and b are integers, integer arithmetic is performed, resulting in the loss of the fractional part of the result. Use a static cast if the fractional part of the result is required. For example:

    ```
    f = static_cast<float>( a ) / b ;
    ```

Quick syntax reference

At the end of each chapter the most important features of the C++ syntax covered in the text are briefly summarised. While not covering the strict definition of the syntax, which can be complex for a beginner, it should prove to be a useful "memory jog" while writing programs.

	Syntax	Examples

Start of program	`#include <iostream>`
	`using namespace std ;`
	`void main()`
	`{`	

Defining variables	`char variables ;`
	
	`int variables ;`
	
	`float variables ;`
	
	`long int variables ;`
	
	`double variables ;`
	
	`unsigned variables ;`
		`char ch, reply ;`
		
		`int count ;`
		
		`float average, vat, sales ;`
		
		`long int employee_no ;`
		
		`double number, remainder ;`
		
		`unsigned int i, j ;`

Assignment	`=`	`number = 59.75 ;`

Comments	`//`
	or
	`/*   */`
		`// A one line comment.`
		`/* A comment split`
		`       over`
		`    more than one line. */`

Arithmetic operators	`+`
	`-`
	`*`
	`/`
	`%`
		`vat = sales * 0.21 ;`
		
		`remainder = number % 10 ;`
		
		`average = ( n1 + n2 ) / 2 ;`

Display to screen	`cout <<`	`cout << "vat = " << vat ;`

Increment and decrement	`++`
	`--`
		`int n1, n2, n3, n4 ;`
		
		`n1++ ;`
		`n2-- ;`
		`n3 = ++n1 ;`
		`n4 = n2-- ;`

Combined operators	`+=`
	`-=`
	`*=`
	`/=`
	`%=`
		`n1 += 10 ;`
		`n2 *= n1 ;`

Casting	`static_cast<type>`	`int n ;`
		
		`static_cast<float>( n )`

End of program	`}`	

Exercises

1. Which of the following are valid C++ variable names? If valid, do you think the name is a good mnemonic (i.e. reminds you of its purpose)?

    (a) `stock_code`
    (b) `money$`
    (a) `Jan_Sales`
    (b) `X-RAY`
    (c) `int`
    (d) `xyz`
    (e) `1a`
    (f) `invoice_total`
    (g) `John's_exam_mark`

2. Which of the following are valid variable definitions?

    (a) `integer account_code ;`
    (b) `float balance ;`
    (c) `decimal total ;`
    (d) `int age ;`
    (e) `double int ;`

3. Write variable definitions for each of the following:

    (a) integer variables `number_of_transactions` and `age_in_years`
    (b) floating-point variables `total_pay`, `tax_payment`, `distance` and `average`
    (c) long integer variables `record_position` and `count`
    (d) a character variable `account_type`
    (e) a double variable `gross_pay`.

4. Construct a variable definition for each of the following:

    (a) a number of students
    (b) an average price
    (c) the number of days since 1 January 1900
    (d) a percentage interest rate.

5. Assuming the following

    ```
    int i ;
    char c ;
    ```

    which of the following are valid C++ statements?

    ```
    c = 'A' ;
    i = "1" ;
    i = 1 ;
    c = "A" ;
    c = '1';
    ```

6. Write a C++ program to assign values to the variables in exercise 3 and display the value of each variable on a separate line.

7. Write a C++ program to display your name and address on separate lines.

8. Convert the following mathematical equations into valid C++ statements:

(a) $m = \dfrac{y_1 - y_2}{x_1 - x_2}$

(b) $y = mx + c$

(c) $a = \dfrac{b}{c} - \dfrac{d}{e}$

(d) $C = \dfrac{5(F - 32)}{9}$

(e) $s = ut + \frac{1}{2}at^2$

9. Assuming the following variable definitions,

```
int a = 1, b = 10, c = 5 ;
int d ;
```

what is the value of d after each of the following statements?

(a) d = b / c + 1 ;
(b) d = b % 3 ;
(c) d = b - 3 * c / 5 ;
(d) d = b * 10 + c - a * 5 ;
(e) d = (a + b - 1) / c ;
(f) d = ((-a % c) + b) * c ;
(g) d = --a ;

10. Assuming the same variable definitions as in exercise 9, correct the errors in the following C++ statements:

(a) d = 2 (b + C)   ;
(b) d = 5b + 9c ;
(c) d = b - 3 X 19 ;
(d) d = b.c + 10 ;
(e) d = (a + b) / c ;

11. Wiite suitable statements to perform the following:

(a) add 1 to num1, placing the result in num1
(b) add 2 to num1, placing the result in num2
(c) add 2 to num2, placing the result in num2
(d) subtract 1 from num1, placing the result in num1
(e) subtract 2 from num2, placing the result in num2

12. Assuming the following,

```
int a = 12, b = 0, c = 3, d ;
```

what is the value of a, b, c and d after each of the following statements?

(a) a++ ;
(b) b-- ;
(c) d = ++c ;
(d) d = c-- ;
(e) d = a++ - 2 ;
(f) d = a++ + b++ - c-- ;

13. Assuming the following,

```
int a = 1, b = 2, c = 3 ;
```

what is the value of a, b and c after each of the following statements?

(a) a += b ;
(b) a /= 3 ;
(c) a *= c ;
(d) a %= 2 ;
(e) a += b+1 ;
(f) a += ++b ;

14. Place parentheses around the following expressions to indicate the order of evaluation as given in the C++ operator precedence table in appendix B.

(a) a = 1 - 2 * 3 + 4 / 5 ;
(b) a = 5 % b + c - d / 10 ;
(c) a = ++b * -10 / 5 ;

15. Assuming the following,

```
char ch_val ;   int int_val ; long long_val ;
float float_val ;   double double_val ;
unsigned int unsigned_int_val ;
```

which of the following may lose data because of demotion?

(a) int_val = long_val ;
(b) int_val = ch_val ;
(c) double_val = float_val ;
(d) long_val = float_val ;
(e) int_val = unsigned_int_val ;

16. Assuming the following,

```
int a = 5, b = 4 ;
float c = 3, d ;
```

what is the value of d after each of the following?

(a) `d = a / b ;`
(b) `d = static_cast<float>( a ) / b ;`
(c) `d = c / b ;`
(d) `d = static_cast<int>( c ) / b ;`
(e) `d = a / 2 ;`
(f) `d = a / 2.0 ;`
(g) `d = static_cast<float>( a ) / 2 ;`
(h) `d = static_cast<int>( c ) % 2 ;`

17. The following statements are supposed to swap the values in the integer variables a and b. Do they? Assume a is 1 and b is 2.

```
a = b ;
b = a ;
```

18. Write a program to compute

(a) the volume and
(b) the surface area

of a box with a height of 10 cm, a length of 11.5 cms, and a width of 2.5 cms.

19. Given the following variables:

```
double purchase_price, selling_price, profit, percentage_profit ;
```

Write a program to

(a) assign a value of fifty pounds to `purchase_price`
(b) assign a value of sixty pounds to `selling_price`
(c) assign to `profit` the value of the difference between `selling_price` and `purchase_price`
(d) assign to `percentage_profit` 100 times the value of `profit` divided by `purchase_price`
(e) display the value of all four variables.

20. Write a program to do the following:

(a) calculate and display the sum of the integers 1 to 5
(b) calculate the average of the floating-point numbers 1.0, 1.1, 1.2 ... 2.0.

CHAPTER THREE

Keyboard Input and Screen Output

In C++, data stream objects are used to perform basic input and output of data to and from various devices such as the keyboard and the screen. A stream is a data communication object connected to an input or output device.

Just as standard output stream cout is automatically associated with the screen, the standard input stream cin (console input) is automatically associated with the keyboard. The insertion operator << is used to write data to cout and the extraction operator >> is used to read data from the keyboard.

Essentially, reading data from the keyboard is the opposite of writing data out to the screen. The opposite of cout is cin and the opposite of << is >>.

3.1 Simple keyboard input

The following program reads a number from the keyboard and stores it in the variable num (for number).

```
1   // Program example P3A
2   // Program to demonstrate keyboard input.
3   #include <iostream>
4   using namespace std ;
5
6   void main()
7   {
8      int num ;
9
10     cout << "Please type a number: " ;
11     cin >> num ;
12     cout << "The number you typed was " << num << endl ;
13  }
```

This program simply asks the user for a number and displays the entered number on the screen.

Line 10 displays the message:

```
Please type a number:
```

Line 11 causes the computer to wait indefinitely until you type a number and press the Enter key.

When you type in a number (e.g. 123) followed by the Enter key, the program continues to line 12 and displays:

```
The number you typed was 123
```

As a memory aid when using cin, think of the data as entering the input stream and flowing in the direction indicated by the arrows >> i.e. towards the memory variable.

Similarly when using cout, think of the data as entering the output stream and flowing in the direction indicated by the arrows << i.e. towards the screen.

The next program inputs two floating-point numbers from the keyboard and displays the result of their addition.

```
1   // Program P3B
2   // Program to input two numbers and display their sum.
3   #include <iostream>
4   using namespace std ;
5
6   void main()
7   {
8      float num1, num2 ;
9
10     cout << "Type in 2 numbers. Press Enter after each number." << endl ;
11     cin >> num1 >> num2 ;
12
13     float sum ;          ←————— A variable can be defined just before it is used.
14     sum = num1 + num2 ;
15     cout << num1 << " + " << num2 << " = " << sum << endl ;
16 }
```

A sample run of this program is:

```
Type in 2 numbers. Press Enter after each number.
1.1
2.2
1.1 + 2.2 = 3.3
```

Line 11 reads the two numbers from the keyboard and line 14 assigns the result of their addition to the variable sum defined on line 13.

As shown in line 13, a variable can be defined at any point in a program, provided it is defined before it is used.

3.2 Manipulators

Manipulators are used to modify input and output data streams. The manipulator endl was used in previous programs to skip to the start of a new line on the screen.

A full list of manipulators is given in appendix E, but this section will look at just five of them: endl, setw, setfill, fixed and setprecision.

A manipulator can appear anywhere in a series of insertion or extraction operations. For example,

```
cout << endl << endl << "endl can be used anywhere" << endl ;
```

This example will skip to the start of a new line, skip another line, display the message in quotes and then skip to the start of the following line.

The manipulator setw is used to set the width of a data field. The width of a data field is the number of columns that the data item occupies on the screen.

```
1  // Program example P3C
2  // Demonstration of the setw manipulator.
3  #include <iostream>
4  #include <iomanip>
5  using namespace std ;
6
7  void main()
8  {
9     int num1 = 123, num2 = 4567 ;
10
11    cout << "Without setw:" << endl ;
12    cout << num1 << num2 << endl ;
13    cout << "With setw:" << endl ;
14    cout << setw( 4 ) << num1 << setw( 7 ) << num2 << endl ;
15 }
```

The output from this program is:

```
Without setw:
1234567
With setw:
 123    4567
```

Line 4 is required for any manipulator, like setw, that has a value in parentheses. Other manipulators, like endl, do not require this line.

Without using setw, the two numbers are displayed beside each other without any intervening space, making it difficult to see where one number ends and the next number starts.

The field width (number of columns) for num1 is set to 4 on line 14 by inserting the manipulator setw(4). Since num1 is only a three-digit number and the field width is set to four, a space precedes the three digits of num1. Similarly the field width for num2 is set to 7, resulting in three spaces preceding its four-digit value.
If the field width is set too small to display a value, the width is automatically expanded so that all the digits in the value are displayed.

The manipulator setfill is used to change the "padding" character from a space to any other character. This is demonstrated in the next program.

```
1  // Program example P3D
2  // Demonstration of the setfill manipulator.
3  #include <iostream>
4  #include <iomanip>
5  using namespace std ;
6
7  void main()
8  {
9    double num = 123.456 ;
10
11   cout << setw( 9 ) << setfill( '*' ) << num << endl ;
12   cout << setw( 9 ) << setfill( '0' ) << num << endl ;
13   cout << setw( 10 ) << num << endl ;
14 }
```

The output from this program is:

```
**123.456
00123.456
000123.456
```

Unlike setw, which applies only to the next data item in the output stream, the setfill manipulator remains in effect for all subsequent data items sent to the output stream. This is shown in line 13 where the fill character remains '0', as set in line 12.

The manipulator setprecision is used to specify the number of digits of a number to display. There are two ways of using this manipulator as shown in the next program.

```
1  // Program example P3E
2  // Program to demonstrate the setprecision and fixed manipulators.
3  #include <iostream>
4  #include <iomanip>
5  using namespace std ;
6
7  void main()
8  {
9    double num = 123.45678 ;
10
11   cout << num << endl ;
12   cout << setprecision( 7 ) << num << endl ;
13   cout << fixed << setprecision( 2 ) << num << endl ;
14 }
```

The output from this program is:

```
123.457
123.4568
123.46
```

By default, the maximum number of digits displayed for a number is six, which includes digits before and after the decimal point. On line 11, num is rounded up so that there is a total of six digits displayed.
On line 12, num is rounded up so that there is a total of seven digits displayed.

In line 13 the manipulator `fixed` precedes the `setprecision` specification. In this case `setprecision` refers to the number of digits after the decimal point. Line 13 therefore displays the value of `num` rounded up to two places of decimals.

Both manipulators `fixed` and `setprecision` remain in effect for subsequent insertions into the output stream.

3.3 Single-character input and output

Unlike pressing keys such as A, B or C on the keyboard, pressing keys such as Tab, Enter and the space bar do not display anything on the screen. These keys generate an invisible blank or white space on the screen and are consequently called whitespace characters. (Of course it is only when the background is white that white spaces are displayed. If the background is black then black spaces are generated. Nevertheless, they are still called whitespace characters.)

The following code segment inputs a character from the keyboard to the variable `ch`, ignoring whitespace characters.

```
char ch ;
cin >> ch ; // Reads the next character,
            // whitespace characters are ignored.
```

Sometimes it is required to read a single character from the keyboard whether it is a whitespace character or not. This can be done by using the manipulator `noskipws` (no skip whitespace).

```
cin >> noskipws >> ch ; // Reads the next character,
                        // a whitespace character may be read.
```

Alternatively, the function `get()` associated with the input stream object `cin` can be used.

```
cin.get( ch ) ; // Also reads the next character,
                // a whitespace character may be read.
```

A function is a block of program code that carries out a specific task.
Functions that are associated with an object are called *member functions* of the object.
In this case the function is pre-written and is available for use by a programmer. Chapters 7 and 8 show how to write functions and member functions.

In addition to displaying a character using >>, the output stream object `cout` has a member function `put()` that can be used to display a character.

```
cout.put( ch ) ; // Display the character ch.
```

Programming pitfalls

1. Do not mix up the insertion operator `<<` and the extraction operator `>>`. The insertion operator is used to insert data into the output stream; the extraction operator is used to read data from the input stream.

2. Some manipulators apply only to the next data field (e.g. `setw`); others (e.g. `setprecision`) stay in effect for all subsequent data fields.

3. The line

   ```
   #include <iomanip>
   ```

   is required for a manipulator that has a value in parentheses, e.g. `setw( 4 )`. Other manipulators, like `endl`, do not require this line.

Quick syntax reference

	Syntax	Examples
Input data from the keyboard	`cin >> variable₁` `>> variable₂` `... >> variableₙ ;`	`float num1, num2, num3 ;` `cin >> num1 >> num2 >> num3 ;`
Input a single character from the keyboard	`cin.get( variable ) ;`	`char char_in ;` `cin.get( char_in ) ;`
Output a single character to the screen	`cout.put( variable ) ;`	`char char_out ;` `cout.put( char_out ) ;`
Set the width of a field	`setw( integer )`	`float num ;` `cout << setw( 5 ) << num ;`
Set the number of decimal places	`fixed << setprecision( integer )`	`cout << fixed << setprecision( 2 )` `<< num ;`
Set a fill character	`setfill( character )`	`cout << setw( 5 ) << setfill( '0' )` `<< num ;`

Exercises

1. Write a program to input four numbers and display them in reverse order.

2. Write a program that inputs a number of hours and displays the equivalent number of weeks, days and hours. For example, an input of 553 should display 3 weeks, 2 days and 1 hour.

3. Assuming the human heart rate is seventy-five beats per minute, write a program to ask a user their age in years and to calculate the number of beats their heart has made so far in their life. Ignore leap years.

4. Write a program to accept a temperature in degrees Fahrenheit and convert it to degrees Celsius. Your program should display the following prompt:

    ```
    Enter a temperature in degrees Fahrenheit:
    ```

    You will then enter a decimal number followed by the Enter key.
    The program will then convert the temperature by using the formula

    $$\text{Celsius} = (\text{Fahrenheit} - 32.0) * (5.0 / 9.0)$$

    Your program should then display the temperature in degrees Celsius using an appropriate message.

5. Make changes to the program developed in exercise 4 to accept the temperature in degrees Celsius and convert it to degrees Fahrenheit.

6. Write a program to accept a distance in kilometres and display the equivalent distance in miles. (1 mile = 1.609344 kilometres.)

7. Write a program to input three floating-point numbers from the keyboard and to calculate

    (a) their sum and
    (b) their average.

    Display the results to three decimal places.

8. Write a program to read in two numbers from the keyboard and to display the result of dividing the second number into the first.

    For example, if the input is 123 and 12, the result should be displayed in the following format:

    ```
    123 divided by 12 = 10   Remainder = 3
    ```

    (Hint: use the modulus operator % to get the remainder 3, and use integer division to get the quotient 123.)

CHAPTER FOUR

Selection and Iteration

All the programs written so far execute one statement after the other, starting at the first statement and finishing at the last. Only the simplest of problems can be solved using this sequential top-to-bottom approach. Selection and iteration program constructs are used to modify this sequential execution of program statements.

4.1 Selection

4.1.1 The if statement

An if statement starts with the keyword if followed by an expression in parentheses. If the expression is found to be true, then the statement following the if is executed. If the expression is untrue, then the statement following the if is not executed. For example:

```
if ( account_balance < 0 )
    cout << "Your account is in the red" << endl ;
```

This statement tests whether the value of account_balance is less than 0 or not. If the value is less than 0, then the message is displayed; otherwise the message is not displayed.

The < is called a *relational operator*. The full list of relational operators is given below.

Operator	Meaning
==	equivalent to
!=	not equal to
<	less than
>	greater than
<=	less than or equal to
>=	greater than or equal to

The next program demonstrates the use of if statements with < and >=.

```
1   // Program example P4A
2   // Program to demonstrate if statements.
3   #include <iostream>
4   using namespace std ;
5
6   void main()
7   {
8     float account_balance ;
9
10    cout << "What is your account balance? " ;
11    cin >> account_balance ;
12
13    if ( account_balance < 0 )
14        cout << "Your account is in the red" << endl ;
```

31

```
15   if ( account_balance >= 0 )
16      cout << "Your account is in the black" << endl ;
17 }
```

When this program is run, it will ask the user to enter an account balance. If the account balance is negative, the statement on line 14 is executed; if it is greater than or equal to 0, then the statement on line 16 is executed.
Here is a sample run of this program:

```
What is your account balance? -100
Your account is in the red
```

4.1.2 The `if-else` statement
With the simple `if` statement there is a choice of either executing a statement or skipping it. With an `if-else` there is choice of executing one or other of two statements.

```
1   // Program example P4B
2   // Program to demonstrate the use of if-else.
3   #include <iostream>
4   using namespace std ;
5
6   void main()
7   {
8      float account_balance ;
9
10     cout << "What is your account balance? " ;
11     cin >> account_balance  ;
12
13     if ( account_balance < 0 )
14        cout << "Your account is in the red" << endl ;
15     else
16        cout << "Your account is in the black" << endl ;
17 }
```

In this program, if the value of account_balance is less than 0, line 14 is executed; otherwise the line 16 is executed.

4.1.3 Compound statements
A *compound statement* is one or more statements enclosed in braces { and }.
A compound statement can be used anywhere a single statement can be used.

```
1   // Program example P4C
2   // Program to demonstrate the formation and use of a
3   // compound statement.
4   #include <iostream>
5   #include <iomanip>
6   using namespace std ;
7
8   void main()
9   {
10     float account_balance, interest ;
11     const float overdraft_rate = 10.0 ;
12
```

```
13   cout << "What is your account balance? " ;
14   cin >> account_balance ;
15
16   if ( account_balance < 0 )
17   {
18     cout << "Your account is in the red" << endl ;
19     interest = -account_balance * overdraft_rate / 100.0 ;
20     cout << "The overdraft charge is "
21            << fixed << setprecision( 2 ) << interest << endl;
22   }
23   else
24   {
25     cout << "Your account is in the black" << endl ;
26     cout << "There is no overdraft charge" << endl ;
27   }
28 }
```

The statements within a compound statement are usually indented for appearance purposes. For example, lines 18 to 21 are two spaces to the right of the opening brace on line 17.

This program will ask for a bank balance and will then calculate an overdraft charge, assuming an overdraft rate of 10 per cent. The balance is tested in line 16. If the balance is less than 0, the statements on lines 18 to 21 are executed. If the balance is not less than 0, then the statements on lines 25 and 26 are executed.

Here is a sample run of this program:

```
What is your account balance? −100
Your account is in the red
The overdraft charge is 10.00
```

4.1.4 Logical operators

There are three logical operators for use in `if` statements:

Logical operator	Meaning
&&	AND
||	OR
!	NOT

The logical operators && (AND) and || (OR) are used to combine tests within an `if` statement. && is used to join two simple conditions together; the resulting compound condition is only true when *both* simple conditions are true.

If || is used to join two simple conditions, the result is true if *either* or *both* are true.
The logical NOT operator ! is used to reverse the result of an `if` statement. If the result is true, then it becomes false, and if it is false, then it becomes true.

Examples:

```
if ( a == 0 && b == 0 )    // Example of &&
   cout << "both a AND b are zero" ;

if ( a == 0 || b == 0 )    // Example of ||
   cout << "a OR b is zero" ;

if ( ! ( a == 0 ) )        // Example of !
   cout << "a is not zero" ;
```

4.1.5 Nested `if` statements

When an `if` statement occurs within another `if` statement it is called a *nested if* statement. For example

```
if ( a == 0 && b == 0 )
   cout << "Both a AND b are zero" ;
```

can be rewritten using a nested `if` as follows:

```
if ( a == 0 )
   if ( b== 0 )
      cout << "Both a AND b are zero" ;
```

4.1.6 The `switch` statement

The `switch` statement provides an alternative to a series of if-else statements, which can become quite complex to follow.

The next program emulates a four-function calculator. For each calculation the user inputs two numbers and an operator. For example, if the input is 5 + 3 then the program will display 8.

```
1   // Program example P4D
2   // Simple four-function calculator.
3   // This program illustrates the use of the switch statement.
4   #include <iostream>
5   using namespace std ;
6
7   void main()
8   {
9      char op ;
10     float num1, num2, answer ;
11
12     cout << "Please enter an arithmetic expression (e.g. 1 + 2) " ;
13     cin >> num1 >> op >> num2 ;
14
15     switch( op )
16     {
17       case '+' :
18         answer = num1 + num2 ;
19         cout << num1 << " plus " << num2 << " equals "
20              << answer << endl ;
21         break ;
22
23       case '-' :
24         answer = num1 - num2 ;
```

```
25        cout << num1 << " minus " << num2 << " equals "
26              << answer << endl ;
27        break ;
28
29     case '*' :
30        answer = num1 * num2 ;
31        cout << num1 << " multiplied by " << num2 << " equals "
32              << answer << endl ;
33        break ;
34
35     case '/' :
36        answer = num1 / num2 ;
37        cout << num1 << " divided by " << num2 << " equals "
38              << answer << endl ;
39        break ;
40
41     default :
42        cout << "Invalid operator" << endl ;
43   }
44 }
```

A sample run of this program will produce the following output:

```
Please enter an arithmetic expression (e.g. 1+2) 5+3
5 plus 3 equals 8
```

The `switch` statement is equivalent to a series of if-else statements. The variable or expression to be tested is placed in parentheses after the keyword `switch`. Unfortunately, this variable or expression can only be of type `char` or `int`, which somewhat limits the usefulness of `switch`. As many cases as are required are then enclosed within braces. Each case begins with the keyword `case`, followed by the value of the variable and a colon. The value of the variable is compared with each case value in turn. If a match is found, then the statements following the matching `case` are executed.

Once a match is found and the appropriate statements are executed, the `break` statement terminates the `switch` statement. Without the `break` statement, execution would continue to the end of the `switch` statement. The `break` can be omitted when the same statements are to be executed for several different cases. For example, in the last program either *, x or X can be used to indicate multiplication by modifying the `switch` statement as follows:

```
case '*' :
case 'x' :
case 'X' :
  answer = num1 * num2 ;
  cout << num1 << " multiplied by " << num2 << " equals "
        << answer << endl ;
  break ;
```

Either *, x or X will execute the same statements.

If no case matches the value of the `switch` variable, the `default` case is executed. In this program the `default` case is used to trap an invalid operator.

4.1.7 The conditional operator ?

The conditional operator ? is a short form of if-else.

The following program reads two values from the keyboard and finds the larger of the two using the ? operator.

```
1   // Program example P4E
2   // Demonstration of the conditional operator ?
3   #include <iostream>
4   using namespace std ;
5
6   void main()
7   {
8      float max, num1, num2 ;
9
10     cout << "Type in two numbers. Press Enter after each number."
11          << endl ;
12     cin >> num1 >> num2 ;
13
14     // Assign max to the larger of the two numbers.
15     max = ( num1 > num2 ) ? num1 : num2 ;
16     cout << "The larger number is " << max << endl ;
17 }
```

Line 15 is just a shorthand way of writing

```
   if ( num1 > num2 )
     max = num1 ;
   else
     max = num2 ;
```

A sample run of this program follows:

```
Type in two numbers. Press Enter after each number.
1
2
The larger number is 2
```

4.2 Iteration

Iterative control statements allow you to execute one or more program statements repeatedly. C++ has three iterative control statements: the while, the do-while and the for statements.

4.2.1 The while statement

The while statement causes one or more statements to repeat as long as a specified expression remains true. The next program demonstrates the while statement by inputting a series of numbers and displaying a running total of the numbers. The program stops when a 0 is input.

```
1   // Program example P4F
2   // Program to demonstrate the use of the while statement.
3   // This program reads in a series of numbers from the
4   // keyboard, prints a running total, and stops when a 0
5   // is entered.
6   #include <iostream>
7   using namespace std ;
```

```
8
9   void main()
10  {
11     float num, total ;
12
13     total = 0 ;
14     num = 1 ;
15
16     while ( num != 0 )
17     {
18        cout << "Please enter a number " ;
19        cin >> num ;
20        total += num ;
21        cout << "The running total is " << total << endl << endl ;
22     }
23
24     cout << "The final total is " << total << endl ;
25  }
```

As long as num *is not 0, this condition is true and the loop continues.*

As long as the condition is true, the statements between { and } are executed.

The statements enclosed within the braces { and } are executed repeatedly while the control expression n != 0 is true. The repeated execution of one or more program statements is called a *program loop*. The braces forming the loop may be omitted if there is only one statement in the loop.

A sample run of this program displays the following:

```
Please enter a number 12
The running total is 12

Please enter a number 6.4
The running total is 18.4

Please enter a number -1.25
The running total is 17.15

Please enter a number 0
The running total is 17.15

The final total is 17.15
```

The statements on lines 18 to 21 are executed repeatedly while the value of the variable num is not 0. When num becomes 0, the loop stops and the statement on line 24 is executed.

The control expression in a while loop is tested before the statements in the loop are executed. The sequence in a while loop is as follows:

1. Evaluate the control expression.

2. If the control expression is true, execute the statements in the loop and go back to 1.

3. If the control expression is false, exit the loop and execute the next statement after the loop.

It is important to note that if the first evaluation of the control expression is false, the statements in the loop are never executed. This is the purpose of giving the variable num a non-zero value in line 14. Line 14 places a value of 1 into num, but any non-zero value would do.

4.2.2 The do-while loop

In a while loop the control expression is tested *before* the statements in the loop are executed. The test in a do-while loop is done *after* the statements in the loop are executed. This means that the statements in a do-while loop are executed at least once. The sequence in a do-while loop is as follows:

1. Execute the statements in the loop.

2. Evaluate the control expression.

3. If the control expression is true then go back to 1.

4. If the control expression is false then exit the loop and execute the next statement after the loop.

The next program replaces the while loop in program P4F with a do-while loop.

```
1   // Program example P4G
2   // Program to demonstrate a do-while loop.
3   // This program will read in a series of numbers from the
4   // keyboard, prints a running total, and stops when a 0
5   // is entered.
6   #include <iostream>
7   using namespace std ;
8
9   void main()
10  {
11    float num, total ;
12
13    total = 0 ;
14
15    do
16    {
17      cout << "Please enter a number " ;      The statements between { and } are
18      cin >> num ;                            executed at least once.
19      total += num ;
20      cout << "The running total is " << total << endl << endl ;
21    }
22    while ( num != 0 ) ;
23
24    cout << "The final total is " << total << endl ;
25  }
```

Using a do-while loop means there is no need to initialise the variable num, because the loop is executed at least once. The output from this program is the same as for program P4F.

4.2.3 The for statement

The for statement is used to execute one or more statements a specified number of times. The general format of the for statement is:

```
for ( initial expression; continue condition; increment expression )
{
  ...
  // one or more statements.
  ...
}
```

The for statement consists of three expressions enclosed in parentheses and separated by semicolons.

The initial expression is executed once at the beginning of the loop. The loop continues while the continue expression is true and terminates when continue expression becomes false. The continue expression is a relational expression. The increment expression is executed at the end of every pass through the loop.

The braces { and } are needed only when there is more than one statement in the loop.

The next program displays a table of squares and cubes from 1 to 5.

```
1   // Program example P4H
2   // Program to display a table of squares and cubes.
3   #include <iostream>
4   #include <iomanip>
5   using namespace std ;
6
7   void main()
8   {
9     cout << "Number    Square    Cube" << endl ;
10    cout << "-----------------------" << endl ;
11
12    for ( int i = 1 ; i < 6 ; i++ )
13    {
14      cout << setw( 3 ) << i
15           << setw( 10 ) << i * i
16           << setw( 8 ) << i * i * i << endl ;
17    }
18  }
```

The output from this program is:

```
Number    Square    Cube
-----------------------
  1         1         1
  2         4         8
  3         9        27
  4        16        64
  5        25       125
```

The statements within the braces on lines 13 and 17 are executed five times. The loop contains only one statement, so the braces may be omitted. However, the braces are useful in that they clearly show the body of the loop.

The variable i is defined within the parentheses on line 12, but it could also be defined before the for statement as in the following:

```
int i ;
for ( i = 1 ; i < 6 ; i++ )
...
```

The for statement on line 12 causes the loop to be executed 5 times, with the variable i starting at 1 and continuing while the value of i is less than 6. Each time the loop is completed the value of i is incremented by 1. When the value of i becomes 6, the loop terminates.

There are many variations you can add to the simple for on line 12. Try modifying the program in each of the following ways:

1. To display the table for numbers from 10 down to 1, change line 10 to:

```
for ( int i = 10 ; i > 0 ; i -- )
```

Here i starts at 10 and is decremented at the end of each pass through the loop until it eventually becomes 0.

2. To display the table for even numbers between 2 and 10, change line 10 to:

```
for ( int i = 2 ; i <= 10 ; i += 2 )
```

In this for statement the variable i is initialised to 2 and increases by 2 each time through the loop, giving i the values 2 4 6 8 10.

Either initial expression or increment expression, or both, may consist of multiple statements separated by commas. For example:

```
for ( int i = 0, int j = 0 ; i < 10 ; i++, j++ )
```

This loop initialises both i and j to 0 and increments both of them at the end of each pass through the loop.

Any or all of the three expressions may be omitted from a for statement, but the two semicolons must always be present in the statement. For example, the statement for(;;) will create an infinite loop, because there is no condition to end the loop.

4.2.4 Nested loops
A for loop can contain any valid statements, including another for loop. When a loop is contained within another loop it is called a *nested loop*.

The next program displays a 12 by 12 multiplication table using a nested loop.

```
 1  // Program example P4I
 2  // Program displays a 12 x 12 multiplication table using a nested
 3  // loop.
 4  #include <iostream>
 5  #include <iomanip>
 6  using namespace std ;
 7
 8  void main()
 9  {
10    int i, j ;
11
12    cout << "     " ;
13
14    for ( i = 1 ; i <= 12 ; i++ )
15    {
16      cout << setw( 5 ) <<  i  ;
17    }
18
19    cout << endl << "    +" ;
20
21    for ( i = 0 ; i <= 60 ; i++ )
22    {
23        cout << '-'  ;
24    }
25
26    for ( i = 1 ; i <= 12 ; i++ )       // Start of outer loop.  <--+
27    {                                   //                          |
28      cout << endl << setw( 2 ) << i << " |" ;   //                 |
29      for ( j = 1; j <= 12 ; j++ )      // Start of inner loop.<-+  |
30      {                                 //                       |  |
31        cout << setw( 5 ) << i * j ;    //                       |  |
32      }                                 // End of inner loop. <--+  |
33    }                                   // End of outer loop.    <--+
34
35    cout << endl   ;
36  }
```

This program will display the following table:

		1	2	3	4	5	6	7	8	9	10	11	12
1	|	1	2	3	4	5	6	7	8	9	10	11	12
2	|	2	4	6	8	10	12	14	16	18	20	22	24
3	|	3	6	9	12	15	18	21	24	27	30	33	36
4	|	4	8	12	16	20	24	28	32	36	40	44	48
5	|	5	10	15	20	25	30	35	40	45	50	55	60
6	|	6	12	18	24	30	36	42	48	54	60	66	72
7	|	7	14	21	28	35	42	49	56	63	70	77	84
8	|	8	16	24	32	40	48	56	64	72	80	88	96
9	|	9	18	27	36	45	54	63	72	81	90	99	108
10	|	10	20	30	40	50	60	70	80	90	100	110	120
11	|	11	22	33	44	55	66	77	88	99	110	121	132
12	|	12	24	36	48	60	72	84	96	108	120	132	144

The loop in lines 14 to 17 displays the numbers 1 to 12 across the screen, and the loop in lines 21 to 24 displays the hyphens beneath them. The remainder of the program uses a nested loop to display the numbers in the table.

The outer loop (lines 26 to 33) starts with i at 1. Line 28 displays a 1 and the vertical stroke character | at the left of the screen.

The inner loop (lines 29 to 32) is then executed to completion, with j starting at 1 and ending when j exceeds 12. Each iteration of the inner loop displays a number in the multiplication table.

When the inner loop is completed, the outer loop regains control, and i is incremented to 2. Line 28 then displays 2 | at the left of the screen, and the inner loop on lines 29 to 32 is executed again.

The program continues until the outer loop is completed when the value of i exceeds 12.

Programming pitfalls

1. There is no ; immediately after an if statement. For example:

```
if ( account_balance < 0 ) ;   // Misplaced semicolon.
   cout << "Your account is in the red" << endl ;
```

should be:

```
if ( account_balance < 0 )
   cout << "Your account is in the red" << endl ;
```

In the first case the message Your account is in the red is always displayed, regardless of the value in account_balance.

2. There is no ; after switch.

3. When testing for equality use ==, not =.

4. Each else is matched with the previous if.

5. For each opening brace { there will be a closing brace }.

6. Braces are necessary to control the execution of a set of statements with an if statement. For example:

```
if ( a == b )
   a = 1 ;
   b = 2 ;
```

In this example, the statement a = 1 is executed only if a and b are equal. However, the statement b = 2 is always executed, regardless of the values of a and b. To execute both statements when a and b are equal the braces are required:

```
if ( a == b )
{
   a = 1 ;
   b = 2 ;
}
```

7. The logical operators (&& and ||) evaluate the smallest number of operands needed to determine the result of an expression. This means that some operands of the expression may not be evaluated. For example, in

```
if ( a > 1 && b++ > 2 )
```

the second operand, b++, is evaluated only if the condition a > 1 is logically true.

8. There is no semicolon immediately after the `while` or `for` statements. For example:

```
for ( i = 0 ; i < 10 ; i++ ) ;   // Misplaced semicolon.
   cout << "The value of i is " << i ;
```

This loop does not contain any statements and will not display the values 0 to 9, as expected. Only the final value of i (=10) will be displayed.

9. Be careful in specifying the terminating condition in a `for` loop. For example:

```
for ( int i = 0 ; i == 10 ; i++ )   // This loop does nothing.
   cout << "The value of i is " << i << endl ;
```

This loop does nothing, because i `==` 10 is false at the start of the loop (i is in fact 0) and the loop terminates immediately. Replace i `==` 10 with i `<` 10 or i `!=` 10 and the loop will execute ten times.

10. There is no semicolon after `while` in a while loop, but there is in a do-while loop. See line 16 of program P4F and line 22 of program P4G.

11. There is a limit to the precision with which floating-point numbers are represented. This is important when testing a floating-point number for equality in an `if` or in a `for` loop. For example, consider the following loop:

```
float f ;
for ( f = 0.0 ; f != 1.1 ; f += 0.1 )
{
   ...
   // statements in the loop.
   ...
}
```

On most computers this will result in an infinite loop. The reason for this is that f may never equal 1.1 exactly. You can allow for this situation by writing the loop as:

```
for ( f = 0.0 ; f <= 1.1 ; f += 0.1 )
{
   ...
   // statements in the loop.
   ...
}
```

Quick syntax reference

	Syntax	Examples
if-else	```if (condition)` `{` ` statement(s) ;` `}` `else` `{` ` statement(s) ;` `}```	```if (n > 0)` `{` ` average = total / n ;` ` cout << average ;` `}` `else` ` average = 0 ;```
?	`variable = (condition) ? v1 : v2 ;`	`max = ( n1 > n2 ) ? n1 : n2 ;`
switch	```switch (expression)` `{` `case value₁ :` ` statement(s) ;` ` break ;` `case value₂ :` ` statement(s) ;` ` break ;` `default :` ` statement(s) ;` `}```	```char traffic_light ;` `...` `switch(traffic_light)` `{` `case 'R':` `case 'r':` ` cout << "Red: STOP" ;` ` break ;` `case 'G':` `case 'g':` ` cout << "Green: GO" ;` ` break ;` `case 'A':` `case 'a':` ` cout << "Amber: READY" ;` ` break ;` `default:` ` cout << "FAULT" ;` `}```
while	```while (condition)` `{` ` statement(s) ;` `}```	```// Read and total until n is 0.` `int n = 1 ;` `int total = 0 ;` `while (n != 0)` `{` ` cin >> n ;` ` total += n ;` `}```
do-while	```do` `{` ` statement(s) ;` `}` `while (condition) ;```	```// Read and total until n is 0.` `int n ;` `int total = 0 ;` `do` `{` ` cin >> n ;` ` total += n ;` `}` `while (n != 0) ;```
for	```for (initial expression ;` ` continue condition ;` ` increment expression)` `{` ` // statement(s)` `}```	```// Read and total 10 numbers.` `int total = 0 ;` `for (int i = 0 ; i < 10 ; i++)` `{` ` cin >> n ;` ` total += n ;` `}```

Exercises

1. Rewrite the following if-else using a switch statement:

    ```
    if ( marriage_status == 'S' )
      cout << "single" ;
    else if ( marriage_status == 'M' )
      cout << "married" ;
    else if ( marriage_status == 'W' )
      cout << "widowed" ;
    else if ( marriage_status == 'E' )
      cout << "separated"  ;
    else if ( marriage_status == 'D' )
      cout << "divorced"  ;
    else
      cout << "error: invalid code" ;
    ```

2. The following program segment displays an appropriate message depending on the values of three integers: n1, n2, and n3.

    ```
    if ( n1== n2 )
    if (n1 == n3 )
    cout <<  "n1, n2 and n3 have the same value" << endl ;
    else
    cout << "n1 and n2 have the same value" << endl ;
    else if ( n1 == n3 )
    cout <<  "n1 and n3 have the same value" << endl ;
    else if ( n2 == n3 )
    cout <<  "n2 and n3 have the same value" << endl ;
    else
    cout << "n1, n2 and n3 have different values" << endl ;
    ```

    Use spaces to improve the readability of this code.
    To test the various branches in this code you will need to construct five sets of test data, each set testing one of the branches. Construct the five sets of test data for n1, n2, and n3.

3. Write a program to read in two integers and check if the first integer is evenly divisible by the second. (Hint: use the modulus operator %.)

4. Input two numbers and find the smaller of the two using the conditional operator ?.

5. In a triangle, the sum of any two sides must be greater than the third side.
    Write a program to input three numbers and determine if they form a valid triangle.

6. Input a person's height in centimetres and weight in kilograms and display a message indicating that they are either underweight, overweight or normal weight. As an approximation, a person is underweight if their weight is less than their height divided by 2.5 and they are overweight if their weight is greater than their height divided by 2.3.

7. Write a program that reads a single numeral from the keyboard and displays its value as a word. For example, an input of 5 will display the word 'five'.

8. Write a program to input a number 1 to 7 from the keyboard, where 1 represents Sunday, 2 Monday, 3 Tuesday, etc. Display the day of the week corresponding to the number typed by the user. If the user types a number outside the range 1 to 7, display an error message.

9. Add the increment operator (I or i) and the decrement operator (D or d) to the simple calculator program P4D.

10. Write a program to input the time of day in Ireland and display the equivalent time in Washington (– 5 hours), Moscow (+ 3 hours), and Tokyo (+ 9 hours). Input the time in the 24-hour format, e.g. 22:35 (11:35 p.m.).

11. Write a program to display the effects of an earthquake based on the Richter scale value:

Richter scale value	Effects
Less than 4	Little.
4.0 to 4.9	Windows shake.
5.0 to 5.9	Walls crack; poorly built buildings are damaged.
6.0 to 6.9	Chimneys tumble; ordinary buildings are damaged.
7.0 to 7.9	Underground pipes break; well-built buildings are damaged.
More than 7.9	Ground rises and falls in waves; most buildings are destroyed.

12. What is the output from the following?

```
for ( int j = 1, int i = 10 ; i > 0 ; i /= 2, j++ )
   cout << i << j ;
```

13. Modify program P4F to calculate the average along with the total of the numbers entered.

14. Rewrite the following using a for loop.

```
int i = 0, total = 0 ;
while ( i < 10 )
{
   cin >> n   ;
   total += n ;
   i++ ;
}
```

15. What is displayed when the following program is run and the number 1234 is entered?

```
int num ;
cout << "Please enter a number "   ;
cin >> num ;
do
{
   cout << num % 10 ;
   num /= 10 ;
}
while ( num != 0 ) ;
```

16. The following program segment is intended to compute $0.1 + 0.2 + 0.3 \ldots + 99.8 + 99.9$. It contains a flaw. What is it, and how would you correct it?

```
float sum = 0.0 ;
float i = 0.1 ;
while ( i != 100.0 )
{
  sum += i ;
  i += 0.1 ;
}
```

17. What is the output from the following?

(a)
```
for (int i = 0 ; i < 5 ; i++ )
  for ( int j = i ; j < 5 ; j++ )
    cout << i << j << endl ;
```

(b)
```
for ( int i = 0 ; i < 5 ; i++ )
  for ( int j = 0 ; j < 5-i ; j++ )
    cout << i << j << endl ;
```

18. Write a `for` loop to

(a) display the numbers 0, 5, 10, 15, ..., 100
(b) display the numbers 1, 2, 4, 8, 16, ..., 1024

19. Write a program to find the sum of all the odd integers in the range 1 to 99.

20. Write a program that outputs all the numbers between 5 and 50 that are divisible by 3 or 5.

21. Write a program to display all the hour and minute values in a 24-hour clock, i.e. 0:00   0:01 ... 23:59.
How would you display the values in fifteen-minute intervals?

22. Write a program to simulate the operation of a supermarket cash register. The program will display an option menu with the following options:

1. Bread 2. Butter 3. Confectionery 4. Fruit 5. Meat 6. Milk 7. Vegetables 8. Other 9. Sub-Total 10. Total 0. Quit

The program should prompt the user for an option number and display an error message if the number is outside the range 0 to 10.

If the user enters 1 to 8, the program will ask for the amount of the purchase and add it to a total. Option 9 will display the total. Option 10 will display the total, ask the user to enter the amount tendered, display the change, and reset the total to 0.

The program stops when the user enters 0 as the option number.

CHAPTER FIVE

Arrays and Structures

5.1 Arrays

5.1.1 Introduction

An array is a group of variables of the same data type, such as ten `ints`, fifteen `chars` or a hundred `floats`. For example, an array of ten integers is defined by:

```
int numbers[10] ; // Defines an array of 10 ints called numbers.
```

The individual values or elements in the array are all held in memory under one name, i.e. the array name. The array name can be any valid variable name.

Visually the array `numbers` is stored in memory like this:

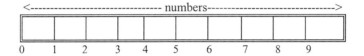

The number of elements in an array is known as the *dimension* of the array. The dimension of the array `numbers` is 10.

Each individual element of the array is accessed by reference to its position in the array relative to the first element of the array. The position of an element in an array is called the *index* or *subscript*. The first element in an array of ten elements has an index value of 0, and the last element has an index value of 9. Note that the index goes from 0 to 9, not 1 to 10.

To refer to a particular element of an array, the array name and the index in brackets is used. In the array `numbers` above the first element is `numbers[0]`, the second element is `numbers[1]`, and so on. For example, `numbers[0]=49`, assigns 49 to the first element of the array and `numbers[2]=52`, assigns 52 to the third element of the array.

Care must be taken when referencing the tenth element – it is `numbers[9]`, not `numbers[10]`.

The next program demonstrates a simple application of an array.

```
1   // Program example P5A
2   // Program to calculate the average age of ten people
3   // using an array.
4   #include <iostream>
5   using namespace std ;
6
7   void main()
8   {
9     int ages[10] ;
10    int total_age = 0 ;
11
12    cout << "Please enter the ages of ten people" << endl ;
13  // Input and total each age.
14    for ( int index = 0 ; index < 10 ; index ++ )
15    {
```

```
16      cin >> ages[index] ;
17      total_age += ages[index] ;
18    }
19    cout << "The average age is " << total_age / 10 << endl ;
20 }
```

A sample run of this program is:

```
Please enter the ages of ten people
41
67
21
7
59
57
41
74
47
68
The average age is 48
```

The statement:

```
int ages[10] ;
```

defines ages as an array of ten integers. An array is defined by stating the type of its elements, its name, and the number of elements in the array. In general, the format is:

```
data_type variable_name[number_of_elements] ;
```

For example:

```
float array_1[50] ; // An array of 50 floats.
long  array_2[20] ; // An array of 20 long ints.
```

The for loop in lines 14 to 18 is used to read in a value for each of the elements of the array and add them to total_age.

The variable index is used to hold the value of the *index* or *subscript* of the array. On the first pass through the loop, index is 0, and line 16 reads in a value for ages[0], i.e. the first array element. Line 17 then adds ages[0] to total_age.

On the second pass through the loop, index has a value of 1, line 16 reads in a value for ages[1], and line 17 adds ages[1] to total_age. The loop continues until the tenth element, ages[9], is read in and added to total_age.

It is a common requirement in programming to find the minimum and maximum values in an array. The next program inputs ten ages and finds the youngest and the oldest. The average age is also computed.

```
1    // Program example P5B
2    // Program to read a series of ages and to find
3    // the youngest, the oldest, and the average.
4    #include <iostream>
5    using namespace std ;
6
7    void main()
8    {
9      const int SIZE = 10 ;
10     int ages[SIZE] ;
11     int i ;
12     int total_age = 0 ;
13     int youngest, oldest ;
14
15     cout << "Please enter " << SIZE << " ages" << endl ;
16     // Input a value for each age.
17     for ( i = 0 ; i < SIZE ; i++ )
18     {
19       cin >> ages[i] ;
20       total_age += ages[i] ;
21     }
22
23     youngest = ages[0] ;
24     oldest = ages[0] ;
25
26     for ( i = 0 ; i < SIZE ; i ++ )
27     {
28       if ( ages[i] > oldest )
29       {
30         oldest = ages[i] ;
31       }
32       if ( ages[i] < youngest )
33       {
34         youngest = ages[i] ;
35       }
36     }
37
38     cout << "The youngest is " << youngest << endl ;
39     cout << "The oldest is " << oldest << endl ;
40     cout << "The average is " << total_age / SIZE << endl;
41   }
```

This program starts by defining a constant integer SIZE on line 9. The const keyword is used in the definition of SIZE to specify that its value cannot be changed in the program. Although any valid identifier can be used for a constant, the identifier is usually written in uppercase. SIZE is known as a *symbolic constant*.

In line 9 SIZE is assigned a value of 10. The symbolic constant SIZE can now be used throughout the program in place of the number 10. Using a symbolic constant variable makes the program easier to modify. For example, to modify the above program to cater for twenty ages rather than ten, change line 9 to:

```
const int SIZE = 20 ;
```

The `for` loop in lines 17 to 21 reads in values into the array `ages` and totals them in `total_age`.

Lines 23 and 24 assign the first element of the array to the variables `youngest` and `oldest`. The `for` loop in lines 26 to 36 compares each element in the array with the values in the variables `youngest` and `oldest`. When an element larger than `oldest` is found, the value of this element is assigned to `oldest`. When an element is found that is less then `youngest`, this element is assigned to `youngest`. When the loop is completed, the smallest element of the array is in `youngest` and the largest is in `oldest`.

The variables `oldest` and `youngest` were initially assigned the value of the first element of the array. Any element of the array can be used, not necessarily the first.

5.1.2 Initialising an array
The next program demonstrates array initialisation by asking the user to enter a month and displaying the number of days in that month (leap years excepted).

```
1   // Program example P5C
2   // Program to display the number of days in a month.
3   #include <iostream>
4   using namespace std ;
5
6   void main()
7   {
8     const int NO_OF_MONTHS = 12 ;
9     int days [NO_OF_MONTHS] =
10            { 31, 28, 31, 30, 31, 30, 31, 31, 30, 31, 30, 31 } ;
11    int month ;
12
13    cout << "Please enter a month (1 = Jan., 2 = Feb., etc.) " ;
14    do
15    {
16      cin >> month ;
17    }
18    while ( month < 1 || month > 12 ) ;
19
20    cout << endl << "The number of days in month " << month
21         << " is " << days [month-1] << endl ;
22 }
```

A sample run of this program is:

```
Please enter a month (1 = Jan., 2 = Feb., etc.) 9

The number of days in month 9 is 30
```

Lines 9 and 10 of this program define and initialise an array `days`. The initial values in the array are separated by commas and placed between braces.

When the list of initial values is less than the number of elements in the array, the remaining elements are initialised to 0. For example,

```
float values[5] = { 2.3, 5.8, 1.3 } ;
```

initialises the first three elements with the values specified within the braces. The remaining two elements of the array are initialised to 0.

If an array is defined without specifying the number of elements and is initialised to a series of values, the number of elements in the array is taken to be the same as the number of initial values. This means that

```
int numbers[] = { 0, 1, 2, 3, 4, 5, 6, 7, 8 } ;
```

and

```
int numbers[9] = { 0, 1, 2, 3, 4, 5, 6, 7, 8 } ;
```

are equivalent definitions of the array numbers.

5.1.3 Two-dimensional arrays

So far, only one-dimensional arrays, i.e. arrays with just one row of elements, have been used. A two-dimensional array has more than one row of elements. For example, to record the number of students using one of five computer laboratories over a week, the data could be recorded in a table of the form:

| | ← Computer laboratory number → | | | | |
	1	2	3	4	5
Day 1	120	215	145	156	139
Day 2	124	231	143	151	136
Day 3	119	234	139	147	135
Day 4	121	229	140	151	141
Day 5	110	199	138	120	130
Day 6	62	30	37	56	34
Day 7	12	18	11	16	13

This table has a row for each day of the week and a column for each computer laboratory. This is an example of a two-dimensional array. To define two-dimensional arrays, enclose each dimension of the array in brackets. For example,

```
int usage[7][5] ;
```

defines an integer array of seven rows and five columns.

To access an element of a two-dimensional array, you specify the row and the column. Note that the row number starts at 0 and ends at 6, and the column number starts at 0 and ends at 4. For example:

```
usage[0][0] is 120    i.e. row 0, column 0
usage[0][4] is 139        row 0, column 4
usage[6][0] is  12        row 6, column 0
usage[6][4] is  13        row 6, column 4
```

The row number is in the first set of square brackets and the column number is in the second set of square brackets.

The next program reads in the number of students using the five laboratories over seven days into a two-dimensional array usage and calculates the average usage for each laboratory. Run this program and study the code to see how it works.

```
1  // Program example P5D
2  // Program to read in number of students using five computer labs
3  // over seven days and to display the average usage for each lab.
4  #include <iostream>
5  using namespace std ;
6
7  void main()
8  {
9     const int NO_OF_DAYS = 7 ;
10    const int  NO_OF_LABS = 5 ;
11    int usage[NO_OF_DAYS][NO_OF_LABS] ;
12    int day, lab, total_usage, average ;
13
14    // Read each lab's usage for each day.
15    for ( day = 0 ; day < NO_OF_DAYS ; day++ )
16    {
17      cout << "Enter the usage for day " << ( day + 1 ) << endl ;
18      for ( lab = 0 ; lab < NO_OF_LABS ; lab++ )
19      {
20        cout << " Lab number " << ( lab + 1 ) << ' ' ;
21        cin >> usage[day][lab] ;
22      }
23    }
24
25    // Calculate the average usage for each laboratory.
26    for ( lab = 0 ; lab < NO_OF_LABS ; lab++ )
27    {
28      total_usage = 0 ;
29      for ( day = 0 ; day < NO_OF_DAYS ; day++ )
30      {
31        total_usage += usage[day][lab] ;
32      }
33      average = total_usage / NO_OF_DAYS ;
34      cout << endl << "Lab number " << ( lab+1 )
35           << " has an average usage of " << average << endl ;
36    }
37 }
```

5.1.4 Initialising a two-dimensional array

A two-dimensional array, like a one-dimensional array, is initialised by enclosing the initial values in braces. For example,

```
int vals[4][3] = { 4, 9, 5, 2, 11, 3, 21, 9, 32, 10, 1, 5 } ;
```

initialises the first row of vals with 4, 9, and 5. The second row is initialised with 2, 11, and 3. The third row is initialised with 21, 9, and 32; and the fourth row is initialised with 10, 1, and 5.

Readability is improved if you place the initial values of each row on a separate line, as follows:

```
int vals[4][3] = { 4,   9, 5,
                   2, 11, 3,
                  21,   9, 32,
                  10,   1, 5 } ;
```

Additional braces may also be used to separate the rows, as follows:

```
int vals[4][3] = {  { 4,   9, 5  },
                    { 2, 11, 3  },
                    { 21, 9, 32 },
                    { 10, 1, 5 }  } ;
```

As with one-dimensional arrays, you can omit the first dimension and let the compiler calculate the number of rows from the initial values in the braces. Therefore you can rewrite the above definition of `vals` as:

```
int vals[][3]  =  {  { 4,   9, 5  },
                     { 2, 11, 3  },
                     { 21, 9, 32 },
                     { 10,  1, 5 }  } ;
```

As with one-dimensional arrays, missing values are initialised to 0. For example, the definition

```
int vals[4][3] = {  { 4,   9 },
                    {  2  }  } ;
```

will result in

```
vals[0][0] = 4, vals[0][1] = 9 and vals[1][0] = 2
```

with all the remaining elements being 0. Note that the first dimension is required here or the compiler will assume it to be 2, as there are only two rows of initial values.

5.1.5 Multi-dimensional arrays
You can define arrays with any number of dimensions. For example, if in program P5D you wanted to store the usage in the five laboratories for each day in three different terms, the array `usage` would be defined as:

```
const int NO_OF_TERMS = 3 ;
const int NO_OF_DAYS = 7 ;
const NO_OF_LABS = 5 ;
int usage[NO_OF_TERMS][NO_OF_DAYS][NO_OF_LABS] ;
```

The elements of this array are accessed by using three subscripts. For example,
`usage[0][2][4]` is the usage in the first term of day 3 in laboratory number 5.

5.2 Structures

5.2.1 Introduction

The items of information that make up an array have all the same data type (int, float etc.) and are logically related in some way. For example, a student's test scores may be integer values that are logically related to the student. In this case it makes sense to store the test scores together in an array. In short, arrays are suitable for storing sets of homogeneous data.

However, there are items of information that are logically related but each item may have a different data type. A student's number and test scores, for example, are logically related to the student, but the number may be an integer, while the test scores may be floating-point values.

Logically related items of information that may have different data types can be combined into a *structure*. Unlike an array, the data items in a structure may be of different types.

5.2.2 Declaring a structure

The first step in defining a structure is to declare a *structure template*:

```
struct student_rec
{
  int number ;           // Student number.
  float scores[5] ;      // Scores on five tests.
} ;
```

A structure template consists of the reserved keyword struct followed by the name of the structure. The name of the structure is known as the *structure tag*. In the example above, student_rec is a structure tag.

After the structure tag, each item within the structure is declared within the braces { and }. Each item in a structure is called a *structure member*. A structure member has a name and a data type. Any name can be used for a structure member, provided it is a valid C++ identifier (see page 5).

Declaring a structure template does not allocate memory to the structure. All that has been done at this stage is to define a new data type consisting of other previously defined data types. Once you have defined the new data type you can then define variables with that type. For example,

```
struct student_rec student1, student2 ;
```

defines the variables student1 and student2 to be of the type struct student_rec. Both student1 and student2 are structure variables with two structure members, i.e. number, and scores.

student1:

student2:

The members of a structure variable can be accessed with the member selection operator ".
" (a dot). For example, we can assign values to the member number of the variables student1 and student2 with the statements:

```
student1.number = 1234 ;          student2.number = 13731 ;
```

The two variables student1.number and student2.number are used in the same way as any other integer variable.

The next program inputs values for each member of a structure and displays it on the screen.

```
1    // Program example P5E
2    // Introduction to structures: assigning values to structure
3    // members.
4    #include <iostream>
5    #include <iomanip>
6    using namespace std ;
7
8    void main()
9    {
10     int i ;
11
12     // Declare the structure template.
13     struct student_rec
14     {
15       // Declare the members of the structure.
16       int number ;
17       float scores[5] ;
18     } ;
19
20     // Define two variables having the type struct student_rec.
21     struct student_rec student1, student2 ;
22
23     // Read in values for the members of student1.
24     cout << "Number: " ;
25     cin >> student1.number ;
26     cout << "Five test scores: " ;
27
28     for ( i= 0 ; i < 5 ; i++ )
29       cin >> student1.scores[i] ;
30
31     // Now assign values to the members of student2.
32     // The assignments are not meant to be meaningful and
33     // are for demonstration purposes only.
34     student2.number = student1.number + 1 ;
35     for ( i = 0 ; i < 5 ; i++ )
36       student2.scores[i] = 0 ;
37
38     // Display the values in the members of student1.
39     cout << endl << "The values in student1 are:" ;
40     cout << endl << "Number is " << student1.number ;
41     cout << endl << "Scores are:" ;
42     cout << fixed << setprecision( 1 ) ;
43     for ( i = 0 ; i < 5 ; i++ )
```

```
44      cout << setw(5) << student1.scores[i] ;
45
46    // Display the values in the members of student2.
47    cout << endl << endl << "The values in student2 are:" ;
48    cout << endl << "Number is " << student2.number ;
49    cout << endl << "Scores are:" ;
50    for ( i = 0 ; i < 5 ; i++ )
51      cout << setw(5) << student2.scores[i] ;
52
53    cout << endl ;
54 }
```

A sample run of this program is shown below.

```
Number: 1234
Five test scores: 4.5    6.0    5.5    6.5    7.5

The values in student1 are:
Number is 1234
Scores are:   4.5   6.0   5.5   6.5   7.5

The values in student2 are:
Number is 1235
Scores are:   0.0   0.0   0.0   0.0   0.0
```

The structure tag student_rec in line 13 of program P5E is optional. The structure template and the structure variables can be defined together:

```
// Declaring a structure template without a structure tag.
struct    // No tag name after struct.
{
  int number ;
  float scores[5] ;
} student1, student2 ; // Variables follow immediately after the }.
```

5.2.3 Initialising a structure variable
The members of a structure variable can be initialised by placing their initial values in braces.

Example:

```
struct student_rec
{
  int number ;
  int scores[5] ;
} ;

struct student_rec student = { 1234,
                               { 50, 60, 45, 65, 75 }
                             } ;
```

The first member of the structure (student.number) is initialised to 1234, the second member (student.scores) is an integer array and is initialised to the values enclosed in the inner set of braces. The initial values are on separate lines for visual purposes only, to make it easy to relate a structure member with its initial value.

5.2.4 Nested structures

A *nested structure* is a structure that contains another structure as one of its members. For example, a company personnel record might consist of, among other things, the employees' date of birth and date of joining the company. Both these dates can be represented by a structure with members day, month and year.

First declare the structure template for a date as follows:

```
struct date      // Structure template for a date.
{
  int day ;
  int month ;
  int year ;
} ;
```

Next, the template for the structure `personnel` is declared in terms of the previously declared structure template `date`.

```
struct personnel       // Structure template for an employee.
{
  int number ;   // Employee number.
                 // and various other structure members, e.g. pay.
  struct date dob ;    // The data type of dob is struct date.
  struct date joined ; // joined is also of type struct date.
} ;
```

Finally, define a variable `person` of the type `struct personnel`, as in:

```
struct personnel person ;
```

Graphically, the personnel structure looks like this:

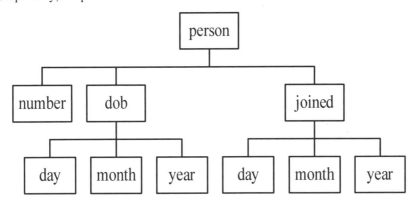

The expressions

```
person.dob    and   person.joined
```

will access the date of birth and date of joining members, respectively. Furthermore,

```
person.dob.day    person.dob.month   and   person.dob.year
```

will access the day, month and year of birth, respectively. Similarly,

    person.joined.day   person.joined.month   and   person.joined.year

will access the day, month and year of the date the person joined the company.

5.3 The `typedef` statement

`typedef` allows you to define a synonym for a built-in or a programmer-defined data type. From the personnel example on the previous pages, we had the following structure templates:

```
struct date            // Structure template for a date.
{
  int day ;
  int month ;
  int year ;
} ;

struct personnel       // Structure template for an employee.
{
  int number ;   // Employee number.
                 // and various other structure members, e.g. pay.
  struct date dob ;    // The data type of dob is struct date.
  struct date joined ; // joined is also of type struct date.
} ;
```

The following statement uses `typedef` to define a synonym DATE for `struct date`:

```
typedef struct date DATE ;
```

The personnel structure template can now be written as:

```
struct personnel
{
  int number ;   // Employee number
                 // and various other structure members.
  DATE dob ;
  DATE joined ;
} ;
```

Going a step further, a synonym EMPLOYEE can be written for `struct personnel`:

```
typedef struct personnel EMPLOYEE ;
```

The variable `person` can now be conveniently defined as:

```
EMPLOYEE person ;
```

5.4 Arrays of structures

Continuing with the personnel example used in the previous sections:

```
struct personnel persons[5] ;
```

or

```
EMPLOYEE persons[5] ;
```

defines a five-element array `persons`. Each element of this array is of the type `struct personnel`, with members `number`, `dob` and `joined`. The members `dob` and `joined` are themselves structures and have members `day`, `month` and `year`.

Note that `persons[0].number` will access the employee number of the first employee and `persons[4].joined.year` will access the year of joining of the fifth employee.

5.5 Enumerated data types

An enumerated data type is used to describe a set of integer values. For example:

```
enum response { no, yes, none } ;
enum response answer ;
```

These statements declare the data type `response` to have one of three possible values: `no`, `yes`, or `none`. The variable `answer` is defined as an enumerated variable of type `response`. This is similar to the way in which a structure template and a structure variable are defined.

The names enclosed in the braces { and } are integer constants. The first name (`no`) has a value of 0, the second name (`yes`) has a value of 1, and the third name (`none`) has a value of 2. The variable `answer` can be assigned any of the possible values: `no`, `yes`, or `none`.

For example:

```
answer = none ;
```

or:

```
answer = no ;
```

The variable `answer` can also be used in an `if` statement. For example:

```
if ( answer == yes )
{
  // statement(s)
}
```

The purpose of the enumerated data type is to improve the readability of the program. In the example above, using `yes`, `no` and `none` rather than 0, 1 and 2 makes the program more readable.

In this example, `response` is called the *enumeration tag*. Like a structure tag, the enumeration tag is optional. For example, the variable `answer` could also be defined as:

```
enum { no, yes, none } answer ;
```

Arrays can also be used. For example:

```
enum response answers[200] ;
```

Values other than 0, 1, and 2 can also be used. For example:

```
enum response { no = -1, yes = 1, none = 0 } ;
```

To add another possible value to response, include the new value within the braces. For example:

```
enum response { no = -1, yes = 1, none = 0, unsure = 2 } ;
```

Programming pitfalls

1. The dimensions of an array are placed between brackets [ ] and not between parentheses ( ).

2. The range of a subscript is 0 to the number of elements in an array less one. It is a common error to define an array with, for example, ten elements and then attempt to use a subscript value of 10. The subscripts in this case range from 0 to 9. For example:

   ```
   int i, a[10] ;
   for ( i = 0 ; i <= 10 ; i++ )
     a[i] = 0 ;
   ```

   This may cause an infinite loop. When i is 10, a[i]=0. However, a[10] does not exist, so 0 is stored in the memory location immediately after a[9]. If the variable i happens to be stored after a[9], then i becomes 0, and so the loop starts again.

3. You cannot compare structure variables in an if statement, even if they have the same structure template. For example, if s1 and s2 are defined as:

   ```
   struct
    {
      int a ;
      int b ;
      float c ;
      } s1, s2 ;
   ```

   The two variables s1 and s2 cannot be tested for equality with the statement:

   ```
   if ( s1 == s2 )     // Invalid.
   ```

   To test s1 and s2 for equality you must test each member of each structure for equality, as in the statement

   ```
   if ( s1.a == s2.a && s1.b == s2.b && s1.c == s2.c )
   ```

Quick syntax reference

	Syntax	Examples

Defining arrays	`type array[d₁][d₂]...[dₙ] ;`
	
	Dimensions $d_1,d_2...d_n$ are integer constants.
		`int a[10] ;`
		
		`float b[5][9] ;`

Array subscripts	`array[i₁][i₂]...[iₙ]`
	
	indexes or subscripts $i_1,i_2...i_n$ are integer constants or variables.
		`a[0] // 1st  element.`
		`a[9] // 10th element.`
		`b[0][0] // Row 1, col 1.`
		`b[4][8] // Row 5, col 9.`

Declaring a structure template	`struct structure_tag_name`
	`{`
	`   type variable₁ ;`
	`   type variable₂ ;`
	`   ...`
	
	`} ;`
		`struct date`
		`{`
		`   int day ;`
		`   int month ;`
		`   int year ;`
		`} ;`

Defining structure variables	`struct struct_name variable₁,`
	`                    variable₂,`
	`                    ...      ;`
		`struct date dob ;`

Accessing structure members	Member selection operator . (Dot operator)	`dob.day ;`

Exercises

1. What are the subscript ranges of the following arrays?
    (a) `int array1[6] ;`
    (b) `float array2[] = { 1.3, 2.9, 11.8, 0 } ;`
    (c) `int array3[6][3] ;`
    (d) `int array4[][4] = { { 6, 2, 1, 3 }, { 7, 3, 8, 1 } } ;`

2. Write statements to define each of the following:
    (a) a one-dimensional array of floating-point numbers with ten elements
    (b) a one-dimensional array of characters with five elements
    (c) a two-dimensional array of integers with seven rows and eight columns
    (d) a 10 by 5 two-dimensional array of double precision numbers
    (e) a 10 by 8 by 15 three-dimensional array of long integers.

3. What is the output from the following program?

    ```
    int i, c1 = 0, c2 = 0 ;
    int a[] = { 6, 7, 3, 13, 11, 5, 1, 15, 9, 4 } ;
    for ( i = 0 ; i < 10 ; i++ )
    {
      if ( i % 2 == 0 )
        c1++ ;
      if ( a[i] % 2 == 0 )
        c2++ ;
    }
    cout << "c1 = " << c1 << "c2 = " << c2 ;
    ```

4. Write a program to read in fifteen numbers from the keyboard and display them as follows:

    (a) each number on a separate line
    (b) on one line, each number separated by a single space
    (c) as in (b) but in the reverse order to which they were input.

5. Write a program to input numbers to two one-dimensional arrays, each having five elements, and display the result of multiplying corresponding elements together.

6. The number of customers entering a shop per hour is recorded for each of the nine hours the shop is open. Write a program to display a report of the form:

Time	Number of customers	Percentage of total
9:00 - 10:00	153	10
10:00 - 11:00	189	12
...	...	...
17:00 - 18:00	135	9

7. The following two arrays represent the fixed and variable costs involved in producing each of eight items:

    ```
    float fixed[]   = { 11.31, 12.12, 13.67, 11.91, 12.30,
                        11.8, 11.00, 12.00 } ;
    ```

```
float variable[] = {  1.12, 1.13, 3.14, 1.35, 2.20, 1.28,
                      1.00, 2.10 } ;
```

Write a program to input an item number in the range 1 to 8 along with the number of units produced. The program should then display the cost of producing that number of units.

8. Use two for loops to set all the diagonal elements of a 9 by 9 integer array to 1 and all the elements not on a diagonal to 0.

9. Write a program to input values to a 4 by 5 array, search the array for values that are less than 0 and display these values along with their row and column indices.

10. Write a program to input ten integer values into an array unsorted. Your program should then loop through unsorted ten times, selecting the lowest value during each pass. For each pass through the loop, the element in unsorted containing the lowest value is replaced with a large value (e.g. 9999) after copying it into the next available element of another integer array sorted.
    This is illustrated below:

    unsorted at the start: 14 22 67 31 89 11 42 35 65 49
        sorted at the start:

    unsorted after the first pass: 14 22 67 31 89 9999 42 35 65 49
        sorted after the first pass: 11

    unsorted after the second pass: 9999 22 67 31 89 9999 42 35 65 49
        sorted after the second pass: 11   14

    etc.

    Display the values in sorted. (Hint: see program P5B to determine the smallest value.)

11. In a magic square the rows, columns and diagonals all have the same sum. For example:

17	24	1	8	15
23	5	7	14	16
4	6	13	20	22
10	12	19	21	3
11	18	25	2	9

and

4	9	2
3	5	7
8	1	6

Write a program to read in a two-dimensional integer array and check if it is a magic square.

12. It is required to scale a ten element floating-point array a so that the maximum element in the array becomes 1, the minimum element becomes 0 and the other elements are scaled to between 0 and 1 according to their values. The following statement computes the scaled value of element a[i]

```
a[i] = ( a[i] - min_value ) / ( max_value - min_value ) ;
```

where `min_value` and `max_value` are the minimum and maximum values in the array a.

Write a program to read in values for the elements of a and display the elements of a scaled to values between 0 and 1.

13. Write a structure template for each of the following:

(a) the time of day using the twenty-hour format, i.e. hours, minutes and seconds
(b) a playing card, such as the five of diamonds or the three of spades. The structure members will be an integer to represent the card value and a character to represent the suit
(c) a transaction record consisting of a transaction type (1 character), the date of the transaction (3 integers), and the amount of the transaction (long int)
(d) the longitude and latitude co-ordinates of a geographical position consisting of degrees (float), and direction ('N', 'S', 'E' or 'W').

14. Given the following definition,

```
struct
{
  int stock_no ;
  float price ;
  long qty ;
} stock ;
```

write statements to

(a) initialise `stock` with values of your choice
(b) input a value to each member of `stock`
(c) display the value of each member of `stock`.

15. Create an enumerated data type for each of the following:

(a) the days of the week: Monday, Tuesday, Wednesday, and so on
(b) the months of the year
(c) monetary denominations
(d) the suits in a pack of cards
(e) the points on a compass.

CHAPTER SIX

Strings

6.1 C-strings

In the C programming language, a string is an array of characters (elements of type `char`) with the null character `'\0'` in the last element of the array. Because it comes from C, this type of string is called a C-string. C-strings are used in many instances in C++.

A C-string is an array of characters and can be initialised in the same way as any other array. For example:

```
char greetings[6] = {'H', 'e', 'l', 'l', 'o', '\0'} ;
```

This statement initialises a six-element `char` array `greetings` with the character constants that spell the word `"Hello"`. Note that the last element of the array `greetings` is the null character (`'\0'`). Without the null character `greetings` is a character array but not a proper C-string.

An easier way to initialise `greetings` is:

```
char greetings[] = "Hello" ;
```

This statement shows that it is not necessary to specify the number of characters in the array or to initialise each element individually. In the definition of the array `greetings`, the compiler determines the size of the array by the number of characters in the array plus 1 (for the null character `'/0'`).

A sequence of characters enclosed in double quotation marks is called a *string literal*. The compiler automatically inserts the null character `'\0'` after the last character of a string literal. The string literal `"Hello"`, for example, actually contains six, rather than five, characters.

Just as with other array types, the individual elements of `greetings` can be accessed using subscripts:

```
greetings[0] is 'H'
greetings[1] is 'e'
```

If you specify the size of the array and the string is shorter than this size, the remaining elements of the array are initialised with the null character `'\0'`. For example

```
char greetings[9] = "Hello" ;
```

initialises `greetings` to:

'H'	'e'	'l'	'l'	'o'	'\0'	'\0'	'\0'	'\0'

To include a double quote inside a string precede the quote with a back slash (`\`). For example,

```
char greetings[] = "\"Hello\", I said." ;
cout << greetings ;
```

will display

```
"Hello", I said.
```

The \\ " is an example of an escape sequence. Further examples of escape sequences are given in appendix F.

The newline ('\n') escape sequence can be used in place of endl to advance to a new line. For example,,

```
cout << "some text\n"
```

is equivalent to

```
cout << "some text" << endl ;
```

If a string is too long to fit onto a single program line, it can be broken up into smaller segments. For example,

```
char long_string[] = "This is the first half of the string "
                     " and this is the second half."
```

6.2 C-string input and output

C-strings may be read and displayed in much the same way as for any other data. There is, however, an important consideration to keep in mind when using C-strings and that is to allow for sufficient storage to hold the string. Remember that the number of elements in the char array must be one more than the number of characters in the string.

The next program is a simple demonstration of C-string input and output. The program inputs a name from the keyboard and displays it on the screen.

```
1  // Program example P6A
2  // Program to read in a string of characters from the keyboard
3  // and to display it on the screen.
4  #include <iostream>
5  using namespace std ;
6
7  void main()
8  {
9    const int MAX_CHARACTERS = 10 ;
10   char first_name[ MAX_CHARACTERS + 1 ] ;
11
12   cout << "Enter your first name (maximum "
13        << MAX_CHARACTERS << " characters) " ;
14   cin >> first_name ;
15   cout << "Hello " << first_name << endl ;
16 }
```

A maximum of 10 characters plus 1 for '\0' is stored in first_name.

The following is a sample run of this program:

```
Enter your first name (maximum 10 characters) John
Hello John
```

Another sample run of this program is:

```
Enter your first name (maximum 10 characters) John Paul
Hello John
```

What happened to Paul? Why was it not displayed?

The extraction operator >> read the characters up to, but not including, the space character after John. The remaining characters (Paul) are left in the input stream and are not extracted.

If the user does not follow the instructions and types in more than 20 characters, the array first_name will overflow, the excess characters will overwrite other areas of memory, and the program will probably malfunction. To allow for this possibility and also to allow for whitespace characters in the input, the getline() function can be used.

```
1   // Program example P6B
2   // Program to read in a string of characters containing whitespaces
3   // from the keyboard and to display it on the screen.
4   #include <iostream>
5   using namespace std ;
6
7   void main()
8   {
9     const int MAX_CHARACTERS = 10 ;
10    char first_name[ MAX_CHARACTERS + 1 ] ;        ◄──── Same number as the
11                                                          dimension of the array.
12    cout << "Enter your first name(maximum "
13         << MAX_CHARACTERS << " characters) " ;  ◄
14    cin.getline( first_name, MAX_CHARACTERS + 1, '\n' ) ;
15    cout << "Hello " << first_name << endl ;
16  }
```

Line 14 reads characters from cin until either the user presses the Enter (or newline) key '\n' or 10 characters have been read. The newline character '\n' is called the delimiter and signifies the end of the input from cin to first_name. The delimiter can be any character. If the delimiter is omitted, it is assumed to be '\n', so line 14 can also be written as

```
   cin.getline( first_name, MAX_CHARACTERS + 1 ) ;
```

The characters are stored in the character array first_name with the null character '\0' automatically added by getline.

Since '\0' is automatically added to the end of an extracted string, the maximum number of characters extracted from the stream by getline is 1 less than specified. The number of characters specified should not be more than the number of elements in the character array or the array will overflow into other areas of memory.

The function getline() is a member function of the input stream object cin. It is more powerful than the extraction operator >>, since it allows the input of characters to stop after a specified delimiter is read.

There is another problem that can arise when inputting data from the keyboard. The following program inputs a student number and a name from the keyboard and displays it on the screen.

```
1  // Program example P6C
2  // Program to read in a student number and name from the keyboard.
3  #include <iostream>
4  using namespace std ;
5
6  void main()
7  {
8    const int MAX_CHARACTERS = 20 ;
9    char student_name[ MAX_CHARACTERS + 1 ] ;
10   int student_number ;
11
12   cout << "Enter student number: " ;
13   cin >> student_number ;
14   cout << "Enter student first name and surname (maximum "
15        << MAX_CHARACTERS << " characters) " ;
16   cin.getline( student_name, MAX_CHARACTERS + 1 ) ;
17   cout << endl << "Data Entered:" << endl
18        << "Student Number: " << student_number << endl
19        << "Student Name: " << student_name << endl ;
20 }
```

A sample run of this program follows:

```
Enter student number: 12345  ◄──────── Enter pressed here is read as the name.
Enter student first name and surname (maximum 20 characters)
Data Entered:
Student Number: 12345
Student Name: ◄──────────────────────────
```

The prompt on line 14 is displayed correctly but line 16 seems to be skipped and no name is read in from the keyboard.

The problem is as follows:

Line 13 stops reading into the numeric variable `student_number` as soon as a non-numeric character is read.

The Enter key that is pressed after typing 12345 is left in the input stream, which is then read by `getline()` on line 16 into `student_name`.

That's why the program didn't wait for the user to enter a name and why line 19 displayed an empty string.

One solution to this problem is to read the newline character `'\n'` into a 'dummy' character variable. For example, after line 13 include the line:

```
char dummy ; cin.get( dummy ) ;
```

This will work provided the user doesn't type any superfluous characters (e.g. spaces) after the student number before pressing Enter. If a space is typed after the student number, then it will be read into `dummy` and the `'\n'` will remain in the input stream.

The complete solution to the problem is to discard or ignore all characters in the input stream up to and including the newline character `'\n'`. Only then should `getline()` be used to read data into `student_name`.

This can be accomplished by using the `ignore()` function, as shown in the next program.

```
1  // Program example P6D
2  // Corrected program to read in a student number
3  // and name from the keyboard.
4  #include <iostream>
5  using namespace std ;
6
7  void main()
8  {
9    const int MAX_CHARACTERS = 20 ;
10   char student_name[ MAX_CHARACTERS + 1 ] ;
11   int student_number ;
12
13   cout << "Enter student number: " ;
14   cin >> student_number ;
15   cout << "Enter student first name and surname (maximum "
16        << MAX_CHARACTERS << " characters) ";
17   cin.ignore( 80,'\n' ) ;
18   cin.getline( student_name, MAX_CHARACTERS + 1 ) ;
19   cout << endl << "Data Entered:" << endl
20        << "Student Number: "<< student_number << endl
21        << "Student Name: "<< student_name << endl ;
22 }
```

Execution of cin.ignore(80, '\n') on line 17 removes at most 80 characters up to and including the newline character '\n' from the input stream. The maximum number of characters to remove is usually set to 80 for keyboard input, but this may be changed if required.

6.3 Accessing individual characters of a C-string
As a C-string is an array of characters, each character of a C-string can be accessed using an index. The next program displays each character of the string "hello" on separate lines.

```
1  // Program example P6E
2  // Accessing each character of a C-string.
3  #include <iostream>
4  using namespace std ;
5
6  void main()
7  {
8    char greetings[6] = "Hello" ;
9    // Display each character of greetings on a new line.
10   for ( int i = 0 ; i < 5 ; i++ )
11     cout << greetings[i] << endl ;
12 }
```

This program will display the following lines:

```
H
e
l
l
o
```

6.4 C-string functions

C++ has inherited a library of C-string functions from the C programming language. To use any of these functions it is necessary to include the following line in the program;

```
#include <cstring>
```

6.4.1 Finding the length of a C-string

The standard library function `strlen()` returns the number of characters in a C-string, excluding the null character `'\0'`.

Example:

```
char name1[]    = "Sharon";
char name2[10] = "Mark";
int len ;
len = strlen( name1 ) ;
cout << setw( 3 ) << strlen( name1 )
     << setw( 3 ) << strlen( name2 )
     << setw( 3 ) << strlen( "Rob" )
     << setw( 3 ) << len ;
```

This will display:

```
 6   4   3   6
```

The general format of the `strlen()` function is:

```
len = strlen( str )
```

where `str` is a null-terminated string and `len` is an integer. (A null-terminated string is a string of characters ending with the null character `'\0'`.)

6.4.2 Copying a C-string

The C-string copy function, `strcpy( str1, str2 )`, copies the contents of a C-string `str2` to another C-string `str1`.
Example:

```
char name1[] = "Sharon" ;
char name2[10] = "Mark" ;
// Copy the contents of name1 to name2.
strcpy( name2, name1 ) ;
// Restore the original name.
strcpy( name2, "Mark" ) ;
```

The general format of `strcpy()` is:

```
strcpy( destination, source ) ;
```

where the source string is copied to the destination string. The source string must be null-terminated, i.e. a `'\0'` must be at the end of the string. The `strcpy()` function assumes that the destination string is big enough to hold the string being copied to it. No checking is performed, so beware!

6.4.3 C-string concatenation

The function strcat(str1, str2) concatenates a C-string str2 to the end of the C-string str1. Both str1 and str2 must be null-terminated. Enough memory must be allocated to str1 to hold the result of the concatenation.

Example:

```
char str1[15] = "first & " ;
char str2[] = "second" ;
strcat( str1, str2 ) ; // str1 is now "first & second".
                       // str2 is unchanged.
```

6.4.4 Comparing C-strings

The function strcmp(str1, str2) compares two null-terminated C-strings str1 and str2. This function returns a negative value if the string in str1 is less than the string in str2, 0 if the string in str1 is equal to the string in str2, and a positive value if the string in str1 is greater than the string in str2.

The next program demonstrates strcmp().

```
1  // Program example P6F
2  // Program to demonstrate strcmp() for comparing C-strings.
3  #include <iostream>
4  using namespace std ;
5
6  void main()
7  {
8    char password[7] = "secret" ;
9    char user_input[81] ;
10   cout << "Enter Password: " ;
11   cin >> user_input ;
12   if ( strcmp( password, user_input ) == 0 )
13     cout << "Correct password. Welcome to the system ..." << endl ;
14   else
15     cout << "Invalid password" << endl ;
16 }
```

In this program the user types in a password, which is stored in user_input. Line 12 compares the user_input with the internal password "secret" held in password. The function strcmp() will return 0 if there is an exact match and a welcome message is displayed; otherwise an error message is displayed.

6.4.5 Other C-string functions

```
strncat( str1, str2, n )
```
Appends the first n characters of the C-string str2 to the C-string str1.

```
strncmp( str1, str2, n )
```
Identical to strcmp(str1, str2), except that at most, n characters are compared.

```
strncpy( str1, str2, n )
```
Copies n characters of str2 into str1.

6.4.6 Converting numeric C-strings to numbers

Each character of the string "123" is stored in one byte of memory in the ASCII representation, as shown below.

Character:	'1'	'2'	'3'	'\0'
ASCII value in decimal:	49	50	51	0
ASCII value in binary:	00110001	00110010	00110011	00000000

This is very different from the way in which an integer value of 123 is stored. Integer values are held in binary, not ASCII format. An integer value of 123 is represented in binary as:

00000000	01111011

The functions `atoi()`, `atol()` and `atof()` convert a numeric C-string to its binary equivalent. To use any of these functions, include the preprocessor directive:

```
#include <cstdlib>
```

at the beginning of the program.

Example:

```
char str[] = "123" ;
int int_number ;
long long_number ;
double double_number ;

int_number = atoi( str ) ;    // C-string to an integer.
long_number = atol( str ) ;   // C-string to a long integer.
double_number = atof( str ) ; // C-string to a double float.
```

These functions will ignore any leading whitespace characters and stop converting when a character that cannot be part of the number is reached. For example, `atoi()` will stop when it reaches a decimal point, but `atof()` will accept a decimal point, because it can be part of a decimal number.

6.5 C++ strings

The C-strings discussed above can be awkward to use and tend to be error-prone. Common errors include attempting to access elements outside the array bounds, not using the function `strcpy()` to one C-string to another and not using `strcmp()` to compare two C-strings.

In addition to using C-strings, the newer and more convenient C++ strings can also be used. This doesn't mean that C-strings can be completely ignored. On the contrary, C-strings are still important because of the large quantity of software written in C++ using C-strings.

The next program demonstrates C++ strings by prompting the user for a password and checking it against the correct password held in memory.

```
1  // Program example P6G
2  // Program to demonstrate the C++ string type.
3  #include <iostream>
4  #include <string>
5  using namespace std ;
6
7  void main()
8  {
9    string password = "secret" ;
10   string user_input ;
11   cout << "Enter Password: " ;
12   cin >> user_input ;
13   if ( password == user_input )
14     cout << "Correct password. Welcome to the system ..." << endl ;
15   else
16     cout << "Invalid password" << endl ;
17 }
```

A sample run of this program follows.

```
Enter Password: secret
Correct password. Welcome to the system ...
```

To use C++ strings, the program must contain the line 4:

```
#include <string>
```

The string data type is not built into C++ like other data types such as int, float and char. In C++ the string data type is defined by a class. Although classes are not discussed until chapter 8, it is not necessary to know the details of a class in order to use it. This, in fact, is one of the strengths of a class. Suffice for the moment to say that a class introduces a new data type into a language. The new data type can then be used like any of the built-in data types.

Line 9 defines a string called password and initialises it to the correct password "secret". This is analogous to defining and initialising a variable of a built-in data type.
Line 10 defines another string called user_input with no initial value assigned.

Line 12 reads a value for user_input and line 13 checks if this value is identical to the correct password "secret", held in the string variable password. Note that there is no need for strcmp() when comparing C++ strings as there is when comparing C-strings. C++ strings are compared using the same relational operators (=, <, >, etc) as the built-in (int, float etc) data types.

Compare this program with the equivalent program P6F to see how much easier it is to use C++ strings rather than C-strings.

There are many useful functions associated with C++ strings, making them more powerful and convenient than C-strings. These functions are called string member functions. The following programs demonstrate a selection of string member functions.

6.5.1 `string` initialisation and assignment

```
1   // Program example P6H
2   // Program to demonstrate C++ string initialisation and assignment.
3   #include <iostream>
4   #include <string>
5   using namespace std ;
6
7   void main()
8   {
9       // String initialisation examples.
10      string str1 = "ABCDEFGHI" ; // Define a string and initialise it.
11      string str2( 11, '-' ) ;    // Define a string of 11 dashes.
12      string str3 = "This is the first part"
13                    " and this is the second part." ;
14      string str4 = str2 ;  // Initialise str4 with str2.
15      string str5 ; // str5 has no initial value.
16
17      cout << "After initialisations:" << endl
18          << "  str1=" << str1 << endl
19          << "  str2=" << str2 << endl
20          << "  str3=" << str3 << endl
21          << "  str4=" << str4 << endl
22          << "  str5=" << str5 << endl ;
23
24      // String assignment examples.
25      str1 = "ABCD" ;
26      str2.assign( 3, '.' ) ; // Assign 3 dots to str2.
27      cout << "After the 1st and 2nd assignments:" << endl
28          << "  str1=" << str1 << endl
29          << "  str2=" << str2 << endl ;
30      // Can also assign a part of another string (a sub-string).
31      // Assign 3 characters, starting at the character with index 1.
32      // The index starts at 0, so index 1 is the 2nd character.
33      str5.assign( str1, 1, 3 ) ;  // Assign "BCD" to str5.
34      cout << "After the 3rd assignment:" << endl
35          << "  str5=" << str5 << endl ;
36
37      // Swapping strings.
38      cout << "Before swapping str1 and str2:"  << endl
39          << "  str1=" << str1 << endl
40          << "  str2=" << str2 << endl ;
41      str1.swap( str2 ) ; // swap str1 and str2.
42      cout << "After swapping str1 and str2:"  << endl
43          << "  str1=" << str1 << endl
44          << "  str2=" << str2 << endl ;
45  }
```

The output from this program is:

```
After initialisations:
  str1=ABCDEFGHI
  str2=-----------
  str3=This is the first part and this is the second part.
  str4=-----------
```

```
  str5=
After the 1st and 2nd assignments:
  str1=ABCD
  str2=...
After the 3rd assignment:
  str5=BCD
Before swapping str1 and str2:
  str1=ABCD
  str2=...
After swapping str1 and str2:
  str1=...
  str2=ABCD
```

Line 10 defines and initialises a C++ string str1.
Line 11 shows how to assign a C++ string with a number of identical characters.
As shown on lines 12 and 13, the string that is being assigned can be on two or more lines. This is useful for assigning a long string of characters to a C++ string.
Line 14 shows how to define and initialise a C++ string with a previously defined C++ string.
On line 15, str5 is defined but is not given an initial value; str5 is called an empty string.

Line 25 is a simple assignment of a character string to str1.
Line 26 uses the string member function assign() to give str2 a value of "...".
Line 33 uses assign() to assign part of str1 to str5. The values in parentheses are the string to assign from, the starting position and the number of characters to assign. The position in the C++ string starts at 0, so that the first character is in position 0, the second character is in position 1 etc.

Line 41 demonstrates the string member function swap() by swapping the two strings str1 and str2. The same can be achieved by the following:

```
  string temp = str1 ;
  str1 = str2;
  str2 = temp ;
```

6.5.2 string concatenation

```
1   // Program example P6I
2   // Program to demonstrate C++ string concatenation.
3   #include <iostream>
4   #include <string>
5   using namespace std ;
6
7   void main()
8   {
9      string str1 = "ABCD", str2, str3 ;
10
11     str2.assign( 3, '.' ) ; // Assign 3 dots to str2.
12
13   // Concatenate str2 to str1 and assign to str3.
14     str3 = str1 + str2 ;  // With strings, + means concatenate.
15     cout << "After the 1st concatenation:" << endl
16          << "   str1=" << str1 << endl
17          << "   str2=" << str2 << endl
```

```
18              << " str3=" << str3 << endl ;
19
20    // Can also use += to concatenate.
21    str3 += "etc." ;    // same as str3 = str3 + "etc."
22    cout << "After the 2nd concatenation:" << endl
23              << " str3=" << str3 << endl ;
24
25    // Can also use append to concatenate.
26    str3.append ( ", etc., etc." ) ;
27    cout << "After the 3rd concatenation:" << endl
28              << " str3=" << str3 << endl ;
29
30    // Can also append a sub-string.
31    string str4 = "It is near the end of the program." ;
32    str3 = "This is " ;
33    // Append 7 characters, starting at the 12th character position.
34    str3.append( str4, 11, 7 ) ;  // Append "the end" to str3.
35    cout << "After the 4th concatenation:" << endl
36              << " str3=" << str3 << endl ;
37
38    // Finally append a repetition of a character.
39    str3.append( 3, '.' ) ;  // Append 3 dots.
40    cout << "After the 5th concatenation:" << endl
41              << " str3=" << str3 << endl ;
42 }
```

The output from this program is:

```
After the 1st concatenation:
  str1=ABCD
  str2=...
  str3=ABCD...
After the 2nd concatenation:
  str3=ABCD...etc.
After the 3rd concatenation:
  str3=ABCD...etc., etc., etc.
After the 4th concatenation:
  str3=This is the end
After the 5th concatenation:
  str3=This is the end...
```

6.5.3 `string length`, `string` indexing and sub-strings

```
1  // Program example P6J
2  // Program demonstrates
3  // (a) how to get the length of a  C++ string
4  // (b) how to access each individual character of a C++ string
5  // (c) how to get a part (a sub-string) of a string using substr().
6  #include <iostream>
7  #include <string>
8  using namespace std ;
9
10 void main()
11 {
12    string str1 = "ABCDEFGH" ;
```

```
13    int len1 ;
14
15    len1 = str1.length() ;  // Store the length of str1 in len1.
16
17    // Can access each character of a string - like C-strings
18    // e.g. change the first and last characters.
19    str1[0] = '*' ;
20    str1[len1-1] = '*' ;
21    // Index start at 0 and ends at (len1-1).
22    // No index checking is done using [].
23
24    // It is much safer to check the index value to ensure it is
25    // not out of range by using the string member function at().
26    str1.at( 0 ) = 'A' ;
27    str1.at( len1 - 1 ) = 'H' ;
28
29    // Display a space between each character of str1.
30    cout << str1 << " with a space between each character:" << endl ;
31    for ( int i = 0 ; i < len1 ; i++ )
32      cout << str1.at( i ) << ' ' ;
33     cout << endl ;
34
35    // Demonstration of substr() to extract part of a C++ string.
36    // The 1st argument is a starting position and the 2nd
37    // argument is the number of characters to extract.
38    string str2 = "ABCDEFGH" ;
39    cout << "Demonstration of substr:" << endl << "   " ;
40    cout << "The first four characters of " << str2<< " are "
41         << str2.substr( 0, 4 ) << endl << "   "
42         << "The middle two characters of " << str2 << " are "
43         << str2.substr( 3, 2 ) << endl << "   "
44         << "The last three characters of " << str2 << " are "
45         << str2.substr( 5,3 ) << endl ;
46 }
```

The output from this program is:

```
ABCDEFGH with a space between each character:
A B C D E F G H
Demonstration of substr:
   The first four characters of ABCDEFGH are ABCD
   The middle two characters of ABCDEFGH are DE
   The last three characters of ABCDEFGH are FGH
```

6.5.4 string replace, erase, insert and empty strings

```
1  // Program example P6K
2  // Program to demonstrate replace, erase, insert and empty.
3  #include <iostream>
4  #include <string>
5  using namespace std ;
6
7  void main()
8  {
9    string str1 = "ABCDE" ;
```

```
10    string str2 = "abcdefghij" ;
11
12    // Replace 3 characters from str1
13    // starting at the 2nd character position with 4 characters
14    // from str2, starting at the 3rd character position.
15    // N.B. character at position 0 is the first character.
16    str1.replace( 1, 3, str2, 2, 4 ) ;
17    cout << "After the 1st replacement:" << endl
18         << "  str1=" << str1 << endl ;
19
20    // Replace 3 characters from str1
21    // starting at the 2nd character position
22    // with all the characters from str2.
23    str1 = "ABCDE" ;
24    str1.replace( 1, 3, str2 ) ;
25    cout << "After the 2nd replacement:" << endl
26         << "  str1=" << str1 << endl ;
27
28    // Erase from the 10th character position to the end of str1.
29    str1.erase( 9 ) ;
30    cout << "After the 1st erase:" << endl
31         << "  str1=" << str1 << endl ;
32
33    // Erase 2 characters starting at the 5th character position.
34    str1.erase( 4, 2 ) ;
35    cout << "After the 2nd erase:" << endl
36         << "  str1=" << str1 << endl ;
37
38    // Erase the entire string.
39    str1.erase() ;
40    cout << "After the 3rd erase:" << endl
41         << "  str1=" << str1 << endl ;
42
43    // Are any characters in str1?
44    if ( str1.empty() )   // empty returns TRUE or FALSE
45      cout << "str1 is empty" << endl ;
46    else
47      cout << "str1 is not empty" << endl ;
48 }
49    // Starting at the 2nd character of str2, insert 6 characters
50    // at the 5th character position of str1.
51    str1 = "ABCDEFG" ;
52    str1.insert( 4, str2, 1, 6 ) ;
53    cout << "After the 1st insert:" << endl
54         << "  str1=" << str1 << endl ;
55
56    // Insert the entire str2
57    // at the 4th character position of str1.
58    str1 = "ABCDEFG" ;
59    str1.insert( 3, str2 ) ;
60    cout << "After the 2nd insert:" << endl
61         << "  str1=" << str1 << endl ;
62 }
63
```

The output from this program is:

```
After the 1st replacement:
  str1=AcdefE
After the 2nd replacement:
  str1=AabcdefghijE
After the 1st erase:
  str1=Aabcdefgh
After the 2nd erase:
  str1=Aabcfgh
After the 3rd erase:
  str1=
str1 is empty
After the 1st insert:
  str1=ABCDbcdefgEFG
After the 2nd insert:
  str1=ABCabcdefghijDEFG
```

6.5.5 string searching

```
1   // Program example P6L
2   // Program to demonstrate string searching.
3   #include <iostream>
4   #include <string>
5   using namespace std ;
6
7   void main()
8   {
9     string str1 = "ABCDEFABCDEF" ;
10    int p ;
11
12    // Find the first occurrence of "CDE" in str1.
13    p = str1.find( "CDE" ) ;
14    // The variable p holds the position of the
15    // first occurrence of "CDE" in str1.
16    // If "CDE" is not in str1, p = -1.
17    cout << "Results of 1st search:" << endl << "  " ;
18    if ( p == -1 )
19      cout << "CDE Not Found in str1" << endl ;
20    else
21      cout << "First Occurrence of CDE Found at " << p << endl ;
22
23    // Reverse find - the last occurrence of "CDE"
24    p = str1.rfind( "CDE" ) ;
25    cout << "Results of 2nd search:" << endl << "  " ;
26    if ( p == -1 )
27      cout << "CDE Not Found" << endl ;
28    else
29      cout << "Last Occurrence of CDE Found at " << p << endl ;
30
31    // Find the first occurrence of any one of a number of characters.
32    p = str1.find_first_of( "ED" ) ; // Find either E or D.
33    cout << "Results of 3rd search:" << endl << "  " ;
34    if ( p == -1 )
35      cout << "E or D Not Found in str1" << endl ;
```

```
36    else
37      cout << "E or D First Found at " << p << endl ;
38
39    // Find the last occurrence of any one of a number of characters.
40    p = str1.find_last_of( "ED" ) ;
41    cout << "Results of 4th search:" << endl << "  ";
42    if ( p == -1 )
43      cout << "E or D Not Found in str1" << endl ;
44    else
45      cout << "E or D Last Found at " << p << endl ;
46
47    // Find the first occurrence of any character that is not
48    // one of a number of characters.
49    p = str1.find_first_not_of( "ABC" ) ;
50    cout << "Results of 4th search:" << endl << "  " ;
51    if ( p == -1 )
52      cout << "No Characters Other than A, B or C Found in str1"
53            << endl ;
54    else
55      cout << "A Character Other than A, B or C First Found at "
56            << p << endl ;
57
58    // Find the last occurrence of any character that is not
59    // one of a number of characters.
60    p = str1.find_last_not_of( "ABC" ) ;
61    cout << "Results of 5th search:" << endl << "  " ;
62    if ( p == -1 )
63      cout << "No Characters Other Than A, B or C Found in str1"
64            << endl ;
65    else
66      cout << "A Character Other Than A, B or C Last Found at "
67            << p << endl ;
68 }
```

The output from this program is:

```
Results of 1st search:
  First Occurrence of CDE Found at 2
Results of 2nd search:
  Last Occurrence of CDE Found at 8
Results of 3rd search:
  E or D First Found at 3
Results of 4th search:
  E or D Last Found at 10
Results of 4th search:
  A Character Other than A, B or C First Found at 3
Results of 5th search:
  A Character Other Than A, B or C Last Found at 11
```

6.5.6 string comparisons

```
1   // Program example P6M
2   // Program to demonstrate string comparisons.
3   // Strings are compared on the basis of the ASCII codes of their
4   // individual characters.
5   #include <iostream>
6   #include <string>
7   using namespace std ;
8
9   void main()
10  {
11     string str1 = "ABCDEFGH" ;
12     string str2 = "BCD" ;
13     int result ;
14
15     result= str1.compare( str2 ) ;
16     // result is < 0 if the first differing character in str1 is less
17     // than the character in the same position in str2.
18     // result = 0 if all the characters of str1 and str2
19     // are equal and the two strings are the same length.
20     // Otherwise result is > 0.
21     cout << "After the 1st compare:" << endl << "  " ;
22     if ( result == 0 )
23       cout << "str1 and str2 are equal" << endl ;
24     if ( result < 0 )
25       cout << "str1 is less than str2" << endl ;
26     if ( result > 0 )
27       cout << "str1 is greater than str2" << endl ;
28
29     // Can also compare a sub-string with a string.
30     // For example, compare the 3 character sub-string of str1
31     // starting at the second character, with all characters of str2.
32     result = str1.compare( 1, 3, str2 ) ;
33     cout << "After the 2nd compare:" << endl << "  " ;
34     if ( result == 0 )
35       cout << "Characters 2,3 and 4 of str1" << endl <<
36               "  and all the characters of str2 are equal" << endl ;
37     if ( result < 0 )
38       cout << "Characters 2,3 and 4 of str1 are less than" << endl <<
39               "  all the characters of str2" << endl ;
40     if ( result > 0 )
41       cout << "Characters 2,3 and 4 of str1 are greater than"
42             << endl << "  all the characters of str2" << endl ;
43
44     // Can also compare sub-strings.
45     // For example, compare the 2 character sub-string of str1
46     // starting at the second character,
47     // with the 2 character sub-string of str2,
48     // starting at the first character.
49     result = str1.compare( 1, 2, str2, 0, 2 ) ;
50     cout << "After the 3rd compare:" << endl << "  " ;
51     if ( result == 0 )
52       cout << "Characters 2 and 3 of str1 " << endl <<
53               "  and characters 1 and 2 of str2 are equal" << endl ;
```

```
54   if ( result < 0 )
55     cout << "Characters 2 and 3 of str1 are less than" << endl <<
56            "  characters 1 and 2 of str2" << endl ;
57   if ( result > 0 )
58     cout << "Characters 2 and 3 of str1 are greater than"
59           << endl << "  characters 1 and 2 of str2" << endl ;
60 }
```

The output from this program is:

```
After the 1st compare:
  str1 is less than str2
After the 2nd compare:
  Characters 2,3 and 4 of str1
  and all the characters of str2 are equal
After the 3rd compare:
  Characters 2 and 3 of str1
  and characters 1 and 2 of str2 are equal
```

6.5.7 **string input**

```
1    // Program example P6N
2    // Program to demonstrate C++ string input.
3    #include <iostream>
4    #include <string>
5    using namespace std ;
6
7    void main()
8    {
9      string str1, str2 ;
10
11     // getline reads all characters up to a delimiter.
12     cout << "Demonstration of getline:" << endl ;
13     cout << "  Type a string and press Enter:" ;
14     getline( cin, str1, '\n' ) ;
15     // The 3rd argument is the delimiter. If omitted the delimiter
16     // is assumed to be '\n'. The above can also be written as
17     // getline( cin, str1 ) ;
18     cout << "  You typed:" << str1 << endl ;
19
20     // Demonstration of input stream operator >>
21     // >> skips any leading whitespace characters,
22     // then reads input until a whitespace character is read
23     // i.e. >> reads a word.
24     cout << "Demonstration of >>:" << endl ;
25     cout << "  Type a string and press Enter:" ;
26     cin >> str2 ;
27     cout << "  You typed:" << str2 << endl ;
28 }
```

A sample run of this program follows.

```
Demonstration of getline:
  Type a string and press Enter:This is a string with whitespaces
  You typed:This is a string with whitespaces
```

```
Demonstration of >>:
  Type a string and press Enter:    This is a string
  Type a string a
  You typed:This
```

6.5.8 string conversions

```
1    // Program example P60
2    // Program to demonstrate C++ string conversions to and from
3    // C-strings.
4    #include <iostream>
5    #include <string>
6    using namespace std ;
7
8    void main()
9    {
10     char c_string[6] ;
11     string cpp_string  = "ABCDE" ;
12     int len ;
13
14     len = cpp_string.length() ;
15     // Convert a C++ string to a C-string.
16     cpp_string.copy( c_string, len ) ;
17     // C-strings have a '\0' at the end.
18     c_string[len] = '\0' ;
19     cout << "Results of 1st conversion:" << endl << "   " ;
20     cout << "The C-string is:" << c_string << endl ;
21
22     // Convert the 2 character sub-string of cpp_string
23     // starting at the first character.
24     cpp_string.copy( c_string, 2, 0 ) ;
25     c_string[2] = '\0' ;
26     cout << "Results of 2nd conversion:" << endl << "   " ;
27     cout << "The C-string is:" << c_string << endl ;
28
29     strcpy ( c_string, "abcde" ) ;
30
31     // Convert a C-string to a standard c++ string.
32     // A simple assignment is all that is required.
33     cout << "Results of 3rd conversion:" << endl << "   " ;
34     cpp_string = c_string ;
35     cout << "The C++ string is:" << cpp_string << endl ;
36     // Note: A string literal such as "ABCDE" is in fact a C-string,
37     // so line 11 is another example of converting a C-string to a
38     // C++ string.
39   }
```

The output from this program is:

```
Results of 1st conversion:
  The C-string is:ABCDE
Results of 2nd conversion:
  The C-string is:AB
Results of 3rd conversion:
  The C++ string is:abcde
```

6.6 Arrays of strings

Just like any other data type, arrays of C-strings and arrays of C++ strings can be defined. Arrays of C++ strings are much easier to work with and are demonstrated in the next program.

```
1   // Program example P6P
2   // Program to demonstrate an array of C++ strings.
3   #include <iostream>
4   #include <string>
5   using namespace std ;
6
7   void main()
8   {
9       // Define an array of twelve strings.
10      string months[12] = { "January", "February", "March",
11                            "April", "May", "June", "July",
12                            "August", "September", "October",
13                            "November", "December" } ;
14
15      // Display the months of the year.
16      cout <<  "The months of the year are:" << endl ;
17      for ( int i = 0 ; i < 12 ; i++ )
18        cout << months[i] << endl ;
19  }
```

Lines 10 to 13 define and initialise an array of C++ strings. The first element of the array, months[0], contains "January", the second element, months[1], contains "February", and so forth.

The loop in lines 17 to 18 displays each element of the array.

6.7 Character classification

There are a number of C++ functions that can be used to test the value of a single character. These functions return a true (non-zero integer) value or a false (zero integer) value depending on whether or not the character belongs to a particular set of characters.

Function	Character set
isalnum	Alphanumeric character: A–Z, a–z, 0–9
isalpha	Alphabetic character: A–Z, a–z
isascii	ASCII character: ASCII codes 0–127
iscntrl	Control character: ASCII codes 0–31 or 127
isdigit	Decimal digit: 0–9
isgraph	Any printable character other than a space
islower	Lowercase letter: a–z
isprint	Any printable character, including a space
ispunct	Any punctuation character

isspace	Whitespace character: \t,\v,\f,\r,\n or space ASCII codes 9–13 or 32
isupper	Uppercase letter: A–Z
isxdigit	Hexadecimal digit: 0–9 and A–F

Example:

```
char ch ;
cin >> ch ;

if ( isupper( ch ) )
   cout<< ch << " is an uppercase character" << endl ;
```

C++ has also two further functions that are used to covert the case of a character: tolower and toupper.

Function	Purpose
tolower	Converts an uppercase character to lowercase.
toupper	Converts a lowercase character to uppercase.

Example:

```
char ch = 'a' ;
ch = toupper( ch ) ;
cout << "Convert to uppercase " <<  ch << endl ;
ch = tolower( ch ) ;
cout << "Back to lowercase " << ch << endl ;
```

As a practical example, the following program inputs a name and displays the name with the first letter of the forename and surname capitalised. The program assumes that the forename and surname are separated by at least one space.

```
1   // Program example P6Q
2   // Program to input a name and capitalise the first letter
3   // of the forename and surname.
4   #include <iostream>
5   #include <string>
6   using namespace std ;
7
8   void main()
9   {
10    string in_name ;
11
12    cout << "Type a name and press Enter: " ;
13    getline( cin, in_name ) ;
14
15    // Capitalise the first character.
16    in_name[0] = toupper( in_name[0] ) ;
```

```
17
18    int i = 1 ;
19    // Ignore all characters until a space is reached.
20    while( !isspace( in_name[i] ) )
21      i++ ;
22
23    // Ignore all characters until the first letter of the surname
24    // is reached.
25    while( !isalpha( in_name[i] ) )
26      i++ ;
27
28    // Capitalise the first letter of the surname.
29    in_name[i] = toupper( in_name[i] ) ;
30
31    cout << "Formatted Name: " << in_name << endl ;
32 }
```

A sample run of this program is:

```
Type a name and press Enter: john smith
Formatted Name: John Smith
```

Programming pitfalls

1. Double quotation marks (") are used for string literals; single quotation marks (') are used for character constants. For example, "abcd" and 'e'.

2. When you allocate space for a C-string you must allow for the terminating null character '\0'. For example, to store a C-string of twenty characters you must define a character array with twenty-one elements.

3. When using strcpy(str1, str2) to copy C-strings, the string str2 is copied to the string str1, and not the other way around.

4. To compare two C-strings use strcmp(). For example, if str1 and str2 are C- strings, then the statement

    ```
    if ( str1 == str2 ) // OK for C++ strings, not for C strings.
    ```

    is incorrect. The correct statement is

    ```
    if ( strcmp(str1, str2 ) == 0 )
    ```

5. Accessing a character in a string that is outside the bounds of the array. To avoid this error use the string member function at().

Quick syntax reference

	Syntax	Examples

To define a C-string	`char c_string[n+1] ;`
	
	`// n is the number of characters`
	`// in the string.`
		`char c_str[11] ;`
		`// c_str can hold ten`
		`// characters plus the`
		`// null character '\0'.`

C-string input	`cin >> c_string ;`
	
	`cin.getline( c_string, n+1, delim ) ;`
	`// n is the number of characters`
	`// in the string.`
	`// delim is the delimiter,`
	`// default value is '\n'`
		`cin >> c_str ;`
		
		`cin.getline( c_str, 11 ) ;`

C-string length	`size = strlen( c_string ) ;`	`len = strlen( c_str ) ;`

Comparing C-strings	`strcmp( c_string1, c_string2 )`	`if ( strcmp(c_str1,c_str2)`
		`    == 0 )`
		`    cout << "Identical" ;`

Copying a C-string	`strcpy( destination, source ) ;`	`// Copy c_str2 to c_str1.` `strcpy( c_str1, c_str2 ) ;`
To define a C++ string	`string variable_name ;`	`string cpp_str ;`

C++ string input	`cin >> variable_name ;`
	
	`getline( cin, variable_name, delim ) ;`
	`// delim is the delimiter,`
	`// default value is '\n'.`
		`cin >> cpp_str ;`
		
		`getline( cin, cpp_str ) ;`

C++ string length	`size = variable_name.length() ;`	`len = cpp_str.length() ;`

Exercises

1. What is the output from the following program segment?

    ```
    char str1[] = "abc" ;
    char str2[] = "ABCD" ;
    cout << str1 << endl << strlen( str1 ) << endl ;
    if ( strcmp( str1, str2 ) == 0 )
      cout << str1 << "==" << str2 << endl ;
    else
      if ( strcmp( str1, str2 ) < 0 )
        cout << str1 << "<" << str2 << endl ;
    else
      if ( strcmp( str1, str2 ) > 0 )
        cout << str1 << ">" << str2 << endl ;
    char str3[8] ;
    strcpy( str3, str1 ) ;
    strcat ( str3, str2 ) ;
    cout << str3 << endl << strlen( str3 ) << endl ;
    str3[6] = 'x' ;
    cout << str3 << endl ;
    ```

2. Modify exercise 1 to use C++ strings rather than C-strings.

3. Given the following,

    ```
    char c_str1[18] ;
    char c_str2[6] = "abcde" ;
    ```

    what is in c_str1 after each of the following?

    (a) strcpy(c_str1, "A string") ;
    (b) strcat(c_str1, " of text.") ;
    (c) strncpy(c_str1, c_str2, 1) ;

4. Write a program to input a C-string from the keyboard and replace each space in the string with the character '_'.

5. What is the output from the following program segment?

    ```
    string str = "ABCDEFGHIJ" ;
    cout << str << endl << str.length() << endl ;
    str.replace( 4, 2, "123456" ) ;
    str.at( 3 ) = '0' ;
    cout << str << endl << str.length() << endl ;
    str.erase( 10, 2 ) ;
    cout << str << endl << str.length() << endl ;
    cout << str.substr( 3, 7 ) << endl ;
    str += "KLMN" ;
    cout << str << endl << str.length() << endl ;
    str.insert( 10, "7890" ) ;
    cout << str << endl << str.length() << endl ;
    cout << str.find( "0" ) << endl ;
    ```

6. Read in three names from the keyboard and display them in alphabetical order.

7. Write a program to read in a line of text from the keyboard and calculate the average length of the words in that line. Assume each word in the line is separated from the next by at least one space. Allow for punctuation marks. Use C++ strings.

8. Modify exercise 7 to display the number of words in the line with lengths of
   (a) 1
   (b) 2 to 5
   (c) 6 to 10
   (d) 11 to 20
   (e) 21 and above.

9. Write a program to ask a user for their name. The user's name is then compared with a list of names held in an array in memory. If the user's name is in this list, display a suitable greeting; otherwise display the message "Name not found".

10. Write a program to input a string. If every character in the string is a digit ('0' to '9'), then convert the string to an integer, add 1 to it, and display the result. If any one of the characters in the string is not a digit, display an error message.

11. The following is a list of countries and their capital cities.

Australia	Canberra
Belgium	Brussels
Denmark	Copenhagen
England	London
France	Paris
Greece	Athens
Ireland	Dublin
Scotland	Edinburgh
Wales	Cardiff

Write a program to input a country and display the capital city of that country.

12. Initialise an array of strings with the following quotations:

"There is no reason for any individual to have a computer in their home."
"Computers are useless. They can only give you answers."
"To err is human, but to really foul things up requires a computer."
"The electronic computer is to individual privacy what the machine gun was to the horse cavalry."

Input a word from the keyboard and display all quotations, if any, containing that word.

13. Input two strings from the keyboard and check if they are anagrams of each other. Hint: Take each character of the first string and check that it exists in the second string. If it doesn't then the strings are not anagrams of each other. If the character does exist in the second string, remove it and continue to the next character of the first string. When all the characters of the first string have been processed, the second string should be empty. If it is, then the two strings are anagrams of each other. Use C++ strings.

CHAPTER SEVEN

Functions

7.1 Introduction

The programs used in previous chapters are relatively small programs used to demonstrate a particular topic in C++. Typical commercial programs have hundreds or even thousands of lines of code. In order to reduce the complexity involved in writing such large programs, they have to be broken into smaller, less complex parts. Functions, along with classes that are covered in chapter 8, enable the programmer to do this. Functions and classes are the building blocks of a C++ program.

A function is a block of statements called by name to carry out a specific task, such as displaying headings at the top of every page of a report, reading a file, or performing a series of calculations.

C++ has a variety of built-in, pre-written, functions in the standard library. The next program demonstrates one such function, sqrt(), that calculates the square root of a number. By convention, when referring to a function the name of the function is followed by parentheses.

```
1   // Program example P7A
2   // Program to demonstrate the built-in function sqrt().
3   #include <iostream>
4   #include <string>
5   #include <cmath>
6   using namespace std ;
7
8   void main()
9   {
10    for ( int n = 1 ; n < 11 ; n ++ )
11      cout << sqrt( n ) << endl ;
12  }
```

Line 11 *calls* the function sqrt() to calculate the square root of the value in the variable n, which successively is assigned the values 1, 2, 3, ... 10 by the for statement on line 10.

Line 5 is required to use any of the mathematical functions. The mathematical functions have been adopted from the C programming language, hence the c in <cmath>.

Although the standard library is extensive, it does not include every function that a programmer may require. C++ allows a programmer to write functions to add to those already at hand in the standard library.

The next program displays a string of text surrounded by a box of asterisks. The program includes a programmer-defined function to display a line of asterisks.

```
1   // Program example P7B
2   // Demonstration of a programmer-defined function.
3   #include <iostream>
4   #include <string>
5   using namespace std ;
6
7   void stars( void ) ;            Function declaration or Prototype.
8
9   void main()
10  {
11    string text = "some text" ;
12
13    stars() ;     // Call the function to display the top of the box.
14    cout << endl ;
15    cout <<  '*'  ;        // Left side of the box.
16    cout <<  text  ;       // Text in middle of the box.
17    cout << '*' << endl ; // Right side of the box.
18    stars() ;              // Bottom of the box.
19    cout << endl ;
20  }        ◄──── This is the end of main()
21
22  void stars( void )
23  {
24    for ( int counter = 0 ; counter < 11 ; counter++ )   Function
25      cout << '*' ;                                       definition.
26  }
```

The output from this program is:

```
* * * * * * * * * *
*some text*
* * * * * * * * * *
```

Like variables, functions must be declared before they are used. Line 7 declares `stars` to be a function. The first `void` on line 7 declares the type of the function `stars()`. Functions with type `void` do not return a value to the calling program. Some functions do return a value. For example the `sqrt()` function returns a numeric value, i.e. the square root of a number.

The `void` in the parentheses on line 7 informs the compiler that the function `stars` will not receive any data from the calling program. Some functions do receive data when called. For example, with `sqrt()` a number or a numeric variable is placed in the parentheses.

In summary,

$$\text{void stars(void) ;}$$

↑   ↑

Returns nothing.   Receives nothing.

The function declaration on line 7 is also called the *prototype* of the function `stars()`.
Lines 13 and 18 call the function `stars()`, resulting in the top and bottom lines of stars being displayed.
Lines 22 to 26 define the function. Line 22 is called the *function header*, the remainder of the function enclosed in the braces { and } is called the *function body*.

In both lines 7 and 22 the void in the parentheses is optional. The function prototype on line 7 can therefore be written as:

```
void stars() ;
```

and the function header on line 22 can also be written as

```
void stars()
```

7.2 Function arguments

The function stars(), as written in P7B, displays eleven asterisks every time it is called. It would be useful to have a function to display a variable number of asterisks, not just eleven. This new function could be used for displaying boxes of different sizes.

The next program modifies the function stars() to take a value passed to it and to display the number of asterisks specified in that value.

```
1    // Program example P7C
2    // Demonstration of function arguments.
3    #include <iostream>
4    #include <string>
5    using namespace std ;
6
7    void stars( int ) ; // Function prototype.
8
9    void main()
10   {
11      string text = "some text" ;          11 is passed to num
12
13      stars( 11 ) ;    // Call the function to print 11 *s - top of box.
14      cout << endl ;
15      stars( 1 ) ;     // Left side of box  - 1 * only.
16      cout << text ;   // Display text in the middle of the box.
17      stars( 1 ) ;     // Right side of box - 1 * only.
18      cout << endl ;
19      stars( 11 ) ;    // Bottom of the box - 11 *s.
20      cout << endl ;
21   }
22
23   void stars( int num )
24   {
25      for ( int counter = 0 ; counter < num ; counter++ )
26        cout << '*' ;
27   }
```

Calls to the function stars() in lines 13, 15, 17 and 19 now have a number between the parentheses (and). This number is called an *argument* and is received by the *parameter* num declared as an integer in line 23.

The parameters of a function are known only within the function. Therefore, variables with the same name can be used in main() or in any other function without a conflict occurring.
Line 25 of the function stars() now uses the variable num to decide how many times * is displayed.

Since the function is now receiving an integer value when it is called from `main()`, the function prototype on line 7 now has `int` in the parentheses.

An even more useful function than `stars` would be one where you could specify not only the number but also the character to display. The next program includes such a function: `disp_chars()`. The program displays

```
+++++++++++
+some text+
+++++++++++
```

in the middle of the screen.

```
1   // Program example P7D
2   // Demonstration of a function with two parameters.
3   #include <iostream>
4   #include <string>
5   using namespace std ;
6
7   void disp_chars( int num, char ch ) ;          Function interface.
8   // Purpose   : To display any number of any character.
9   // Parameters: The number of times to display a character and
10  //             the character to display.
11
12  void main()
13  {
14     string text = "some text" ;
15                                  35 is passed to num and a space is passed to ch
16     // Top of box.
17     disp_chars( 35, ' ' ) ; // Display 35 spaces
18     disp_chars( 11, '+' ) ; // and eleven +s.
19     cout << endl ;
20     // Left side of box.
21     disp_chars( 35, ' ' ) ; // Display 35 spaces
22     disp_chars( 1, '+' ) ;  // and a +.
23     // Display text.
24     cout << text ;
25     // Right side of box.
26     disp_chars( 1, '+' ) ;  // Display a +.
27     cout << endl ;
28     // Bottom of the box.
29     disp_chars( 35, ' ' ) ; // Display 35 spaces
30     disp_chars( 11, '+' ) ; // and eleven +s.
31     cout << endl ;
32  }
33
34  void disp_chars( int num, char ch )
35  {
36     for ( int counter = 0 ; counter < num ; counter++ )
37       cout << ch ;
38  }
```

The function `disp_chars()` uses two parameters: `num` (the number of times to display a character) and `ch` (the character to display). Different values are passed to these parameters when the function is called in lines 17, 18, 21, 22, 26, 29, and 30.

The function prototype on line 7 informs the compiler that the function `disp_chars` will receive an `int` and a `char` from the calling program. The compiler checks that the type and number of arguments used in the function calls match the function prototype.

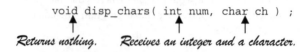

```
void disp_chars( int num, char ch ) ;
```

Returns nothing.   Receives an integer and a character.

The variable names `num` and `ch` are included in the function prototype on line 7. This is optional but can help in describing the function parameters.

The variable names used in the prototype can be any valid variable names and need not be defined. In practice, the names are often the same as those used for the parameters in the function header. This means that the prototype (line 7) is often the same as the function header (line 34), but the prototype ends with a semicolon.

It is good practice to place comments after the function prototype to describe the function and its parameters. The prototype and the comments should provide another programmer with enough information on how to use the function. The prototype and the accompanying comments are called the *function interface*.

7.3 Default argument values

Some or all of the arguments in a function call can be omitted, provided a default value is assigned to each missing argument.

Function arguments are assigned default values in the prototype of the function.

For example, to give default values to the arguments of `disp_chars()` in program P7D, the prototype on line 7 is modified to:

```
void disp_chars( int num = 1, char ch = ' ' ) ;
```

The prototype now assigns a default value of 1 to the first argument and a space to the second argument..

For example, the statement

```
disp_chars( 35 ) ; // The second argument is omitted.
```

is equivalent to

```
disp_chars( 35, ' ' ) ;
```

Similarly, the statement

```
disp_chars() ;      // Both arguments are omitted.
```

is equivalent to

```
disp_chars( 1, ' ' ) ;
```

Only trailing arguments can have default values. This means that it is illegal to have an argument with a default value followed by an argument without a default value. For example,

```
void disp_chars( int num = 1, char ch ) ;    // Illegal.
void disp_chars( int num, char ch = ' ' ) ; // Legal.
```

7.4 Returning a value from a function

To demonstrate the returning of a value from a function, the next program calls a function with two integer values as arguments and returns the minimum of the two values.

```
1   // Program example P7E
2   // Demonstration of the return statement.
3   #include <iostream>
4   using namespace std ;
5
6   int minimum( int num1, int num2 ) ;
7   // Purpose   : returns the minimum of two integers.
8   // Parameters: two integer values num1 and num2.
9   // Returns   : the minimum of num1 and num2.
10
11  void main()
12  {
13    int val1, val2, min_val ;
14
15    // Read in two integer values from the keyboard.
16    cout << "Please enter two integers: " ;
17    cin >> val1 >> val2 ;
18    // Find the minimum of these two values.
19    min_val = minimum( val1, val2 ) ;
20
21    cout << "Minimum of " << val1 << " and " << val2
22         << " is " << min_val << endl ;
23  }
24
25  int minimum( int num1, int num2 )
26  {
27    if ( num1 < num2 )
28      return num1 ;
29    else                   Return a value to min_val
30      return num2 ;
31  }
```

A sample run of this program is:

```
Please enter two integers: 1 2
Minimum of 1 and 2 is 1
```

Because `minimum()` returns an integer value, you must tell the compiler this in two places in the program. The first place is in the function prototype on line 6, and the second place is in the function header on line 25.

$$\text{int minimum(int num1, int num2)}$$

Returns an integer.　　*Receives two integers.*

The `return` statement in lines 28 and 30 does two things: it terminates the function and returns the value of either `num1` or `num2` to the integer variable `min_val` in line 19.

The general format of the `return` statement is:

```
return expression ;
```

Examples:

```
return 10.3 ;          // Return a constant value.
return ;               // No return value, just exit the function.
return variable ;      // Return the value of a variable.
return variable + 1 ;  // Return the value of an expression.
```

Lines 27 to 30 of `minimum()` could also be written as

```
return ( num1 > num2 ) ? num1 : num2
```

A function call can be used anywhere in a program where a variable can be used. For example, in the program P7E the variable `min_val` in line 22 may be replaced with the function call, as in:

```
cout << "Minimum of " << val1 << " and " << val2
     << " is " << minimum( val1, val2 ) << endl ;
```

7.5 Inline functions

Calling a function, passing argument values to a function and returning a value from a function all involve some processing overheads. For a large function that contains a lot of statements, the overheads involved are small in comparison with the processing done by the function itself. However, for small functions, like `minimum()` in program P7E, the overheads are relatively large in comparison with the small number of statements in the function. In this case it would be advantageous to make `minimum()` an `inline` function.

To make a function `inline`, precede the function prototype with the keyword `inline`. When an `inline` function is used in a program, the compiler replaces every call to the function with the program statements in the function, thereby eliminating the function overheads.

In general, consider inlining a function when the function contains one to three lines of code. To make `minimum()` an `inline` function, change line 6 in program P7E to

```
inline int minimum( int num1, int num2 ) ;
```

No other changes to the program are necessary.

7.6 Passing arguments by value

In the functions of the previous programs, a *copy* of the argument values is passed to the function parameters. This is known as *passing by value*.

As only a copy of an argument is sent to the function, the value of the argument cannot be changed within the function.

```
1  // Program example P7F
2  // Demonstration of passing arguments by value.
3  #include <iostream>
4  using namespace std ;
5
6  void any_function( int p ) ;
```

```
7
8  void main()
9  {
10   int a = 1 ;
11   cout << "a is " << a << endl ;
12
13   any_function( a ) ;
14
15   cout << "a is still " << a << endl;
16 }
17
18 void any_function( int p )
19 {
20   cout << "p is " << p << endl ;
21   p = 2 ;
22 }
```

A copy of the value of a *is passed to* p

Changing the value of the parameter p *has no effect on the argument* a.

When you run this program you will get the following result:

```
a is 1
p is 1
a is still 1
```

This program changes the value of the parameter p in line 21 without having any effect on the argument a. Line 15 displays the value of the argument a, showing it to be unchanged.

The value of the parameter can be prevented from change within a function by making it a constant. To do this, place the keyword const before the parameter in lines 6 and 18.

```
6  void any_function( const int p ) ;
   ...
18 void any_function( const int p )
```

Line 21 will now cause the compiler to display an error message.

7.7 Passing arguments by reference
A reference is a synonym or an alias for an existing variable. For example, if a variable n is defined as

```
int n = 1 ;
```

a reference variable r for n can be defined by the statement:

```
int& r = n ; // r is a reference to n. r is any valid identifier.
```

A reference to a variable is defined by adding & after the variable's data type.
After this definition n and r both refer to the same value, as if they were the same variable. The contents of n can be accessed by either n or r.
Note that r is not a copy of n, but is merely another name for n. Both n and r refer to the same storage location.

A change to n will also result in a change to r and vice versa. For example,

```
n = 2 ;   // Changes both n and r.
```

will result in both n and r having the value 2.

A reference must always be initialised when it is defined, since it doesn't make sense to have a reference to nothing.

```
int& r ;   // Illegal: a reference must be initialised.
```

References are commonly used as function parameters. As an example, the next program modifies program P7F to use a reference as a function parameter.

```
1   // Program example P7G
2   // Program to demonstrate passing an argument by reference.
3   #include <iostream>
4   using namespace std ;
5
6   void any_function( int& p ) ;
7
8   void main()
9   {
10    int a = 1 ;
11    cout << "a is " << a << endl ;
12
13    any_function( a ) ;
14
15    cout << "a is now " << a << endl ;
16  }
17
18  void any_function( int& p )
19  {
20    cout << "p is " << p << endl ;
21    p = 2 ;
22  }
```

a *and* p *refer to the same storage location.*

Changing the value of the parameter p *also changes the value of the argument* a.

The output from this program is:

```
a is 1
p is 1
a is now 2
```

Line 18 now declares the parameter p on line 18 to be a reference and the function prototype on line 6 is also changed accordingly. The argument a on line 13 is now *passed by reference* to the parameter p on line 18.

Line 21 changes the value of the parameter p and hence the value of the argument a also changes. Line 15 displays the value of a, showing that it has changed from 1 to 2.

The next program is a further demonstration of passing arguments by reference. This program has a function swap_vals() that has two reference parameters. This function swaps its two parameter values around and in so doing swaps the argument values around.

```
1   // Program example ·P7H
2   // Demonstration of passing two arguments by reference.
3   #include <iostream>
4   using namespace std ;
5
6   void swap_vals( float& val1, float& val2 ) ;
7   // Purpose   : To swap the values of two float variables.
8   // Parameters: References to the two float variables.
9
10  void main()
11  {
12    float num1, num2 ;
13
14    cout << "Please enter two numbers: " ;
15    cin >> num1 ;
16    cin >> num2 ;
17    // Swap values around so that the smallest is in num1.
18    if ( num1 > num2 )
19      swap_vals( num1, num2 ) ;
20    cout << "The numbers in order are "
21         << num1 << " and " << num2 << endl ;
22  }
23
24  void swap_vals( float& val1, float& val2 )
25  {
26    float temp = val1 ;
27
28    val1 = val2 ;
29    val2 = temp ;
30  }
```

Arguments passed by reference.

A sample run of this program is:

```
Please enter two numbers: 12.1  6.4
The numbers in order are 6.4 and 12.1
```

No value is returned from swap_vals(), so line 6 declares the function as type void.
Line 24 declares the parameters val1 and val2 as references to the arguments num1 and num2
on line 19.

The statement

```
  temp = val1 ;
```

in line 26 stores the value of val1 (which is a reference to num1) in the variable temp (temp is
now 12.1).

The statement

```
  val1 = val2;
```

on line 28 is equivalent to

```
  num1 = num2 ;
```

because val1 is a reference to num1 and val2 is a reference to num2. Therefore, num1 gets the value 6.4.

Finally, the statement

```
val2 = temp ;
```

on line 29 assigns the value of temp (12.1) to val2, and in doing so also assigns the same value to num2.

The net result is that the values in num1 and num2 are swapped around.

The variable temp defined on line 26 is a *local* variable to the function swap_vals(). Local variables are known only within the function where they are defined. If a variable of the same name is defined in main() or in another function, C++ regards the two variables as different and not related in any way.

7.8 Passing a one-dimensional array to a function

To avoid the overhead of copying all the elements of an array, that passing by value would entail, arrays can only be passed by reference to a function.

The next program contains a function sum_array() that sums the elements of an integer array passed to it from main().

```
1   // Program example P7I
2   // Demonstration of a one-dimensional array as a function argument.
3   #include <iostream>
4   using namespace std ;
5
6   int sum_array( int array[], int no_of_elements ) ;
7   // Purpose   : Sums the elements of a 1-D integer array.
8   // Parameters: An array and the number of elements in the array.
9   // Returns    : The sum of the array elements.
10
11  void main()
12  {
13    int values[10] = { 12, 4, 5, 3, 4, 0, 1, 8, 2, 3 } ;
14    int sum ;
15
16    sum = sum_array( values, 10 ) ;
17    cout << "The sum of the array elements is " << sum << endl ;
18  }
19
20  int sum_array( int array[], int no_of_elements )
21  {
22    int total = 0 ;
23
24    for ( int index = 0 ; index < no_of_elements ; index++ )
25      total += array[index] ;
26    return total ;
27  }
```

Running this program will display:

```
The sum of the array elements is 42
```

Line 16 calls `sum_array()` to calculate the sum of the values in the array `values`, placing the result of the calculation in the variable `sum`. The arguments are the name of the array and the number of elements in the array.

Line 20 declares the function parameters `array` and `no_of_elements`. Although there is no `&` after the data type, `array` is a reference to `values`. Because arrays can only be passed by reference, `&` is not required.
The square brackets `[` and `]` are necessary to indicate that the parameter is a reference to an array. For a one-dimensional array, the number of elements is not required in the brackets. This allows the same function to be used to process arrays of different sizes without the function being modified.

The loop in lines 24 and 25 calculates the sum of the array elements and line 26 returns the result to `sum` on line 16.

Because the array argument can only be passed by reference, the values of the elements in the array can be changed from within the function.
For example, placing a statement such as

```
array[0] = 0 ;
```

in the function will also assign `0` to the first element of the array `values`.

If required, the array may be prevented from modification by placing the keyword `const` in lines 6 and 20.

```
6   int sum_array( const int array[], int no_of_elements ) ;
```

```
20 int sum_array( const int array[], int no_of_elements )
```

These statements inform the compiler that within the function `sum_array()`, `array` is read-only and should not be modified.

7.9 Passing a multi-dimensional array to a function
When a multi-dimensional array is passed to a function, the function parameter list must contain the size of each dimension of the array, except the first. Consider the following program, which sums the elements of a two-dimensional array.

```
1   // Program example P7J
2   // Demonstration of a two-dimensional array as a function argument.
3   #include <iostream>
4   using namespace std ;
5
6   int sum_array( const int array[][2], int no_of_rows ) ;
7   // Purpose   : Sums the elements of a 2-D integer array.
8   // Parameters: A 2-D array and the number of rows in the array.
9   // Returns    : The sum of the array elements.
```

```
10
11 void main()
12 {
13   int values[5][2] = { { 31, 14 },
14                        { 51, 11 },
15                        {  7, 10 },
16                        { 13, 41 },
17                        { 16, 18 } } ;
18   int sum ;
19
20   sum = sum_array( values, 5 ) ;
21   cout << "The sum of the array elements is " << sum << endl ;
22 }
23 int sum_array( const int array[][2], int no_of_rows )
24 {
25   int total = 0 ;
26
27   for ( int row = 0 ; row < no_of_rows ; row++ )
28   {
29       for ( int col = 0 ; col < 2 ; col++ )
30           total += array[row][col] ;
31   }
32   return total ;
33 }
```

The elements of a two-dimensional array are stored row by row in contiguous memory locations. A sketch of memory would look like this:

31	14	51	11	7	10	13	41	16	18

Any element `array[i][j]` has an offset $i*2 + j$ from the starting memory location of `array[0][0]`. For example, `array[3][1]` (= 41) has an offset of 7 (= 3 * 2 + 1). In order to calculate the offset, the number of columns (= 2) is required; hence the need for the compiler to know the value of the second dimension in line 21.

7.10 Passing a structure variable to a function

When you pass a structure variable to a function, you pass a copy of the member values to that function. This means that the values in the structure variable cannot be changed within the function. As with any variable, the values in a structure variable can only be changed from within a function if the variable is passed by reference to the function.

The next program demonstrates passing a structure variable by value and passing a structure variable by reference to two different functions. In the function get_student_data() the argument is passed by reference and in display_student_data() the argument is passed by value.

```
1   // Program example P7K
2   // Demonstration of using a structure as a function argument.
3   // Program reads data for a student and then displays it.
4   #include <iostream>
5   #include <iomanip>
6   using namespace std ;
```

```
 7
 8  void display_student_data( struct student_rec student_data ) ;
 9  // Purpose   : This function displays student data.
10  // Parameter: A student record structure variable.
11
12  void get_student_data( struct student_rec& student_ref ) ;
13  // Purpose   : This function reads student data from the keyboard.
14  // Parameter: A reference to a student record structure variable.
15
16  struct student_rec  // Student structure template.
17  {
18    int number ;
19    float scores[5] ;
20  } ;
21
22  void main()
23  {
24    struct student_rec student ;
25
26    get_student_data( student ) ;
27    display_student_data( student ) ;
28  }
29
30  void display_student_data( struct student_rec student_data )
31  {
32    cout << endl << "The data in the student structure is:" << endl ;
33    cout << "  Number is " << student_data.number << endl ;
34    cout << "  Scores are:" ;
35    cout << fixed << setprecision( 1 ) ;
36    for ( int i = 0 ; i < 5 ; i++ )
37      cout << setw( 5 ) << student_data.scores[i] ;
38    cout << endl ;
39  }
40
41  void get_student_data( struct student_rec& student_ref )
42  {
43    cout << "Number: " ;
44    cin >> student_ref.number ;
45    cout << "Five test scores: " ;
46    for ( int i = 0 ; i < 5 ; i++ )
47      cin >> student_ref.scores[i] ;
48  }
```

A sample run of this program is:

```
Number: 1234
Five test scores: 75 80 65 45 68

The data in the student structure is:
  Number is 12345
  Scores are: 75.0 80.0 65.0 45.0 68.0
```

The structure template is declared outside `main()` on lines 16 to 20. When a structure template is defined outside `main()`, it makes the structure template *global*. This means that the structure template is known in `main()` and in the functions `display_student_data()` and `get_student_data()`. There is no need, therefore, to declare the structure template in each function.

Line 26 passes the structure variable `student` by reference to `get_student_data()`.
Line 27 passes the value of the structure variable `student` to `display_student_data()`.
When a structure variable is passed by value to a function, the entire structure data must be copied to the function parameter. For a large structure, this is a significant overhead and it is preferable, therefore, to use a reference. If the argument isn't changed by the function, the `const` keyword should be used.

To avoid the overhead involved in copying the student data in program P7K, lines 8 and 30 are modified to:

```
8   void display_student_data( const struct student_rec& student_data ) ;

30 void display_student_data( const struct student_rec& student_data)
```

7.11 Passing a string to a function
The same considerations should be kept in mind when using strings as arguments as when using structure variables as arguments, i.e. passing a string by value means copying all the characters of the string to a function parameter. To avoid this overhead it is preferable to pass strings by reference.

7.11.1 Passing a C++ string to a function
The next program demonstrates passing a C++ string by `const` reference to a function that counts the number of vowels in the string.

```
1   // Program example P7L
2   // Demonstration of using a C++ string as a function argument.
3   #include <iostream>
4   #include <string>
5   using namespace std ;
6
7   int vowel_count( const string& str ) ;
8   // Purpose   : Finds the number of vowels in a C++ string.
9   // Parameter: A C++ string.
10  // Returns   : The number of vowels in the string.
11
12  void main()
13  {
14     string s = "This string contains vowels" ;
15     int n = vowel_count( s ) ;
16     cout << "The number of vowels in \"" << s <<"\" is "<< n << endl ;
17  }
18
19  int vowel_count( const string& str )
20  {
21     int str_len = str.length() ;
22     char ch ;
23     int vowel_count = 0 ;
24
25     for ( int i = 0 ; i< str_len ; i++ )
26     {
```

```
27    ch = str.at( i ) ;
28    if ( ch == 'A' || ch == 'a' ||
29          ch == 'E' || ch == 'e' ||
30          ch == 'I' || ch == 'i' ||
31          ch == 'O' || ch == 'o' ||
32          ch == 'U' || ch == 'u' )
33        vowel_count++ ;
34    }
35    return vowel_count ;
36 }
```

The output from this program is:

```
The number of vowels in "This string contains vowels" is 7
```

7.11.2 Passing a C-string to a function

To use C-strings instead of C++ strings in program P7L, the following modifications must be made to the program:

Since a C-string is an array of characters, line 14 changes to
```
char s[] = "This string contains vowels" ;
```

The function argument s on line 15 is now a character array. This means that line 19 must change to
```
int vowel_count( const char str[] )
```

The prototype on line 7 must also change to correspond to the function header on line 19.
```
int vowel_count( const char str[] ) ;
```

Within the function vowel_count(), two changes are required. Line 21 changes to
```
int str_len = strlen( str ) ;
```

and line 27 changes to
```
ch = str[ i ] ;
```

7.12 Function overloading

Function overloading is used when there is a need for two or more functions to perform similar tasks, but each function requires different arguments.

Program P7I used the function sum_array() to calculate the sum of the elements in a one-dimensional array and program P7J used a different function with the same name, sum_array(), to calculate the sum of the elements in a two-dimensional array.

If required, both versions of sum_array() can be used in a program. Using different functions with the same name in a program is called *function overloading* and the functions are called *overloaded functions*.

Function overloading requires that each overloaded function have a different parameter list, i.e. a different number of parameters or at least one parameter with a different data type.

```
1  // Program example P7M
2  // Demonstration of function overloading.
3  #include <iostream>
4  using namespace std ;
5
```

```
6  int sum_array( const int array[], int no_of_elements ) ;
7  // Purpose    : Sums the elements of a 1-D integer array.
8  // Parameters: An array and the number of elements in the array.
9  // Returns    : The sum of the array elements.
10 int sum_array( const int array[] [2], int no_of_rows ) ;
11 // Purpose    : Sums the elements of a 2-D integer array.
12 // Parameters: A 2-D array and the number of rows in the array.
13 // Returns    : The sum of the array elements.
14
15 void main()
16 {
17    int one_d_array[5] = { 0, 1, 2, 3, 4 } ;
18    int sum ;
19
20    sum = sum_array( one_d_array, 5 ) ;
21    cout << "The sum of the 1-D array elements is "
22         << sum << endl ;
23
24    int two_d_array[3] [2] = { { 0, 1 },
25                               { 11, 12 },
26                               { 21, 22 } } ;
27
28    sum = sum_array( two_d_array, 3 ) ;
29    cout << "The sum of the 2-D array elements is " << sum << endl ;
30 }
31
32 int sum_array( const int array[], int no_of_elements )
33 {
34    int total = 0 ;
35
36    for ( int index = 0 ; index < no_of_elements ; index++ )
37      total += array[index] ;
38    return total ;
39 }
40
41 int sum_array( const int array[] [2], int no_of_rows )
42 {
43    int total = 0 ;
44
45    for ( int row = 0 ; row < no_of_rows ; row++ )
46    {
47       for ( int col = 0 ; col < 2 ; col++ )
48             total += array[row] [col] ;
49    }
50    return total ;
51 }
```

The output from this program is:

```
The sum of the 1-D array elements is 10
The sum of the 2-D array elements is 67
```

The compiler decides which of the two sum_array() functions to call based on their parameters. This means that line 20 calls sum_array()on lines 32 to 39, because the argument and parameter types on lines 20 and 32 are the same, i.e. a one-dimensional array and an integer. Similarly, line 28 calls `sum_array()` on lines 41 to 51, because the argument and parameter types on lines 28 and 41 are a two-dimensional array and an integer.

7.13 Storage classes `auto` and `static`

7.13.1 `auto`

The variables defined inside a function are `auto` (automatic) by default. Every time a function (including `main()`) is entered, storage for each `auto` variable is allocated. When the function is completed, the allocated storage is freed, and any values in the `auto` variables are lost. Such variables are known as *local* variables and are known only within the function in which they are defined. If you do not specify a storage class, `auto` is assumed by default.

For example:

```
void any_function()
{
  auto int var1 ;
  auto float var2[10] ;
  ...// Body of function follows.
}
```

The variables `var1` and `var2` have been defined with the storage class `auto`. As `auto` is the default, the keyword `auto` may be omitted.

Automatic variables permit efficient use of storage, because the storage used by `auto` variables is released for other purposes when a function terminates.

7.13.2 `static`

`static` variables, like `auto` variables, are local to the function in which they are defined. However, unlike `auto` variables, `static` variables are allocated storage only once and so retain their values even after the function terminates.

The next program illustrates the differences between `auto` and `static` variables.

```
1   // Program example P7N
2   // Demonstration of the difference between static and auto.
3   #include <iostream>
4   using namespace std ;
5
6   void any_func( void ) ;
7
8   void  main()
9   {
10    for ( int i = 0 ; i < 10 ; i++ ) // Call a function ten times.
11      any_func() ;
12  }
13
14  void any_func()
15  {
16    int auto_var = 0 ;
17    static int static_var = 0 ;
18
19    static_var++ ;  // Increment the static variable.
20    auto_var ++ ;   // Increment the auto  variable.
21    cout << "auto_var = " << auto_var << " "
22        <<  "static_var = " << static_var << endl ;
23  }
```

The output from this program is:

```
auto_var = 1 static_var = 1
auto_var = 1 static_var = 2
auto_var = 1 static_var = 3
auto_var = 1 static_var = 4
auto_var = 1 static_var = 5
auto_var = 1 static_var = 6
auto_var = 1 static_var = 7
auto_var = 1 static_var = 8
auto_var = 1 static_var = 9
auto_var = 1 static_var = 10
```

The output from this program shows that the variable static_var was initialised only once and retained its value between each function call. However, the auto variable auto_var was created and initialised to 0 every time the function was entered.

7.14 The scope of a variable

The scope of a variable refers to the part of the program in which a variable can be accessed. There are two types of scope: *block scope* and *global scope*.

7.14.1 Block scope

A *block* is one or more statements enclosed in braces { and } that also includes variable declarations. A variable declared in a block is accessible only within that block.

The following program segment illustrates block scope.

```
    void f( int x ) ;

    void main()
    {
      float f = 0 ;
      ...
      if ( f > 0 )
      {
        // f is accessible everywhere in this block.
        char c ; // c is accessible from here to the end of this block.
        if ( f == 1 )
        {
          double d ; //
          ...
        } // d is destroyed.
        // f and c are accessible, d is not.
        ...
      } // c is destroyed at the end of the block.
      // f is still accessible here, but c is not.
      ...
    }// f is destroyed at the end of the program.

    void f( int x )
    {
      // x is accessible here.
      int y ;
      ...
      if ( x == 1 )
```

```
{
  int z ;
  // x, y and z are accessible here.
  ...
} // z is destroyed here.
// x and y are accessible here, but z is not.
...
} // x and y are destroyed when the function terminates.
```

Variables declared inside the parentheses of a for are accessible within the parentheses, as well as in the statement(s) contained in the for loop.
For example,

```
for ( int i = 0 ; i < 10 ; i++ ) // i is declared inside the ().
{                                 // i is accessible inside the ().
  // i is also accessible here.
  ...
  cout << i ;
  ...
} // i is destroyed at the end of the block.
// i is no longer accessible.
...
for ( int j = 0 ; i < 10 ; i++ )
  cout << j ;  // The for loop controls only 1 statement.
// j is destroyed and is no longer accessible.
...
```

7.14.2 Global scope
A variable declared outside main() is accessible from anywhere within the program and is known as a global variable. For example:

```
int g ;  // g is a global variable.

void f1() ;
void f2() ;

void main()
{
  int a ;
  // a and g are accessible here.
  ...
} // Program ends, a and g are destroyed.

void f1()
{
  int b ;
  // b and g are accessible here.
  ...
} // Function ends, b is destroyed.

void f1()
{
  // g is accessible here.
  ...
}
```

Because global variables are known, and therefore can be modified, within every function, they can make a program difficult to debug and maintain. Global variables are not a substitute for function arguments. Strictly speaking, apart from its own local variables, a function should have access only to the data specified in the function parameter list.

7.14.3 Reusing a variable name
It is permissible to give a variable the same name as another variable in another block. This is known as *name reuse*.

The next program demonstrates name reuse and shows its effect on the scope of a variable.

```
1   // Program P70
2   // Demonstration of variable scope and name reuse.
3   #include <iostream>
4   using namespace std ;
5
6   int i = 1 ;  // i is a global variable.
7
8   void f() ;
9
10  void main()
11  { // Start of program block.
12
13     cout << "Global variable i = " << i << endl ;
14
15     int i = 2 ; // i is reused here.
16     cout << "Variable i declared in main() = " << i << endl ;
17
18     // The global variable i can be accessed by using ::
19     cout << "Global variable i = " << ::i << endl ;
20
21     char c = 'x' ;
22     cout << "Variable c declared in main() = " << c << endl ;
23     { // Start of a statement block.
24       int c = 3 ;  // c is reused.
25
26       cout << "Variable c declared in statement block = " << c << endl ;
27       // variable c declared in main() is not accessible here.
28     } // End of statement block.
29
30     cout << "Variable c declared in main() = " << c << endl ;
31     // Variable c declared in the statement block is not accessible here.
32
33     f() ;
34
35     cout << "Variable i declared in main() = " << i << endl ;
36
37     cout << "Global variable i = " << ::i << endl ;
38
39  }  // End of program block.
40
41  void f()
42  { // Start of a function block.
43
44     cout << "Global variable i = " << i << endl ;
```

```
45
46    char i = 'y' ;
47    cout << "Variable i declared in f() = " << i << endl ;
48
49    cout << "Global variable i = " << ::i << endl ;
50
51  } // End of function block.
```

The output from this program is:

```
Global variable i = 1
Variable i declared in main() = 2
Global variable i = 1
Variable c declared in main() = x
Variable c declared in statement block = 3
Variable c declared in main() = x
Global variable i = 1
Variable i declared in f() = y
Global variable i = 1
Variable i declared in main() = 2
Global variable i = 1
```

If a variable is declared in an inner block and if a variable with the same name is declared in a surrounding block, the variable in the inner block *hides* the variable of the surrounding block. For example, the declaration of i on line 15 hides the global variable i declared on line 6. Similarly, the declaration of c on line 24 hides the declaration of c on line 21.

If a global variable is hidden by a local variable, the global variable can still be accessed using the unary scope resolution operator : : (two colons), as shown on line 19.

7.15 Mathematical functions

To use any of the mathematical functions place the statement

```
#include <cmath>
```

at the start of the program.

7.15.1 Some trigonometric functions

Function	Description
cos(x)	Cosine of angle x in radians. x is a double value. Returns a double value.
sin(x)	Sine of angle x in radians. x is a double value. Returns a double value.
tan(x)	Tangent of angle x in radians. x is a double value. Returns a double value.

The next program demonstrates sin(), cos() and tan() functions.

```
1   // Program example P7P
2   // Demonstration of the functions sin(), cos(), and tan().
3   #include <iostream>
4   #include <iomanip>
5   #include <cmath>
6   using namespace std ;
7
8   void main()
9   {
10    const double RADIANS_IN_A_DEGREE = 57.29578 ;
11
12    double degrees, radians ;
13
14    cout <<  "Input the angle in degrees: " ;
15    cin >> degrees ;
16    radians = degrees / RADIANS_IN_A_DEGREE ;
17    cout << fixed << setprecision( 3 )
18         << "sin(" << degrees << ")=" << sin( radians ) << endl
19         << "cos(" << degrees << ")=" << cos( radians ) << endl
20         << "tan(" << degrees << ")=" << tan( radians ) << endl ;
21  }
```

A sample run of this program follows:

```
Input the angle in degrees: 60
sin(60.000)= 0.866
cos(60.000)= 0.500
tan(60.000)= 1.732
```

7.15.2 Pseudo-random number functions

To use the pseudo-random generating functions rand() and srand(), place the statement

```
#include <cstdlib>
```

at the start of the program.

Function	Description
rand()	Returns a pseudo-random integer value. Each call to rand() will produce a pseudo-random integer value. However, each time the program is executed the same sequence of integer values will be returned, unless a different seed value is used with the srand() function.
srand(n)	Use this function to set the seed (starting value) for pseudo-random numbers generated by rand(). The seed value, n, is an unsigned int.

The next program demonstrates the use of the random number functions.

```
1   // Program example P7Q
2   // Demonstration of the random number functions.
3   #include <iostream>
4   #include <cstdlib>
5   #include <ctime>
6   using namespace std ;
7
8   void main()
9   {
10    time_t t ;   // Define t as variable of type time_t.
11
12    t = time( 0 ) ; // Current time in seconds.
13    // Use the time to initialise the random number generator.
14    srand( t ) ; // Set the seed to the time.
15    // Generate five random numbers between 0 and 20.
16    cout << "Five random numbers in the range 0-20" << endl ;
17    for ( int i = 0 ; i < 5 ; i++ )
18    {
19      int r = rand() % 20 ;   // %20 ensures a number between 0 and 20.
20      cout << r << endl ;
21    }
22  }
```

A sample run of this program is:

```
Five random numbers in the range 0-20:
9
8
17
18
17
```

The statement

```
  t = time( 0 ) ;
```

on line 12 assigns to t the current time (measured in seconds since midnight on 1 January 1970, GMT) which is used as the random number seed on line 14.

Without line 14, the program displays the same sequence of random numbers every time the program is run.

Programming pitfalls

1. Parameters and arguments must agree in number and type. For example, if you call a function with two `int`s and a `float` as arguments, then the function must have two `int`s and a `float` as parameters.

2. Be aware of the difference between passing arguments by value and passing arguments by reference. When you pass an argument by value, the value of that argument cannot be changed from within the function. To change the value of an argument from within a function, the argument must be passed by reference to the function.

3. Parentheses ( ) are used to enclose function arguments and parameters; brackets [ ] are used for the subscripts of an array.

4. There is no semicolon after a function header, but there is one after a function prototype.

5. The angle in the trigonometric and hyperbolic functions is measured in radians, not degrees.

6. If you omit a function prototype, C++ assumes the function will return an integer value. If the function is returning a data type other than integer, the compiler will give an error message.
    Avoid the error message by always including a prototype for every function in the program.

Quick syntax reference

	Syntax	Examples
Function prototype	```type function_name (type parameter₁, type parameter₂, ... type parameterₙ) ;```	```float average (float a[], int n) ;```
Function definition	```type function_name (type parameter₁, type parameter₂, ... type parameterₙ) { local variables ; executable statements ; return expression ; }```	```float average (float a[], int n) { int i ; float sum = 0, average ; for (i = 0 ; i < n ; i++) sum += a[i] ; average = sum / n ; return average ; }```
Function call	```variable = function_name(argument₁, argument₂, ... argumentₙ) ;```	```float array[10], n ; float avg ; ... avg = average(array, n) ;```

Exercises

1. (a) Write function prototypes for the following functions:

Function	Parameter(s)	Return value
f1	int	char
f2	char	char
f3	an int	int
f4	two integers	none
f5	string reference	int
f6	none	bool
f7	an integer array	float
f8	a double array	void
f9	none	none

For example, the function prototype for the function `f1()` is:

```
char f1( int variable_name ) ;   or  char f1( int ) ;
```

(b) Write a statement to call each of the above functions.
For example, to call function `f1()` :

```
char c_val ;
int i_val ;
c_val = f1( i_val ) ;
```

2. What is wrong with each of the following functions?

```
(a) void max(a, b) ;        (b)  bool test(int)           (c)  float min()
      if ( a > b )               {                              int a, b ;
         return a ;               for(int i=1;i< n;i++)         if ( a < b )
      else                           cout << "x";                 return a
         return b ;             }                                 return b ;
                                                             }
```

3. Find the errors in this program:

```
#include <iostream>
using namespace std ;

int f1() ;
void f2( int a ) ;

void main()
{
  int v1 ;
  float v2 ;
  long v3 ;

  v1 = f1[ 1 ] ;
  v2 = f1() ;
  v3 = f2() ;
  v2 = f2( 1, 2, 3 ) ;
}
```

```
    }

    void f1( int a )
    {
      // Body of function f1.
    }

    void f2( int a, b )
    {
      // Body of function f2.
    }
```

4. What is the output from the following?

```
    #include <iostream>
    using namespace std ;

    int f( int val1, int val2 = 0 ) ;

    void main()
    {
      int var ;

      var = f( 1, 2 ) + 1 ;
      var = f( var + 1 ) ;
      var = f( f( 1, 2 ), f( 3, var ) ) ;
      cout << "The value of var is " << var << endl ;
    }

    int f( int val1, int val2 )
    {
      if ( val1 > val2 )
        return ( val1 - val2 ) ;
      else
        return ( val2 - val1 ) ;
    }
```

5. What is the output from the following?

```
    #include <iostream>
    using namespace std ;

    void f( int val1, int val2 = 2 ) ;
    void f( string& s ) ;
    void f( char c ) ;

    void main()
    {
      string str = "this is a string" ;

      f( 1 ) ;
      f( str ) ;
      f( 'a' ) ;
    }
```

```
void f ( int i, int j )
{
  cout << "i = " << i << " j = " << j << endl ;
}

void f ( string& s )
{
  cout << "s = " << s << endl ;
}

void f ( char c )
{
  cout << "c = " << c << endl ;
}
```

6. Write a function to return the minimum of three integer values.

7. (a) Write a function to return the minimum value in an integer array of ten elements.
    (b) Modify the function to take the number of elements in the array as a parameter.

8. Write a function to test whether an integer lies within a range of values. The function prototype will be:

    ```
    bool range_test ( int val, int low = 1, int high = 10 ) ;
    ```

    where val is the value to be tested, low is the lower value in the range, and high is the higher value in the range. The function will return the bool value true if the value is in the specified range, otherwise it will return the bool value false.

9. Write a function to convert hours, minutes and seconds to seconds.

10. Write a function to convert seconds to hours, minutes, and seconds.

11. (a) Write a function to return the minimum value in an integer array.
    (b) Overload the function in (a) with a function to return the minimum value in a floating-point array.

12. Write a function to count the number of words in a string.
    (Assume that every word is separated by at least one whitespace character.)

13. Write a function that has four parameters: a starting number, an ending number, an increment (default 1) and the number of numbers to be displayed per line (default 10).

14. Write a function to capitalise all the letters in a string.

15. Write a function to determine the frequency of each of the vowels in a string.

16. Write a function to reverse a string.

17. A palindrome is a word that you can spell forwards or backwards. For example, the word 'madam' is a palindrome. Write a function to check whether a word is a palindrome or not. The function should return a `bool` value of `true` or `false` as appropriate.

18. Write a function to determine whether a string is palindromic or not.
An example of a palindromic string is:

"rats live on no evil star"

Each word in the string is separated by one or more whitespace characters.
The function should return a `bool` value of `true` or `false` as appropriate.

19. (a) What is the output from the following?

```
#include <iostream>
using namespace std ;

void any_function(void) ;

void main()
{
  int i ;
  for ( i = 0 ; i < 10 ; i++ )
    any_function() ;
}
void any_function()
{
  static int var = 10 ;
  cout << var << endl ;
  var += 10 ;
}
```

(b) What would be the effect of replacing the function `any_function()` with the following:

```
void any_function()
{
  static int var ;
  var = 10 ;
  cout << var << endl ;
  var += 10 ;
}
```

20. Write a function that will return the letter A the first time it is called, B the second time it is called, C the third time it is called, and so on. (Hint: use a `static` data type.)

21. Write a program to generate a set of lotto numbers, using `srand()` and `rand()`.

CHAPTER EIGHT

Objects and Classes

8.1 What is an object?

An object is a component of a program that knows how to perform certain actions and knows how to interact with other parts of the program. An object consists of one or more data values, which define the state or properties of the object, and functions that can be applied to the object. The functions associated with an object represent what can be done to the object and how the object behaves. An object can be anything such as a person, a computer or even an intangible such as a bank account.

Consider a computer adventure game. Among the objects in the game might be:

> You, the player,
> Your enemies e.g. dragons
> Your weapons
> Obstacles such as locked doors, rivers, etc.
> The prize e.g. a fair maiden

A player will have data values to represent certain attributes, e.g. the state of their health or the weapons they possess. A player must be able to perform functions such as walk, run, attack an enemy, and rescue the fair maiden to win. Behaviour between objects is very important. For example, if you fall into the river loaded with weapons, you drown. If you fatally wound an enemy, then it is out of the game and you have one less enemy to contend with.

8.2 What is a class?

A class is a general category that defines

- The characteristics that an object of that category contains. The characteristics are called properties or class data members.
- The functions that can be applied to objects of that category. The functions are also called class member functions or methods.

That is, a class defines both the type of data and the operations that can be applied to that data. Including both the data and functions into one unit, the class, is called *encapsulation*.

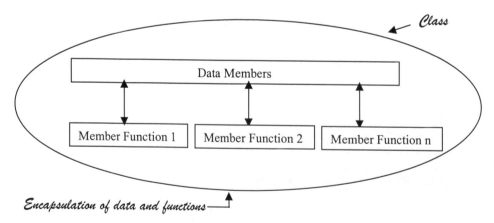

In our computer adventure game a player class may be defined as:

```
class player
{
// functions:
     walk()
     run()
     jump()
     attack()
     rescue()
     ...
//data:
     state_of_health
     type_of_weapon
     ...
} ;
```

Note: This is only a pseudo(not real)-code representation of the class used for explanatory purposes only. Details of the functions and the data types used in the class have been omitted. When writing a class in C++, these details are required.

A dragon class may be defined in pseudo-code as:

```
class dragon
{
//functions:
     walk()
     spit_fire()
     use_claws()
     use_tail()
     die()
     ...

//data:
     size
     number_of_claws
     state_of_health
     ...
}
```

There is an important distinction between a class and an instance of the class. A class is a blueprint or a template that can be used to create many instances of the class. An instance of a class is the actual object, created from the template, that can be manipulated by the member functions of the class.

The difference between a class and an instance of a class (an object) is like the difference between a noun and a proper noun. For example, person is a noun, John Smith is a proper noun that represents a specific person. Person is the class and John Smith is the object.

Getting back to the adventure game, the following statement creates an instance of a dragon:

```
  class dragon george( 10, 4 ) ;
```

Here george is an instance or an object of the dragon class. The data in the parentheses represent initial values for some of the data members of george, e.g. size and number_of_claws.

If in the game `george` is required to spit fire, a 'message' is sent to `george` by calling the class member function `spit_fire()`. A class member function is called using the member selection operator (a dot):

```
george.spit_fire() ;
```

Any number of dragon objects can be created. For example,

```
class ivan( 6, 2 ), baby( 1, 0 ) ;
```

In this example, `ivan` is a size 6 dragon with 2 claws and `baby` is a size 1 dragon with no claws.

Each dragon can perform different functions independent of each other:

```
ivan.use_claws() ;     // ivan attacks with claws.
baby.die() ;           // baby dragon dies. sorry!
george.spit_fire() ;   // george attacks with fire.
```

To summarise:
- An object is an instance of a class
- An object has:
    - an identity, i.e. its name
    - a state, i.e. its data members
    - a behaviour, i.e. its member functions.

8.3 Further examples of classes and objects
8.3.1 A book class
A book is an example of a class. Some of the properties (class data members) that define a book are the title, the author, the price, the year of publication, the number of pages in the book, the ISBN, etc. Some of the functions (class member functions or methods) that can be performed on a book are to open the book, go to a specific page in the book, read a word, and close the book. These operations are performed by the member functions of the class. So a book class will have member functions `open_book()`, `read_word()`, `close_book()` and `go_to_page( n )` where n is any number from one to the number of pages in the book. The book class can de defined in pseudo-code as:

```
class book
{
//functions:
    open_book()
    read_word()
    go_to_page( n )
    close_book()
//data:
    title
    author
    price
    year_of_publication
    number_of_pages
    ISBN
}
```

A book object is a specific instance of the book class. Specific books such as *A Guide to C++ Programming* or *The Hitchhiker's Guide to the Galaxy* are instances of the book class. Each of these book class objects has its own title, author, price, year of publication, number of pages and ISBN.

You can use `open_book()` to open a book object and then use `go_to_page( 50 )` to turn to page fifty of the book. Of course, if there are not fifty pages in the book then this operation will not be valid and the member function `go_to_page()` should be able to respond to this invalid data.

8.3.2 A bank account class

In its simplest form, a bank account has an account number and a balance. These are the class data members of a bank account class. Some of the operations that can be done on a bank account class are to open the account with an amount of money and to deposit and withdraw money from the account. These operations will be represented by class member functions such as `open( amount )`, `withdraw( amount )` and `deposit( amount )`, where `amount` represents an amount of money.

```
class bank_account
{
//functions:
        open( amount )
        deposit( amount )
        withdraw( amount )
//data:
        account_number
        balance
}
```

A bank account object is a specific instance of the bank account class. So your bank account will have a unique account number and you will have a specific amount of money in your account.

The following statement creates an instance of a bank account called `my_bank_account`:

```
class bank_account my_bank_account ;
```

To withdraw twenty pounds from `my_bank_account`:

```
my_bank_account.withdraw( 20.00 )
```

8.4 Abstraction

In the computer adventure game, each software object behaves only in some respects as its real-world counterpart. Not all the behaviour or characteristics of the real-world object is necessary in the game. For example, there may be no need for a player to eat, drink or sleep in the game. In effect, each software object is a simplification of its real world counterpart. This is called *abstraction*.

Abstraction is also used in the bank account class. The bank account class as described above doesn't describe all the characteristics and all the operations of a real bank account, but only the characteristics and operations that are relevant for the purposes of the program.

The relevant characteristics and functions of a real bank account have been abstracted to produce a software model of its real world counterpart.

Abstraction is used in our everyday lives. For example, a lecture timetable will contain a subject, a lecturer's name, a room number and a time. On the timetable, the room where the lecture is to be held is represented simply by a number. For the purpose of a student's timetable, details of the room, such as its size, are unnecessary and are therefore not given. However, for a college administrator the size of the room is relevant and so would be included in an abstraction for the purposes of college administration.

A more common example is our use and understanding of a car. It is well known that the engine makes the car go, but technical knowledge of the engine is not necessary in order to drive the car. To drive a car it is necessary to know how the various controls like the gear stick, accelerator and brake are used, but what happens under the bonnet is not entirely necessary. Our understanding of a car is a simplification or abstraction of the real thing.

8.5 Constructing a class in C++

The bank account class of section 8.3.2 can be constructed in C++ as follows:

```
1    // Program example P8A
2    // Demonstration of a C++ class.
3    #include <iostream>
4    #include <iomanip>
5    using namespace std ;
6
7    class bank_account
8    {
9    public:
10     void open( long int acc_no, double initial_balance ) ;
11     void deposit( double amount ) ;
12     void withdraw( double amount ) ;     The class member function prototypes.
13     void display_balance() ;
14   private:
15     long int account_number ;
16     double balance ;                     The class data members.
17   } ;    Don't forget the semicolon.
18
```

On line 7, following the keyword class, the class is given the name bank_account, which can be any valid C++ identifier.
Lines 10 to 13 declare the member functions of the class and lines 15 and 16 declare the data members of the class.

The members of the class are divided into private and public members. The keywords private and public specify the access control level for the data and function members of the class. Data members declared with private access control are accessible only to member functions of the class and unavailable to any functions that are not members of the class. This is called *information hiding* and prevents the data from being changed except from within the class. The only way the private data members of a class can be accessed is through the public functions of the class.

Members declared with public access control are accessible in any part of a program. In the bank_account class all the member functions are public, but a class member function can also have private access control. A public member function can be called from any part of a program, while a private member function can only be called from within member functions of the same class. The public member functions are known as the *public interface* of the class.

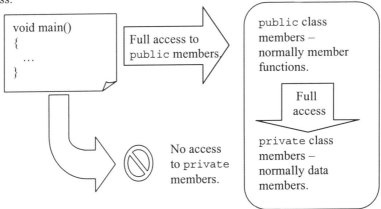

The general format of a class is:

```
class class_name
{
public:
// Details of the public interface of the class.
private:
// Private member functions and data members.
} ;
```

Generally, data members of a class are all private and the member functions of the class are all public.

Although not mandatory, the public section is usually placed at the start of the class before the private section. A programmer who wants to know how to use the class need only read the first part of the class, i.e. the public interface, to see what member functions are available and how to use them.

To complete the class, the class member functions must be defined.

```
19  void bank_account::open( long int acc_no, double initial_balance )
20  {
21    account_number = acc_no ;
22    balance = initial_balance ;
23  }
24
25  void bank_account::deposit( double amount )
26  {
27    balance += amount ;
28  }
29
30  void bank_account::withdraw( double amount )
```

The class member function definitions.

```
31  {
32     balance -= amount ;
33  }
34
35  void bank_account::display_balance()
36  {
37     cout << "Balance in Account " << account_number << " is "
38          << fixed << setprecision( 2 )
39          << balance << endl ;
40  }
```

A class member function has the general format:

```
return_type class_name::function_name( parameter list )
{
// function statements.
}
```

The scope resolution operator `::` is used here to specify that a function is a member of a class.

8.6 Using a class: defining and using objects

To use the `bank_account` class, place the class and member function definitions before `main()`. The objects of the class are defined and used in `main()`.

Program example P8A…continued

```
42  void main()
43  {
44     class bank_account my_account ; // my_account is an object
45                                     // of class bank_account.
46
47     my_account.open( 123, 10.54 ) ; // Open account 123 with 10.54
48
49     my_account.display_balance() ;  // Display account details.
50
51     my_account.deposit( 10.50 ) ;   // Deposit £10.50
52
53     my_account.display_balance() ;
54
55     my_account.withdraw( 20.04 ) ;  // Withdraw £20.04
56
57     my_account.display_balance() ;
58  }
```

Line 44 creates a `bank_account` object called `my_account`.:

my_account	
account_no	balance
?	?

Line 44 can also be written as

```
bank_account my_account ;   // The keyword class is optional.
```

Although `my_account` has been created, the data members `account_no` and `balance` have not been initialised, so their values are unknown.

Line 47 initialises the data members of the class by calling the member function `open()` with values for the `account_no` and `balance`:

my_account	
account_no	balance
123	10.54

Running this program will display the following:

```
Balance in Account 123 is 10.54
Balance in Account 123 is 21.04
Balance in Account 123 is 1.00
```

8.7 Abstract data types

C++ has a set of built-in data types such as `char`, `int` and `float`. Each one of these data types has a unique range of allowable values and a set of allowable operations and functions. For example, the `float` data type has a range of positive and negative values which is different from the range of numbers that can be held with an `int` data type (see appendix D). An allowable operation on both the `int` and `float` data types is the square root function `sqrt()` (see program P7A). A `string` function such as `length()` (see program P6J) is not applicable to either `float` or `int` and is consequently not allowed. The details of how negative numbers are stored or how many bits of storage are used to store a value are not necessary in order to use a `float` or an `int` type variable. All that is required to know is what functions and operations can be used with a particular data type, and what is the range of allowable values for that data type. In other words, the implementation details of the data types are hidden from the programmer. This is called *data abstraction*.

This is very similar to the way in which the bank account class is used in program P8A. The bank account class defines a new data type that is not built into the C++ language. The new data type is called an *abstract data type* (ADT). Once written, to use the new bank account data type it is not necessary to know the details of how each of the class member functions work. It is only necessary to know how to call the public member functions of the class such as `open()`, `deposit()` and `withdraw()`.

In effect, a class object can be regarded as a "black box" where data is entered and results produced without knowing what's happening inside the box.

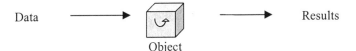

Data ⟶ Object ⟶ Results

8.8 Constructors

Constructors play a critical role in the automatic initialisation of data. A constructor is a class member function that has the same name as the class, and is automatically called when an object of the class is created. A constructor is frequently used to provide the private data members of the object with initial values.

In the bank account class, which doesn't include a constructor, the private data members `account_number` and `balance` are assigned their initial values in the member function `open()`. If `open()` is not explicitly called from `main()` then the private data members do not have initial values and the rest of the program will give spurious results. By including a constructor in a class, it is possible to ensure that the data members of the class are automatically initialised.

In the next program, a constructor is added to the `bank_account` class in place of the `open()` member function.

```
1    // Program example P8B
2    // Demonstration of a class constructor.
3    #include <iostream>
4    #include <iomanip>
5    using namespace std ;
6
7    class bank_account
8    {
9    public:
10      bank_account( long int acc_no, double initial_balance ) ;
11      void deposit( double amount ) ;
12      void withdraw( double amount ) ;
13      void display_balance() ;
14   private:
15      long int account_number ;
16      double balance ;
17   } ;
18
19   bank_account::bank_account( long int acc_no, double initial_balance )
20   {
21      account_number = acc_no ;
22      balance = initial_balance ;
23   }
24
25   void bank_account::deposit( double amount )
26   {
27      balance += amount ;
28   }
29
30   void bank_account::withdraw( double amount )
31   {
32      balance -= amount ;
33   }
34
35   void bank_account::display_balance()
36   {
37      cout << "Balance in Account " << account_number << " is "
```

The class constructor has the same name as the class and has no return type.

```
38              << fixed << setprecision( 2 )
39              << balance << endl ;
40  }
41
```

The class constructor on line 19 has the same name as the class and has no return type. The constructor is never explicitly called and therefore cannot return a value. That's why a class constructor has no return type, not even `void`.

Rewriting `main()` to make use of the class constructor:

```
42  void main()
43  {
44    bank_account my_account( 123, 10.54 ) ;
45
46    my_account.display_balance() ;
47
48    my_account.deposit( 10.50 ) ;
49
50    my_account.display_balance() ;
51
52    my_account.withdraw( 20.04 ) ;
53
54    my_account.display_balance() ;
55  }
```

The class constructor `bank_account()` *is automatically called, assigning the account number a value of* `123` *and the balance a value of* `10.54`

Line 44 of this program creates an object called `my_account` with these values:

my_account	
account_no	balance
123	10.54

Running the program will produce the following output:

```
Balance in Account 123 is 10.54
Balance in Account 123 is 21.04
Balance in Account 123 is 1.00
```

8.9 Default class constructor

Of course there is always the danger that the initial values in line 44 of program P8B are omitted. To allow for such a case, a default constructor can be included in the class. A default class constructor is a constructor that has no parameters.

Rewriting the bank account class to include a default class constructor:

```
1  // Program example P8C
2  // Demonstration of a class default constructor.
3  #include <iostream>
4  #include <iomanip>
```

```
5   using namespace std ;
6
7   class bank_account
8   {
9   public:
10    bank_account() ;
11    bank_account( long int acc_no, double initial_balance ) ;
12    void deposit( double amount ) ;
13    void withdraw( double amount ) ;
14    void display_balance() ;
15  private:
16    long int account_number ;
17    double balance ;
18  } ;
19
20  bank_account::bank_account()
21  {
22    account_number = 0 ;
23    balance = 0.0 ;
24  }
25
26  bank_account::bank_account( long int acc_no, double initial_balance )
27  {
28    account_number = acc_no ;
29    balance = initial_balance ;
30  }
31
32  void bank_account::deposit( double amount )
33  {
34    balance += amount ;
35  }
36
37  void bank_account::withdraw( double amount )
38  {
39    balance -= amount ;
40  }
41
42  void bank_account::display_balance()
43  {
44    cout << "Balance in Account " << account_number << " is "
45         << fixed << setprecision( 2 )
46         << balance << endl ;
47  }
48
```

The default class constructor has no parameters.

Using the default constructor in main() :

Program example P8C ... continued

The default class constructor bank_account()
*is automatically called assigning the account number
a value of* 0 *and the balance a value of* 0.0

```
49  void main()
50  {
51    bank_account my_account ;
52
53    my_account.display_balance() ;
54
```

```
55   my_account.deposit( 10.50 ) ;
56
57   my_account.display_balance() ;
58
59   my_account.withdraw( 20.04 ) ;
60
61   my_account.display_balance() ;
62 }
```

Line 51 creates the object my_account with these values:

my_account	
account_no	balance
0	0.0

Running this program will display the following:

```
Balance in Account 0 is 0.00
Balance in Account 0 is 10.50
Balance in Account 0 is -9.54
```

8.10 Overloading class constructors

The bank_account class of program P8C has now got two constructors. One of the constructors does not have any parameters (the default constructor) and the other constructor has two parameters. There can be several constructors within a class, each with a different number of parameters and so, like any other function, constructors can be overloaded.

The next program extends the bank_account class by adding another constructor that has just one parameter. This parameter is used for setting the value of the bank account number.

```
1   // Program example P8D
2   // Demonstration of overloaded class constructors.
3   #include <iostream>
4   #include <iomanip>
5   using namespace std ;
6
7   class bank_account
8   {
9   public:
10     bank_account() ;
11     bank_account( long int acc_no ) ;
12     bank_account( long int acc_no, double initial_balance ) ;
13     void deposit( double amount ) ;
14     void withdraw( double amount ) ;
15     void display_balance() ;
16   private:
17     long int account_number ;
18     double balance ;
19   } ;
20
```

```
21  bank_account::bank_account()
22  {
23    account_number = 0 ;
24    balance = 0.0 ;
25  }
26
27  bank_account::bank_account( long int acc_no )
28  {
29    account_number = acc_no ;
30    balance = 0.0 ;
31  }
32
33  bank_account::bank_account( long int acc_no, double initial_balance )
34  {
35    account_number = acc_no ;
36    balance = initial_balance ;
37  }
38
39  void bank_account::deposit( double amount )
40  {
41    balance += amount ;
42  }
43
44  void bank_account::withdraw( double amount )
45  {
46    balance -= amount ;
47  }
48
49  void bank_account::display_balance()
50  {
51    cout << "Balance in Account " << account_number << " is "
52          << fixed << setprecision( 2 )
53          << balance << endl ;
54  }
55
56  void main()
57  {
58    bank_account my_account( 123 ) ;
59
60    my_account.display_balance() ;
61  }
```

Because there is only one argument given when the object my_account is being created, the class constructor on lines 27 to 31 is called, assigning 123 to the account number and 0.0 to the balance.

my_account	
account_no	balance
123	0.0

8.11 Constructor initialisation lists

The data members, `account_number` and `balance`, of the `bank_account` class are initialised using assignment statements, e.g. lines 35 and 36.

A data member initialisation list is frequently used in constructors in place of assignment statements. For example, the constructor on lines 33 to 37 can be re-written as:

```
bank_account::
bank_account( long int acc_no, float initial_balance ) :
            account_number( acc_no ), balance( initial_balance )
{
}
```

This is an example of a constructor initialisation list. In a constructor initialisation list, a colon follows the constructor function header. The data member `account_number` is initialised with the value of `acc_no` and the data member `balance` is initialised with the value of `initial_balance`.

In this case, the initialisation list performs all the initialisations required of the constructor. Hence, there are no statements left in this constructor. Note, however, that the chain brackets {} are still required.

8.12 Default argument values in a constructor

In chapter 7, default argument values were used in standalone non-class functions. Since constructors are also functions, default arguments can also be used in constructors.

Instead of using the two overloaded constructors in lines 27 to 37 of program P8D, the data member `balance` can be assigned a default value of `0.0`. This is demonstrated in the next program:

```
1   // Program example P8E
2   // Demonstration of default arguments in a class constructor.
3   #include <iostream>
4   #include <iomanip>
5   using namespace std ;
6
7   class bank_account
8   {
9   public:
10    bank_account() ;
11    bank_account( long int acc_no, double initial_balance = 0.0 ) ;
12    void deposit( double amount ) ;
13    void withdraw( double amount ) ;
14    void display_balance() ;
15  private:
16    long int account_number ;
17    double balance ;
18  } ;
19
20  bank_account::bank_account()
21  {
22    account_number = 0 ;
23    balance = 0.0 ;
```

Default argument in a constructor.

```
24 }
25
26 bank_account::
27 bank_account( long int acc_no, double initial_balance ) :
28          account_number( acc_no ), balance( initial_balance )
29 {}              Can use an initialisation list and assignment statements in a constructor.
30
31 void bank_account::deposit( double amount )
32 {
33   balance += amount ;
34 }
35
36 void bank_account::withdraw( double amount )
37 {
38    balance -= amount ;
39 }
40
41 void bank_account::display_balance()
42 {
43    cout << "Balance in Account " << account_number << " is "
44          << fixed << setprecision( 2 )
45          << balance << endl ;
46 }
47
48 void main()
49 {
50   bank_account account1 ( 1 ) ;
51   // The constructor starting on line 26 is called,
52   // assigning the account number a value of 1 and the balance
53   // the default value of 0.0
54
55   bank_account account2 ( 2, 10.55 ) ;
56   // The constructor starting on line 26 is again called,
57   // assigning the account number a value of 2 and the balance
58   // a value of 10.55
59
60   bank_account account3 ;
61   // The default constructor on lines 20 to 24 is called,
62   // assigning the account number a value of 0 and the balance
63   // a value of 0.00
64
65   account1.display_balance() ;
66   account2.display_balance() ;
67   account3.display_balance() ;
68 }
```

The output from this program is:

```
Balance in Account 1 is 0.00
Balance in Account 2 is 10.55
Balance in Account 0 is 0.00
```

8.13 `static` class data members

A `static` class data member is independent of all the objects that are created from that class. Only one copy of a `static` data member exists and is shared by all objects of a particular class. The value of the `static` data member is therefore the same for all the class objects. If even one of the objects of a class modifies the value of a `static` data member, then the value of the `static` data member changes for every object of that class.

The next program uses a `static` data member `next_account_number` that is incremented every time a bank account object is created. Using `next_account_number`, it is possible to automatically assign a bank account number to each new object of the class.

```
1   // Program example P8F
2   // Demonstration of a class static data member.
3   #include <iostream>
4   #include <iomanip>
5   using namespace std ;
6
7   class bank_account
8   {
9   public:
10    bank_account() ;
11    bank_account( long int acc_no ) ;
12    bank_account( long int acc_no, double initial_balance ) ;
13    void deposit( double amount ) ;
14    void withdraw( double amount ) ;
15    void display_balance() ;          static class data member.
16  private:
17    static long int next_account_number ;
18    long int account_number ;
19    double balance ;
20  } ;
21
22  bank_account::bank_account()
23  {
24    account_number = next_account_number++ ;
25    balance = 0.0 ;
26  }
27
28  bank_account::bank_account( long int acc_no )
29  {
30    account_number = acc_no ;
31    balance = 0.0 ;
32  }
33
34  bank_account::bank_account( long int acc_no, double initial_balance )
35  {
36    account_number = acc_no ;
37    balance = initial_balance ;
38  }
39
40  void bank_account::deposit( double amount )
41  {
42    balance += amount ;
43  }
```

```
44
45 void bank_account::withdraw( double amount )
46 {
47    balance -= amount ;
48 }
49
50 void bank_account::display_balance()
51 {
52    cout << "Balance in Account " << account_number << " is "
53         << fixed << setprecision( 2 )
54         << balance << endl ;
55 }
56
57 long int bank_account::next_account_number = 1 ;
58
59 void main()
60 {
61    bank_account account1, account2, account3 ;
62
63    account1.deposit( 25.50 ) ;
64    account2.deposit( 30.50 ) ;
65    account3.deposit( 10.00 ) ;
66    account1.withdraw( 20.04 ) ;
67
68    account1.display_balance() ;
69    account2.display_balance() ;
70    account3.display_balance() ;
71 }
```

A static *data member is initialised outside the class and outside* main().

The output from this program is:

```
Balance in Account 1 is 5.46
Balance in Account 2 is 30.50
Balance in Account 3 is 10.00
```

The new static data member next_account_number is declared on line 17. Since a static data member is independent of objects of the class, it must be assigned a value outside the class. This is done on line 57, before main() is entered. The scope resolution operator :: is used to specify that next_account_number belongs to the class bank_account.

The class data member next_account_number occurs only once and is shared by all objects of the class, regardless of the number of bank account objects that are created. In contrast, the variables account_number and balance exist for every bank account object that is created.

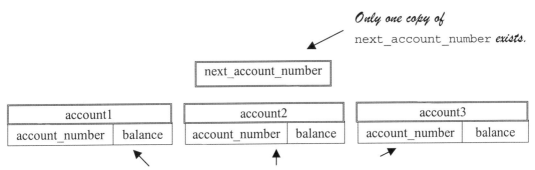

Only one copy of next_account_number *exists.*

Every object has its own copy of the instance variables account_number *and* balance.

Because next_account_number is associated with a class rather than an object, next_account_number is called a *class variable*. The variables account_no and balance are associated with instances of the class and are called *instance variables*.

Line 61 defines three instances of the bank_account class: account1, account2 and account3. The default constructor is called for all three objects.

*   The account number for account1 is assigned the initial value of next_account_number (which is 1) on line 24. After this assignment, next_account_number is incremented to 2.
*   When the constructor for account2 is called the value of next_account_number has remained at 2, because account_number is static and holds its value between calls to the constructor. Line 24 assigns the data member account_number of account2 the value of 2 and increments next_account_no to 3.
*   When the constructor for account3 is called, the data member account_number for this object is assigned the value of 3.

In this way, each instance of the bank_account class is automatically assigned an account number.

8.14 Using return in a member function

The member functions of the bank account class do not have a return statement in them and so are type void. A class member function can, like any function, return a value using a return statement.

The next program calculates the total of the balances in all accounts. To do this a member function get_balance() is added to the bank_account class. This function simply returns the value of the private class data member balance for a bank account object.

```
1   // Program example P8G
2   // Demonstration of a class function that returns a value.
3   #include <iostream>
4   #include <iomanip>
5   using namespace std ;
6
7   class bank_account
8   {
9   public:
10    bank_account() ;
11    bank_account( long int acc_no ) ;
```

```
12    bank_account( long int acc_no, double initial_balance ) ;
13    void deposit( double amount ) ;
14    void withdraw( double amount ) ;
15    void display_balance() ;
16    double get_balance() ;
17  private:
18    static long int next_account_number ;
19    long int account_number ;
20    double balance ;
21  } ;
22
23  bank_account::bank_account()
24  {
25    account_number = next_account_number++ ;
26    balance = 0.0 ;
27  }
28
29  bank_account::bank_account( long int acc_no )
30  {
31    account_number = acc_no ;
32    balance = 0.0 ;
33  }
34
35  bank_account::bank_account( long int acc_no, double initial_balance )
36  {
37    account_number = acc_no ;
38    balance = initial_balance ;
39  }
40
41  void bank_account::deposit( double amount )
42  {
43    balance += amount ;
44  }
45
46  void bank_account::withdraw( double amount )
47  {
48      balance -= amount ;
49  }
50
51  void bank_account::display_balance()
52  {
53      cout << "Balance in Account " << account_number << " is "
54           << fixed << setprecision( 2 )
55           << balance << endl ;
56  }
57
58  double bank_account::get_balance()
59  {
60    return balance ;
61  }
62
63  long int bank_account::next_account_number = 1 ;
64
65  void main()
66  {
67    // Create four accounts.
```

```
68    bank_account account1, account2, account3, account4 ;
69
70    // Put some money into each account.
71    account1.deposit( 125.55 ) ;
72    account2.deposit( 130.75 ) ;
73    account3.deposit( 100.25 ) ;
74    account4.deposit( 300.45 ) ;
75
76    // Calculate the total amount on deposit.
77    float total_balances = account1.get_balance() +
78                            account2.get_balance() +
79                            account3.get_balance() +
80                            account4.get_balance() ;
81
82    cout << "Total Balances = " << fixed << setprecision( 2 )
83         << total_balances << endl ;
84  }
```

The output from this program is:

```
Total Balances = 657.00
```

The member function `get_balance()` is called an *inspector* or *accessor* function. Inspector functions allow `private` data members of a class to be inspected from outside the class. The class member functions `deposit()` and `withdraw()` are examples of *mutator* functions. Mutator functions change the values of the private data members of a class.

8.15 Inline class member functions

Using a member function like `get_balance()` simply to get the value of a data member of an object is a bit costly in terms of the overheads involved in calling a function. Inline functions are useful in cases like this where you want to use a function but don't want the function overheads.

Like the standalone non-class functions of chapter 7, class member functions can be either inline or non-inline. The member functions of a class can be made inline by preceding the function header with the keyword `inline`. For example, to make `get_balance()` inline, change line 16 of program P8G to

```
inline double get_balance() ;
```

An alternative way of making a member function `inline` is to include the function definition in the body of the class. For example,

```
class bank_account
{
public:
  bank_account() ;
  bank_account( long int acc_no ) ;
  bank_account( long int acc_no, double initial_balance ) ;
  void deposit( double amount ) ;
  void withdraw( double amount ) ;
  void display_balance() ;
  double get_balance()
  {
```

`inline` *is implicit for functions defined within the class.*

```
      return balance ;
   }
 private:
   static long int next_account_number ;
   long int account_number ;
   double balance ;
 } ;
```

A disadvantage of making functions inline by moving their definitions into the class is that the class becomes 'crowded' with details. A programmer who wants to use the class will want to know what functions are in the class and how to use them; details of how member functions are implemented may be of no interest.

8.16 Class interface and class implementation

The public interface of a class is a list of the member functions of the class and how they can be used. The public interface starts at `public` and ends at the keyword `private`.

A programmer using a class (the client) should only have to read the public interface in order to use the class; a knowledge of the subsequent details in the `private` section and in the member functions should not be necessary. These details are called the *class implementation* and are of concern only to the programmer who wrote or maintains the class (the implementer).

To make the public interface easier to read, comments should be included explaining the purpose of the functions, their parameters and their return values. For example,

```
1   class bank_account
2   {
3   public:
4   // Constructors.                              Public interface of the class.
5     bank_account() ;
6     // Purpose: Default class constructor.
7     //         First instance of the class is assigned account number
8     //         1, the second instance account number 2, and so on.
9     //         The account balance is set to 0 for each instance.
10
11    bank_account( long int acc_no ) ;
12    // Purpose  : Class constructor to set the account number
13    //            of an instance of the class to the parameter value.
14    // Parameter: An account number.
15
16    bank_account( long int acc_no, double initial_balance ) ;
17    // Purpose  : Constructor to set the account number and balance of a
18    //            class instance to specified values.
19    // Parameters: An account number and a balance.
20
21  // Mutator functions.
22    void deposit( double amount ) ;
23    // Purpose  : Function to add an amount to the account balance.
24    // Parameter: Amount of money.
25
26    void withdraw( double amount ) ;
27    // Purpose  : Function to subtract an amount from the balance.
28    // Parameter: Amount of money.
29
30  // Inspector functions.
```

```
31   void display_balance() ;
32   // Purpose: Displays the account balance.
33
34   inline double get_balance() ;
35   // Purpose: To inspect the account balance of a class instance.
36   // Returns: Private class member account_balance.
37 private:
38   static long int next_account_number ;
39   long int account_number ;
40   double balance ;
41 } ;
42
43 bank_account::bank_account()
44 {
45   account_number = next_account_number ++ ;
46   balance = 0.0 ;
47 }
48
49 bank_account::bank_account( long int acc_no )
50 {
51   account_number = acc_no ;
52   balance = 0.0 ;
53 }
54
55 bank_account::bank_account( long int acc_no, double initial_balance )
56 {
57   account_number = acc_no ;
58   balance = initial_balance ;
59 }
60
61 void bank_account::deposit( double amount )
62 {
63   balance += amount ;
64 }
65
66 void bank_account::withdraw( double amount )
67 {
68   balance -= amount ;
69 }
70
71 void bank_account::display_balance()
72 {
73   cout << "Balance in Account " << account_number << " is "
74        << fixed << setprecision( 2 )
75        << balance << endl ;
76 }
77
78 double bank_account::get_balance()
79 {
80   return balance ;
81 }
82
83 long int bank_account::next_account_number = 1 ;
```

Class implementation details are from the private *section down.*

8.16.1 Separation of class interface and class implementation.

Separating the public interface of a class from its implementation makes sense for a client programmer who is just interested in how to use the class. Unfortunately, it is not possible in C++ to completely separate the public interface of a class from its implementation. In the bank account class, for example, the public interface and the implementation details of the private data members must be enclosed together between braces { and }.

In C++, the class declaration is normally placed in a *header* file (e.g. bank_ac.h) and the member functions are normally placed in a separate file(e.g. bank_ac.cpp).

For example, placing line 1 to 41 of the bank account class declaration in a file bank_ac.h :

```
// Declaration of bank_account class.

#if !defined BANK_AC_H
#define BANK_AC_H

class bank_account
{
public:
// Constructors.
  bank_account() ;
  // Purpose: Default class constructor.
  //          First instance of the class is assigned account number
  //          1, the second instance account number 2, and so on.
  //          The account balance is set to 0 for each instance.
...
private:
  static long int next_account_number ;
  long int account_number ;
  double balance ;
} ;

#endif
```

The lines beginning with a # are standard preprocessor directives used to prevent multiple inclusions of the header file into a program. See appendix G for details.

Placing lines 43 to 83 of the bank account class into bank_ac.cpp:

```
// Member function definitions and static data member initialisation
// code for bank account class.
#include <iostream>
#include <iomanip>
#include "bank_ac.h"
using namespace std ;

bank_account::bank_account()
{
  account_number = next_account_number ++ ;
  balance = 0.0 ;
}
...
long int bank_account::next_account_number = 1 ;
```

Using these two files, program P8G can now be re-written as:

```
1   // Program example P8H
2   // Demonstration of using class header and source code files.
3   #include <iostream>
4   #include <iomanip>
5   #include "bank_ac.h"
6   #include "bank_ac.cpp"
7   using namespace std ;
8
9   void main()
10  {
11    bank_account my_account ;
12
13    my_account.deposit( 12.34 ) ;
14    my_account.display_balance() ;
15  }
```

Lines 5 and 6 are preprocessor directives that incorporate the bank account header and source files into the program. The quotes around the file names on lines 5 and 6 tell the compiler that the files to be included are in the same directory as the program. See appendix G for details.

8.16.2 Use of namespaces in header files
A program may contain many classes and functions #included from many different header files. These header files may have been written by different programmers and may contain many elements such as classes, functions and objects. An element in one of the header files may have inadvertently been given the same name as an element in another header file. This will result in a compiler error.

C++ uses *namespaces* to resolve this problem. A namespace is a named block of statements in a program.

As an example, suppose alpha is one of many classes defined in a class library header file classlib1.h containing the following:

```
#if !defined CLASS_LIB1_H
#define CLASS_LIB1_H

namespace classlib1
{
  class alpha
  {
  private:
    int x, y ;
  public:
    ...
  } ;
  class beta
  {
    ...
  } ;
  ...
}

#endif
```

Another class library header file, classlib2.h, contains a different class with the same name alpha.

```
#if !defined CLASS_LIB2_H
#define CLASS_LIB2_H

namespace classlib2
{
  class alpha
  {
  private:
    int z ;
  public:
    . . .
  } ;
  . . .
}

#endif
```

There are two ways to distinguish between the two versions of alpha in a program. The first way is to use the scope resolution operator (: :).

```
#include "classlib1.h"
#include "classlib2.h"
#include <iostream>
using namespace std ;

void main()
{
  classlib1::alpha o1 ; // o1 is a classlib1 alpha object.
  classlib2::alpha o2 ; // o2 is a classlib2 alpha object.
  . . .
}
```

The second way to distinguish between the two versions of alpha is with the using statement. This statement indicates to the compiler which version of alpha to use.

```
#include "classlib1.h"
#include "classlib2.h"
#include <iostream>
using namespace std ;

void main()
{
  using classlib1::alpha ;
  alpha o1 ;  // o1 is a classlib1 alpha object.
  alpha o2 ;  // o2 is also a classlib1 alpha object.
  . . .
}
```

This form of the using statement provides access to a specific element in a namespace. Access to all the elements of a namespace can be achieved with a second form of the using statement:

```
#include "classlib1.h"
#include "classlib2.h"
#include <iostream>
using namespace std ;

void main()
{
  using namespace classlib1 ;
  // Can access all elements in the classlib1 namespace.
  alpha o1 ; // o1 is a classlib1 alpha object.
  alpha o2 ; // o2 is also a classlib1 alpha object.
  beta o3 ;  // o3 is a classlib1 beta object.
  ...
}
```

The `std` namespace is used throughout the examples in this book. The standard library classes, functions and objects like `cin` and `cout` are defined in this namespace. It is not necessary to use the entire `std` namespace in a program. For example, if a program is just using `cout`, then instead of the statement

```
using namespace std ;
```

the statement

```
using std::cout ;
```

can be used.

Programming pitfalls

1. Don't forget to place a semi-colon after the last } in a class declaration.

2. A constructor has no return type, not even `void`.

3. A class constructor is called automatically when an object of the class is created, it cannot be called explicitly.

4. Do not include parentheses when a default constructor is used. For example,

    ```
    bank_account my_account() ; // Incorrect.
    bank_account my_account ;   // Correct.
    ```

5. Non-inline functions must use the scope resolution operator (`::`).

6. `static` class data members must be initialised before the start of `main()`.

7. The default access of members in a class is `private`. Don't forget to place `public:` before member functions that are intended to be public.

Quick syntax reference

	Syntax	Examples

Declaring a class	```class class_name```
	 ```{```
	 ``` private:```
	 ``` // private data members and```
	 ``` // functions.```
	 ``` public:```
	 ``` // public data members and```
	 ``` // functions.```
	 ```} ;```
		```class bank_account```
		 ```{```
		 ``` private:```
		 ``` int account_number ;```
		 ``` float balance ;```
		 ``` static long int```
		 ``` next_account_number ;```
		 ``` ...```
		 ``` public:```
		 ``` void display_balance() ;```
		 ``` ...```
		 ```} ;```

Creating an instance of a class	```class_name variable₁, variable₂,```
	 ``` ... ;```
		```bank_account ac1,```
		 ``` ac2,```
		 ``` ac3 ;```

Accessing class members	Member selection operator . (Dot operator)	```ac1.display_balance() ;```
Initialising a static class data member	```data type class name::``` ``` variable = a constant value ;```	```long int bank_account::``` ``` next_account_number = 1 ;```

Exercises

1. List the class data members and class member functions for
    (a) a digital alarm clock
    (b) a CD player
    (c) a lift.

2. Briefly answer each of the following:
    (a) What is another name for a class data member?
    (b) What is the name given to a class member function that returns the value of a class data member?
    (c) How many parameters in a default constructor?
    (d) What is the public interface of a class?
    (e) What is the name given to a class member function that modifies the value of a class data member?
    (f) What is another name for a class member function?
    (g) Can a constructor return a value? Explain.
    (h) What is the purpose of the scope resolution operator : : ?

3. Find the errors in the following:

    (a)
    ```
    class class_a
    {
    private
      int a ;
    public::
      class_a( int a_value ) ;
    }
    ```

    (b)
    ```
    class class_b
    {
     private:
       int b1;
       int b2 = 0 ;
       class_b() ;
    } ;
    ```

4. Write a class declaration for each of the following classes. Include the member functions `assign_data()` to assign values to the data members and `display_data()` to display the values of the data members.
    (a) A class `current_date` with integer data members `day`, `month`, and `year`.
    (b) A class `current_time` with integer data members `hours`, `minutes`, and floating point data member `seconds`.
    (c) A class `complex` with floating point data members named `real` and `imaginary`.
    (d) A class `circle` with integer data members named `centre_x` and `centre_y` and an unsigned floating point data member `radius`.
    (e) A class `rectangle` with double data members `length` and `width`.
    (f) A class `cube` with an `unsigned` integer data member `size`.

    Create an object of each of the above classes in `main()`.
    Use `assign_data()` to assign values to the data members of each object.
    Display these values on the screen using `display_data()`.

5. Add a default constructor to each class in exercise 4.

6. Modify the classes developed in exercise 4 as follows:
    (a) Add a member function `increment_date()` to the `current_date` class that adds one day to the current date.
    (b) Add a member function `increment_time( s )` to the `current_time` class that adds s seconds to the current time.
    (c) Add a member function `calculate_magnitude()` to the `complex` class that calculates and returns the magnitude of a complex number.
    (Note: the magnitude of a complex number a + bi is got by calculating the square root of $(a^2 + b^2)$).
    (d) Add a member function `area()` to the `circle` class that calculates and returns the area of a circle.
    (e) Add a member function `perimeter()` to the `rectangle` class that calculates and returns the perimeter of a rectangle.
    (f) Add a member function `volume()` to the `cube` class that calculates and returns the volume of a cube.

7. Modify program P8H to include a `static` class data member `overdrawn_fee` which is added to overdrawn accounts. Assume the overdrawn fee is three pounds.

8. Create an elevator class for an elevator in a building with ten floors.
    (a) The elevator starts at the first floor.
    (b) When + is pressed the elevator goes to the next floor. Ignore this command if the elevator is on the tenth floor.
    (c) When - is pressed the elevator goes to the previous floor. Ignore this command if the elevator is on the first floor.
    (d) When S (shut down) is pressed the elevator should return to the first floor.
    (e) As the elevator moves from floor to floor, the floor number should be displayed along with the bell (ASCII code 7) sounding.

    Test the class in `main()` by creating an elevator object and continually inputting a character from the keyboard until an S (shut down) is entered.

9. The following is a class for recording the position of a motorised robot.

    ```
    class robot
    {
    public:
      // Constructor with default arguments and constructor list.
      robot(float x = 0, float y = 0) : x_coord( x ), y_coord(y)
      {}
      // Inspector function to display the robot's position.
      void display_position()
      {
      cout << "(" << x_coord << "," << y_coord << ")" << endl ;
      }
    private:
      float x_coord, y_coord ;
    } ;
    ```

    The following is a demonstration of `robot`:

```
void main(void)
{
  robot r2d2( 10.0, 8.1 ) ; // Constructor sets the initial
                            // position.

  r2d2.left( 1.3 ) ; // Move robot left 1.3 cms.
                     // New position is (8.7,8.1)
  r2d2.display_position() ;

  r2d2.back(4.21) ; // Move robot back 4.21 cms.
                    // New position is (8.7,12.31)
  r2d2.display_position() ;

  r2d2.right( 3.1 ) ; // Move robot right 3.1 cms.
                      // New position is (11.8,12.31)
  r2d2.display_position() ;

  r2d2.return_to_base() ; // Sets the position to (0,0).

  r2d2.forward( 0.3 ) // Move robot forward 3.1 cms.
                      // New position is (0,0.3).
  r2d2.display_position() ;

  r2d2.goto( 1.5, 4.5 ) ; // New position is (1.5,4.5).

  r2d2.return_to_base() ; // Move to position (0,0).
}
```

Write the member functions `left()`, `right()`, `forward()`, `back()`, `goto()` and `return_to_base()`.

10. Extend exercise 9 to include the following features:

(a) Don't allow the robot to crash into the boundary walls. The corners of the four boundary walls are at the x-y positions (0,0), (0,100), (100,100) and (100,0). These positions will be `static` data members of the class.

If the robot is going to crash into a wall with the next move, it should stop at 0.1 cm from the wall.

(b) Extend the program to allow a speed and a time to be specified. For example, if the robot is at (10,5) then `speed_left(4,2)` will result in the robot moving left at a speed of 4 cm/s for 2 seconds. The robot's new position will then be (2,5).

(c) The robot is fuelled with Xenotoplartogenicplasma (X for short). The robot travels 2000cm per ml of X. If the robot is directed to a position that is so far away from its base that it cannot get back with the remaining fuel, then it should refuse to go.

(d) Use `return` statements in each member function that moves a robot to return to one of the following codes:

0 = move was successful
1 = move failure – fuel shortage
2 = move failure – move is outside a boundary wall

`main()` should now display a message an appropriate message every time the robot is moved.

CHAPTER NINE

Pointers and Dynamic Memory

9.1 Variable addresses

Every variable and object used in a C++ program is stored in a specific place in memory. Each location in memory has a unique address, in the same way that every house in a street has a unique address.

The next program uses & to get the address of a variable and display it on the screen.

```
1   // Program example P9A
2   // Program to display the address of variables.
3   #include <iostream>
4   #include <iomanip>
5   using namespace std ;
6
7   void main()
8   {
9     int var1 = 1 ;
10    float var2 = 2 ;
11
12    cout << "var1 has a value of " << var1
13          << " and is stored at " << &var1 << endl ;
14    cout << "var2 has a value of " << var2
15          << " and is stored at " << &var2 << endl ;
16  }
```

A sample run of this program is:

```
var1 has a value of 1 and is stored at 0012FF88
var2 has a value of 2 and is stored at 0012FF84
```

This is how the variables var1 and var2 are stored in memory:

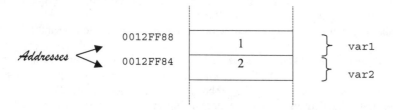

Different computers may give different addresses from the ones above. This is because various computers and operating systems will store variables at different memory locations. The addresses are in hexadecimal (base 16).

154

9.2 Pointer variables

A *pointer* variable is a variable that holds the address of another variable. A pointer variable is defined as follows:

```
data_type* variable_name ;
```

where `data_type` is any data type (such as `char`, `int`, `float`, a `struct`, a `class` and so on) and `variable_name` is any valid variable name. For example:

```
int* int_ptr ;      // int_ptr is a pointer to an int variable.
float* float_ptr ; // float_ptr is a pointer to a float variable.
bank_account* b ;  // b is a pointer to a bank_account object.
```

Whitespace in a pointer definition is not relevant. The pointer variable `int_ptr1`, for example, could also be defined as

```
int * int_ptr ;
```

or

```
int *int_ptr ;
```

or

```
int*int_ptr ;
```

Pointer definitions are read backwards from the variable name, replacing * with the words "is a pointer". Thus, `int* int_ptr` means that `int_ptr` is a pointer to an `int`, and `float* float_ptr` means that `float_ptr` is a pointer to a `float`.

The next program defines and uses two pointer variables.

```
1  // Program example P9B
2  // Demonstration of pointer variables.
3  #include <iostream>
4  using namespace std ;
5
6  void main()
7  {
8    int var1 = 1 ;
9    float var2 = 2 ;
10   int* ptr1 ;
11   float* ptr2 ;
12
13   ptr1 = &var1 ;  // ptr1 contains the address of var1.
14   ptr2 = &var2 ;  // ptr2 contains the address of var2.
15   cout << "ptr1 contains " << ptr1 << endl ;
16   cout << "ptr2 contains " << ptr2 << endl ;
17 }
```

The output from this program is:

```
ptr1 contains 0012FF88
ptr2 contains 0012FF84
```

This is how the program variables are stored in memory:

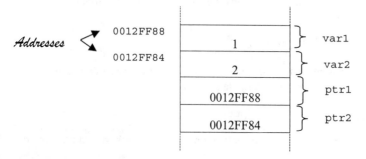

The two variables ptr1 and ptr2 are used to store the addresses of the other two variables, var1 and var2.

9.3 The indirection operator *

The indirection operator * is used to access the value of a variable, whose address is stored in a pointer. For instance, *ptr means the value of the variable at the address stored in the pointer variable ptr.

```
1   // Program example P9C
2   // Demonstration of indirection operator *
3   #include <iostream>
4   using namespace std ;
5
6   void main()
7   {
8      int var =1 ;
9      int* ptr ;
10
11     ptr = &var ; // ptr contains the address of var
12     cout << "ptr contains " << ptr << endl ;
13     cout << "*ptr contains " << *ptr << endl ;
14  }
```

The output from this program will be similar to the following:

```
ptr contains 0012FF88
*ptr contains 1
```

The asterisk (*) is used in two different contexts in the above program. In line 9, the * is used to define ptr as a pointer to an int. In line 13, the * is used to access the value of the memory location, the address of which is in ptr. The two uses of * are not related.

Line 11 of this program assigns the address of the variable var to the pointer variable ptr. Line 12 displays the address contained in the pointer ptr. Line 13 displays the value at the address held in ptr by using the indirection operator *. This is called *dereferencing* the pointer ptr. The value of *ptr is of course the same as the value of var.

9.4 Using `const` with pointers

When defining a pointer, the pointer itself, the value it points to or both can be made constant. The position of `const` in the definition determines which of these three apply.
In each of the following cases, assume two integer variables i and j are defined as:

```
int i, j ;
```

(a)

```
const int* p = &i ; // *p is a constant but p is not.
```

If a pointer definition is read backwards, what is being defined as a constant can be seen. The above definition reads as "p is a pointer to an integer constant". This means that the integer is constant and cannot be changed using pointer p with a statement such as:

```
*p = 5 ; // Illegal: cannot change i using p.
```

Note, however, the value of i can be changed with a statement such as

```
i = 5 ; // Legal: i is not a constant.
```

The pointer may be changed, so the following statement is legal:

```
p = &j ; // Legal: p now points to j.
```

(b)

```
int const* p = &i ;   // *p is a constant; p is not.
```

This definition of p reads as "p is a pointer to a constant integer". Again, this means that the integer is constant and cannot be changed using pointer p. This is an equivalent definition of p in (a) above.

(c)

```
int* const p = &i ;   // p is a constant; *p is not.
```

This definition of p reads, "p is a constant pointer to an integer". This means that the pointer is a constant but not what it points to.

```
*p = 5 ; // Legal: *p can be changed.
p = &j ; // Illegal: p is a constant.
```

(d)

```
const int* const p = &i; // p and *p are constant.
```

This definition of p reads, "p is a constant pointer to an integer constant". This means that both the pointer and the integer it points to are constants.

```
*p = 5 ; // Illegal: *p is a constant.
p = &j ; // Illegal: p is a constant.
```

9.5 Pointers and one-dimensional arrays

Pointers and arrays are directly related to one another. In C++, the name of an array is equivalent to the address of the first element of the array. The name of an array, therefore, is a pointer to the first element of the array. Consider the following array definition:

```
int a[5] ;
```

The elements of this array are: a[0], a[1], a[2], a[3], and a[4]. The name of the array is a, and this is equivalent to the address of the first element; in other words, a is the same as &a[0]. The following program demonstrates this.

```
1    // Program example P9D
2    // Program to show that the name of an array is the same
3    // as the address of its first element.
4    #include <iostream>
5    using namespace std ;
6
7    void main()
8    {
9      int a[5] ;
10
11     cout <<   "a is " << a
12           <<   " and &a[0] is " << &a[0] << endl   ;
13   }
```

The output from this program is:

```
a is 0012FF78 and &a[0] is 0012FF78
```

The actual addresses may be different on your system, but the two addresses will be the same nonetheless.
Just as a is the address of the first element, a + 1 is the address of the second element, a + 2 is the address of the third element, and so on.

As the name of an array is a pointer to the first element of the array, the indirection operator * can be used to access the elements of the array. The next program demonstrates a commonly used technique of displaying the elements of an array using the indirection operator *.

```
1    // Program example P9E
2    // Program to access the elements of an array by using
3    // element addresses rather than subscripts.
4    #include <iostream>
5    using namespace std ;
6
7    void main()
8    {
9      int a[5] = { 10, 13, 15, 11, 6 } ;
10
11     for ( int i = 0 ; i < 5 ; i++ )
12        cout << "Element " << i << " is " << *( a + i ) << endl ;
13   }
```

This program displays the elements of the array as follows:

```
Element 0 is 10
Element 1 is 13
Element 2 is 15
Element 3 is 11
Element 4 is 6
```

If `*( a+i )` in line 12 is changed to `a[i]`, the program would produce the same output. Thus:

```
*( a+0 ) or *a is equivalent to  a[0]
*( a+1 )        is equivalent to  a[1]
*( a+2 )        is equivalent to  a[2], and so on.
```

The parentheses in the expression `*( a+i )` are important. Without them the expression `*a+i` would add the first element of the array `a` and `i` together.

You can use pointers to access the elements of any array, not just an array of integers. If an array of `float`s is defined as

```
float numbers[100] ;
```

then `numbers[i]` is equivalent to `*( numbers + i )`.

Although the name of an array is a pointer to the first element of the array, you cannot change its value; this is because it is a constant pointer. Expressions such as `a++` or `numbers+=2` are invalid, because both `a` and `numbers` are array names. You can, however, assign the name of an array to a pointer variable of the same type. For example:

```
int a[5] ;
int* p ;
p = a ;       // Valid: assignment of a constant to a variable.
a++ ;         // Invalid: the value of a constant cannot change.
p++ ;         // Valid: p is a variable. p now points to
              // element 1 of the array a.
p-- ;         // Valid: p points to element 0 of the array a.
p += 10 ;     // Valid, but p is outside the range of the array a,
              // so *p is undefined. A common error.
p = a - 1 ; // Valid, but p is outside the range of the array.
```

A constant may be added to or subtracted from the value of a pointer, allowing access to different memory locations. However, not all arithmetic operations are permissible on pointers. For example, the multiplication of two pointers is illegal, because the result would not be a valid memory address.

9.6 Pointers and multi-dimensional arrays

As with one-dimensional arrays, you can access the elements of a multi-dimensional array using pointers. However, as the number of dimensions of an array increases, the pointer notation becomes increasingly complex. Consider the following definition of a two-dimensional array a:

```
int a[3][2] ={ { 4, 6 },
               { 1, 3 },
               { 9, 7 } } ;
```

A two-dimensional array is stored as an 'array of arrays'. This means that a is a one-dimensional array whose elements are themselves a one-dimensional arrays of integers.

As with a one-dimensional array, the name of the array is a pointer to the first element of the array. Therefore a is equivalent to &a [0]. a [0] is itself an array of two integers, which means that a [0] is equivalent to &a [0] [0].

a	→	a[0]	→	4	6
		a[1]	→	1	3
		a[2]	→	9	7

a [0], a [1] and a [2] are pointers (data type is int*) and a is a pointer to a pointer (data type is int **).

a [0] is the address of the first element in the first row of the array.
  *a [0] is a [0] [0], which is 4.

a [1] is the address of the first element in the second row.
  *a [1] is a [1] [0], which is 1.

a [2] is the address of the first element in the third row.
  *a [2] is a [2] [0], which is 9.

a [0] +1 is the address of the second element in the first row.
  * (a [0] +1) is a [0] [1], which is 6.

a [1] +1 is the address of the second element in the second row.
  * (a [1] +1) is a [1] [1], which is 3.

a [2] +1 is the address of the second element in the third row.
  * (a [2] +1) is a [2] [1], which is 7.

Using the fact that
            *a is the same as a [0]
      and * (a+1) is the same as a [1]
      and * (a+2) is the same as a [2]

the following can be derived:

1. a [0] [0] is *a [0] is * (*a) or **a

2. a [1] [0] is *a [1] is * (* (a+1))

3. a [2] [0] is *a [2] is * (* (a+2))

4. a [0] [1] is * (a [0] +1) is * (*a+1)

5. a [1] [1] is * (a [1] +1) is * (* (a+1) +1)

6. a [2] [1] is * (a [2] +1) is * (* (a+2) +1)

9.7 Pointers to structures

In addition to defining a pointer to a variable of a built-in data type, it is also possible to define a pointer to a variable of a type defined by `struct` or `class`.

The general format for defining a pointer to a structure is:

```
struct tag_name* variable_name ;
```

where `tag_name` is the structure tag and `variable_name` is the name of the pointer variable. For example, consider the `student_rec` structure used in chapter 5.

```
struct student_rec   // Structure template.
{
  int number ;
  float scores[5] ;
} ;

struct student_rec student ; // Define a structure variable.
```

The following line defines a pointer `ptr` to the `student_rec` structure.

```
struct student_rec *ptr ;
```

A value can be assigned to `ptr` by using the address operator &, as in:

```
ptr = &student ;
```

Note that it is the address of the structure variable `student` and not the address of the structure tag `student_rec` that is assigned to `ptr`.

The members of a structure variable can be referenced by using the dereferencing operator *. For example,

```
(*ptr).number
```

will access the student's number. The parentheses are necessary, because the selection operator `.` has a higher priority than the dereferencing operator *. Without the parentheses `*ptr.number` is attempting to access the memory location given by `ptr.number`. This is invalid, because `ptr` is not a structure and `number` is not a member of `ptr`.

C++ provides a much more convenient notation for accessing the members of a structure. The arrow notation `->` (`-` and `>` together) can be used in place of the dot notation. Thus,

```
ptr -> number    and    (*ptr).number
```

are equivalent. The expression `ptr->number` reads as "the member number of the structure pointed to by `ptr`".

9.8 Pointers to class objects

Defining a pointer to a class object is similar to defining a pointer to a structure variable. The general format for defining a pointer to a class object is:

```
class_name* variable_name ;
```

where class_name is the name of the class and variable_name is the name of the pointer variable.

The next program demonstrates the use of a pointer to an object of the bank account class of program P8H.

```
1   // Program P9F
2   // Demonstration of a pointer to a class object.
3   #include <iostream>
4   #include <iomanip>
5   #include "bank_ac.h"
6   #include "bank_ac.cpp"
7   using namespace std ;
8
9   void main()
10  {
11    bank_account ac ;        // ac is a bank_account object.
12    bank_account* ac_ptr ;   // ac_ptr is a pointer to a bank_account.
13
14    ac_ptr = &ac ;  // ac_ptr contains the address of the object ac.
15    ac_ptr -> deposit( 100 ) ;
16    ac_ptr -> display_balance() ;
17  }
```

The output from this program is:

```
Balance in account 1 is 100.00
```

Line 12 defines ac_ptr as a pointer to a bank_account object and line 14 assigns the address of the bank_account object ac to ac_ptr.

The public members of a class object may be accessed by using the dereferencing operator *. For example,

```
(*ac_ptr).deposit( 100 )
```

will call the public member function deposit().
The parentheses are necessary, because the selection operator . has a higher priority than the dereferencing operator *.

As with structures, the arrow notation -> can be used in place of the dot notation. Thus,

```
ac_ptr -> deposit( 100 ) ;    and    (*ac_ptr).deposit( 100 ) ;
```

are equivalent. Of the two notations, -> is more convenient and common.

9.9 Pointers as function arguments

Like any data type, pointers can be used as function arguments. The next program is a re-write of program P7H, which used reference variables to swap two values. This version of the program uses pointers in place of references.

```
1   // Program example P9G
2   // Demonstration of pointer arguments.
3   #include <iostream>
4   using namespace std ;
5
6   void swap_vals( float* val1, float* val2 ) ;
7   // Purpose   : To swap the values of two float variables.
8   // Parameters: Pointers to the two float variables.
9
10  void main()
11  {
12    float num1, num2 ;
13
14    cout << "Please enter two numbers: " ;
15    cin >> num1 ;
16    cin >> num2 ;
17    // Swap values around so that the smallest is in num1
18    if ( num1 > num2 )
19      swap_vals( &num1, &num2 ) ;
20    cout << "The numbers in order are "
21         << num1 << " and " << num2 << endl ;
22  }
23
24  void swap_vals( float* ptr1, float* ptr2 )
25  {
26    float temp = *ptr1 ;
27
28    *ptr1 = *ptr2 ;
29    *ptr2 = temp ;
30  }
```

Pointer arguments.

A sample run of this program is:

```
Please enter two numbers: 12.1  6.4
The numbers in order are 6.4 and 12.1
```

Line 19 passes the addresses of the two floating-point variables num1 and num2 to the function swap_vals(). These addresses are received by the parameters ptr1 and ptr2, declared as pointers to floats in the function header on line 24.

Line 26 stores the value of num1 (= *ptr1) in the variable temp (temp is now 12.1). The statement

```
  *ptr1 = *ptr2 ;
```

in line 28 is equivalent to

```
  num1 = num2 ;
```

because *ptr1 is the same as num1 and *ptr2 is the same as num2. Therefore, num1 gets the value 6.4.

Finally, the statement

```
*ptr2 = temp ;
```

in line 29 assigns the value of temp (12.1) to num2, because *ptr2 is the same as num2. The result is that the values in num1 and num2 are swapped.

Comparing this program with program P7H, it can be seen that it is easier to use references rather than pointers. When calling the function on line 19, & must be used to pass the address of the variables to the function. Also, within the function the indirection operator * must be used to access the value of each of the numbers. Forgetting to do these two operations is a common error when using pointers as function arguments.

Although references are more convenient to use, pointers are important because of the number of library functions that use them as parameters. One such function is ctime(), which converts the time in seconds to a text string containing the date and time.

```
1   // Program example P9H
2   // Demonstration of ctime() library function.
3   #include <iostream>
4   #include <ctime>
5   #include<string>
6   using namespace std ;
7
8   void main()
9   {
10    time_t current_time ;   // Define a variable of type time_t.
11
12    current_time = time( 0 ) ; // Get the current time in seconds.
13    // Display the current date and time as a text string.
14    cout << "Current date and time: " << ctime( &current_time ) << endl ;
15  }
```

More common examples involve arrays as function parameters. For example, line 20 of program P7I is commonly written as

```
int sum_array( int* array, int no_of_elements )
```

The first argument on line 16 of P7I is the name of an array, which also a pointer to the first element of the array. Therefore, the first parameter on line 20 is a pointer to an integer and can also be written as int* array.

9.10 Dynamic memory allocation

When defining an array, the number of elements in the array must be specified in advance of the program execution. Sometimes, either all the elements specified are not used or more elements than were originally anticipated are required. To avoid these problems, C++ has the ability to allocate memory while a program is executing. This is done using the memory allocation operator new.

9.10.1 Allocating memory dynamically for an array

The new memory operator can be used to allocate a contiguous block of memory for an array of any data type, whether the data type is built-in or is a user-defined structure or class.
The general format of new for allocating memory for an array is:

```
pointer = new data_type[ size ] ;
```

where `pointer` is a pointer to the allocated memory, `data_type` is the data type of the array and `size` is the number of elements in the array. For example:

```
int_ptr = new int[10] ;  // Allocate memory for 10 integers.
ac_ptr = new bank_account[5] ; // Allocate memory for 5 bank a/cs.
```

When allocating memory for an array of class objects, there must be a default constructor for the class so that the elements of the array get initialised.

The next program demonstrates new by allowing the user to specify the number of elements in an integer array while the program is running.

```
1   // Program example P9I
2   // Demonstration of dynamic memory allocation for an array
3   // of integers.
4   #include <iostream>
5   using namespace std ;
6
7   void main()
8   {
9     int* int_array ;
10    int no_els, i ;
11
12    cout << "Enter the number of elements " ;
13    cin >> no_els ;
14    // Allocate the required memory while the program is running.
15    int_array = new int[no_els] ;
16    // Enter the elements into the array.
17    for ( i = 0 ; i < no_els ; i++ )
18    {
19      cout << "Enter element " << i << ": " ;
20      cin >> int_array[i] ;
21    }
22    // Display the element values just entered.
23    for ( i = 0 ; i < no_els ; i++ )
24      cout << "Element " << i << " is " << *( int_array+i ) << endl ;
25    delete[] int_array ; // Free the allocated memory.
26  }
```

The number of array elements required is input from the keyboard on line 13. Line 15 uses new to allocate the exact number of elements required. The operator new stores the starting address of the allocated memory block in the pointer `int_array`.

The elements of the newly allocated array can be accessed using either a pointer or an index. For example, `int_array[0]` and `*int_array` both access the first element of the array and `int_array[1]` and `*( int_array + 1 )` access the second element of the array. The index notation is used on line 20 and the pointer notation is used on line 24.

The allocated memory is freed using the `delete` operator. It is important to remember to include the square brackets `[]` when freeing memory for a previously allocated array. Without the square brackets, only the first element of the array will be deleted.

9.10.2 Initialisation with new
When allocating memory for an array of class objects, the default constructor for the class initialises the elements of the array. For example,

```
ac_ptr = new bank_account[5] ;
```

results in the default constructor for the bank account class being called five times.

No initialisation is done for dynamically allocated arrays of built-in data types. For example,

```
int_ptr = new int[10] ;
```

results in the ten non-initialised integer elements.

Single instances of any data type (built-in, a user-defined structure or a class) can be initialised using a second form of the `new` operator.

The general format of `new` for a single instance of a data type is:

```
pointer = new data_type( initial_value ) ;
```

where `pointer` is a pointer to the allocated memory. The initial value is optional.

```
// Allocate memory for an integer, with an initial value of 100.
int_ptr = new int( 100 ) ;

// Allocate memory for an integer, with no initial value.
int_ptr = new int ;

// Allocate memory for a bank account object. The default
// class constructor is called to do the initialisation.
ac_ptr = new bank_account ;

// Allocate memory for a bank account object. A constructor
// is called to assign initial values to account number
// and balance.
ac_ptr = new bank_account( 1234, 100 ) ;
```

The next program demonstrates the use of `new` with various initialisations.

```
1    // Program example P9J
2    // Demonstration of initialisation with operator new.
3    #include <iostream>
4    #include <iomanip>
5    #include "bank_ac.h"
6    #include "bank_ac.cpp"
7    using namespace std ;
8
9    void main()
10   {
11     int no_of_acs ;
12
13     // Dynamically create an array of bank accounts.
14     // The default constructor is called for each array element.
15     cout << "Enter the number of bank accounts " ;
16     cin >> no_of_acs ;
17     bank_account* accounts = new bank_account[no_of_acs] ;
18     // Display the initialised elements of the array.
19     cout << "Accounts:" << endl ;
20     for ( int i = 0 ; i < no_of_acs ; i++ )
21         accounts[i].display_balance() ;
22     cout << endl ;
23
24     // Create a single instance of a bank account.
25     // The default constructor is called to do the initialisation.
26     cout << "bank_ptr1:" << endl ;
27     bank_account* bank_ptr1 = new bank_account ;
28     bank_ptr1->display_balance() ;
29     cout << endl ;
30
31     // Create a single instance of a bank account.
32     // Initialisation is done by the third constructor in the class.
33     bank_account* bank_ptr2 = new bank_account( 123, 100 ) ;
34     cout << "bank_ptr2:" << endl ;
35     bank_ptr2->display_balance() ;
36     delete[] accounts ;
37     delete bank_ptr1 ;
38     delete bank_ptr2 ;
39   }
```

9.10.3 Allocating memory for multi-dimensional arrays

In C++, multi-dimensional arrays are implemented as 'arrays of arrays'. To fully understand dynamic memory allocation for multi-dimensional arrays, familiarity with section 9.6 is necessary.

The next program illustrates the dynamic allocation of a two-dimensional array of integers.

```
1   // Program P9K
2   // Dynamic allocation of a two-dimensional array.
3   #include <iostream>
4   #include <iomanip>
5   using namespace std ;
6
7   void main()
8   {
9     int no_of_rows, no_of_cols ;
10    int i, j ;
11    float **data ;
12
13    cout<< "Number of rows: " ;
14    cin >> no_of_rows ;
15    cout<< "Number of columns: " ;
16    cin >> no_of_cols ;
17
18    // Allocate requested storage:
19
20    // (a) allocate storage for the rows.
21    data = new float* [no_of_rows] ;
22
23    // (b) allocate storage for each column.
24    for ( j = 0 ; j < no_of_rows; j++ )
25      data[j] = new float[no_of_cols] ;
26
27    // Place some values in the array.
28    for ( i = 0 ; i < no_of_rows ; i++ )
29      for ( j = 0 ; j < no_of_cols ; j++ )
30        data[i][j] = i * 10 + j ;
31
32    // Display elements of the array.
33    for ( i = 0 ; i < no_of_rows ; i++ )
34    {
35      for ( j = 0 ; j < no_of_cols ; j++ )
36        cout << data[i][j] << ' ' ;
37      cout << endl << endl ;
38    }
39
40    // Free the allocated storage:
41
42    // (a) delete the columns.
43    for ( i = 0 ; i < no_of_rows ; i++ )
44      delete[] data[i] ;
45
46    // (b) delete the rows.
47    delete[] data ;
48  }
```

Lines 44 and 47 free the memory allocated in lines 21 and 25. Note that for each pointer returned from new in lines 21 and 25 there is a corresponding call to delete with that pointer in lines 47 and 44.

9.10.4 Out of memory error

In the previous programs, it was assumed that the memory requested with new was allocated, regardless of whether memory was available or not. C++ handles insufficient memory errors produced by new by calling a function specified in set_new_handler().

The next program continually allocates memory in one megabyte blocks until no more memory exists. When new is unable to allocate memory, the function out_of_memory() is called.

```
1   // Program P9L
2   // Demonstration of error handling with the new operator.
3   #include <iostream>
4   using namespace std ;
5
6   void out_of_memory() ;
7
8   void main()
9   {
10    const int ONE_MB = 1024 * 1024 ;
11    int memory_allocated = 0 ;
12    int* ptr ;
13
14    set_new_handler( out_of_memory ) ;
15
16    for ( ; ; )  // Infinite loop.
17    {
18      ptr = new int[ONE_MB] ; // Allocate memory in 1MB blocks.
19      memory_allocated++ ;
20      cout << memory_allocated << " MB allocated..." << endl ;
21    }
22  }
23
24  void out_of_memory()
25  {
26    cerr << "Error:Out of memory" << endl ;
27    exit( 1 ) ;
28  }
```

The function out_of_memory() inserts an error message into the stream cerr rather than into cout. The stream cerr is typically used for error messages while cout is used for displaying the results of a program. Like cout, cerr is, by default, connected to the screen. However, the output for cout is often redirected to a device other than the screen (e.g. a disk file). In this case cout is unsuitable for error messages that may require immediate attention, so cerr is used instead.
Redirecting output streams to different devices is done by the operating system commands, not by C++.

Line 27 terminates the program and exits to the operating system with a status code of 1. A non-zero status code is usually used to indicate an abnormal exit from a program.

Programming pitfalls

1. Consider the following code segment:

```
int a = 1, b = 2, c ;
int* pa = &a, *pb = &b ;

c = *pa/*pb ;
```

The /* in the above assignment is interpreted as the start of a C-style comment. Use parentheses, as in:

```
c = (*pa)/(*pb) ;
```

or use spaces, as in:

```
c = *pa / *pb   ;
```

2. When defining two or more pointers as in

```
int* p1, *p2 ;
```

it is a common error to write the definition as:

```
int* p1, p2 ;
```

In both cases p1 is a pointer to an integer. In the first case p2 is also a pointer to an integer, but in the second case p2 is an integer.

3. Pointers, like any other variable, are not automatically initialised. Do not use a pointer until it has been assigned a value. For example:

```
int* p ;
*p = 100 ; // Where is p pointing to?
```

4. The new operator uses () to initialise a single instance of a data type and [] to allocate memory for an array. For example:

```
int* p = new int(10) ; // Allocate memory for an int with an
                       // initial value of 10.
int* p = new int[10] ; // Allocate memory for an array of 10
                       // integers.
```

5. Use delete if an object was created with new without [] and use delete[] if the object was created with new [].

6. Be careful not to create a *lingering* or *dangling* pointer, i.e. a pointer that points to a memory block that has been de-allocated with delete. For example:

```
int* p1 = new int ( 1 ) ;
int* p2 = p1 ;
delete p1 ;
```

```
cout << *p2 ; // *p2 no longer exists!
```

7. A *memory leak* can occur when an allocated block of memory has no associated pointer.
    For example,

```
int* p = new int ( 1 ) ; // p points to a memory block
                         // with the number 1 in it.
p = new int ( 2 ) ; // p now points to the memory block
                    // with the number 2 in it.
                    // The first memory block is inaccessible.
```

Quick syntax reference

	Syntax	Examples

Defining a pointer	`data_type* variable ;`	`int* pa ;`
		`float* pb, *pc ;`
		`bank_account* bank_ac_ptr ;`

Address	`&variable`	`int a ;` `pa = &a ;`
Indirection *	`*variable`	`a = *pa ;`
The name of an array is a pointer to the first element of the array		`int a[10] ;` `// a is the same as &a[0].`

Memory allocation	`pointer = new [size] ;`
	or
	`pointer = new (value) ;`
		`// Allocate storage for 10`
		`// integers.`
		`int* pi ;`
		`pi = new [10] ;`
		`// Allocate storage for a`
		`// float, initial value 10.`
		`float *pf ;`
		`pf = new float( 10 ) ;`

Free memory	`delete[] pointer ;`
	or
	`delete pointer ;`
		`delete[] pi ;`
		
		`delete pf ;`

Exercises

1. Write a program to define the following variables and to display their addresses:

    ```
    char c = 'a' ;
    int i = 1 ;
    long l = 123456 ;
    float f = 125.5 ;
    double d = 1234.25 ;
    ```

    Draw a diagram to illustrate the memory layout for these variables. How many bytes of main storage are allocated for each of these variables?

2. Given the following:

    ```
    int* i_ptr ;
    float* f_ptr;
    int i = 1, k = 2 ;
    float f = 10.0 ;
    ```

    which of these statements are valid?

    (a) i_ptr = &i ;   (b) f_ptr = &f ;   (c) f_ptr = f ;
    (d) f_ptr = &i ;   (e) k = *i ;   (f) k = *i_ptr ;
    (g) i_ptr = &k ;   (h) *i_ptr = 5 ;   (i) i_ptr = &5 ;

3. What does this program segment display?

    ```
    int a, b ;
    int* p1, *p2 ;
    a = 1 ;
    b = 2 ;
    p1 = &a ;
    p2 = &b ;
    b = *p1 ;
    cout << a << b << endl ;
    cout << *p1 << *p2 << endl ;
    *p1 = 15 ;
    cout << << a << b << endl ;
    *p1 -= 3 ;
    cout << a << b << endl ;
    *p2 = *p1 ;
    cout << a << b << endl ;
    (*p1)++ ;
    cout << << a << *p2 << endl ;
    p1 = p2 ;
    *p1 = 50 ;
    cout << a << b << endl ;
    ```

4. What is wrong with each of the following?

    (a)
```
float a[5] ;
int* p ;
p = a ;
```
    (b)
```
float a[5] ;
float* p ;
p = &a ;
```
    (c)
```
float a[5] ;
float* p ;
p = a ;
```

    (d)
```
int n = new int ;
n = 0 ;
```
    (e)
```
int* p = new float ( 5 ) ;
p[0] = 0 ;
```

5. What is the output from the following?

```
string* sp1 = new string ( "asdfghjk" ) ;
string* sp2 ;
string s = *sp1 ;
string& r = s ; // r is a reference to s.
sp2 = &s ;      // sp2 contains the address of s.
s.at( 0 ) = 'A' ;
sp1 -> erase ( 2, 3 ) ;
cout << s << endl ;
cout << r << endl ;
cout << *sp1 << endl ;
cout << *sp2 << endl ;
```

6. What does this program segment do?

```
int a[5] ;
int *p ;
for ( int i = 0 ; i < 5 ; i++ )
   cin >> (a+i) ;
for ( p = a ; p < a+5 ; p++ )
   cout << *p ;
```

7. What is the value of *p, *p+4 and * (p+4) in each of the following?

    (a)
```
int one_d[] = {1,3,4,5,-1} ;
int *p ;
p = one_d ;
```

    (b)
```
float f[] = { 1.25, 11.0, 9.5, 3.5, 6.5, 1.0 } ;
float *p ;
p = f ;
```

    (c)
```
int two_d[3][6] = { {1, 5, 0,  9,11, -4},
                    {3, 9, 4,  6, 10, 123},
                    {11, 7, 4, -10, 19, 15} } ;
int *p ;
p = two_d[1] ;
```

8. Given the following definitions:

```
int numbers[10] = { 1,7,8,2 } ;
int *ptr = numbers ;
```

what is in the array numbers after each of the following?

(a) `*(ptr+4) = 10 ;`
(b) `*ptr-- ;`
(c) `*(ptr+3) = *(ptr+9) ;`
(d) `ptr++ ;`
(e) `*ptr = 0 ;`
(f) `*(numbers+1) = 1 ;`

9. If a is a 6 by 8 array, which elements of a do the following expressions access?

(a) `*a[2]`
(b) `*(a[2]+7)`
(c) `*(*a)`
(d) `*(*(a+5)+2)`

10. Using new, write a program to input a specified number of integer values into an array and to display the array and the sum of the elements in the array. Use pointers, not subscripts, in the program.

11. Given an array such as

```
int int_array[] = { 1, 2, 9, -1, 4, 0, -2, 8 } ;
```

write a program that replaces all elements less than 0 with 0. Use pointers.

12. Given the following arrays,

```
float   gallons[]  =  {  11.5,   11.21,   12.7,   12.6,   12.4  }  ;
float   miles[]    =  {  471.5,  358.72,  495.3,  453.6,  421.6  }  ;
int mpg[5] ;
```

write a program to calculate and display the value of each element of mpg. Use pointers to access the elements of each array.

CHAPTER TEN

Operator Overloading

10.1 The need for operator overloading

The C++ built-in arithmetic (+, *, \ etc.) and relational operators (>, <, ==, !=) work with built-in data types (int, float, long etc.). However, not all the built-in operators can be used with every data type. For example, multiplication is not a valid operation for strings and % can only be used with integer data types. Of course, it doesn't make sense to multiply two strings together, so the * operator is inappropriate for strings. The + operator, however, is appropriate for strings and is taken to mean concatenation (joining one string of characters to the end of another). This means that the operator + has a different meaning for numeric data types than for string data types.

When you create a new class you may also want to redefine or overload existing operators to work appropriately on objects created from that class.

For example, the addition of an integer to a date such as 31/12/1999 + 1 should result in the date 1/1/2000, not 32/12/1999 nor 31/12/2000. When using dates, the + operator does not mean simple addition and will have to be *overloaded* to work in an appropriate manner for dates.

Although it makes sense to add an integer to a date, it doesn't make sense to add two dates together. However, the subtraction of two dates is meaningful and results in the number of days between the two dates.

Other data types where different meanings are assigned to + and – are time (11:59 + 0:01 = 12:00) and angles (9°10'-20'=8°-50'). Even in the game of snakes and ladders 7+3=16 (a player goes up a ladder at 7) and 15+5=4 (a player goes down a snake at 20).

Existing operators are overloaded for specific use in a class use by writing *operator functions* for the class.

10.2 Overloading the addition operator +

The next program demonstrates the use of an overloaded operator by including an addition operator + function for class objects that store times in the twenty-four hour format.

```
1   // Program example P10A
2   // Demonstration of an overloaded + operator.
3   #include <iostream>
4   using namespace std ;
5
6   class time24      // A simple 24-hour time class.
7   {
8   public:
9     time24( int h = 0, int m = 0, int s = 0 ) ;
10    void set_time( int  h, int  m, int  s ) ;
11    void get_time( int& h, int& m, int& s ) const ;
12    time24 operator+( int secs ) const ;
13  private:
14    int hours ;    // 0 to 23
15    int minutes ; // 0 to 59
16    int seconds ; // 0 to 59
```

```
17 } ;
18
19 // Constructor.
20 time24::time24( int h, int m, int s ) :
21          hours( h ), minutes( m ), seconds( s )
22 {}
23
24 // Mutator function.
25 void time24::set_time( int  h, int m, int  s )
26 {
27   hours = h ; minutes = m ; seconds = s ;
28 }
29
30 // Inspector function.
31 void time24::get_time( int& h, int& m, int& s ) const
32 {
33   h = hours ; m = minutes ;  s = seconds ;
34 }
35
36 // Overloaded + operator.
37 time24 time24::operator+( int secs ) const
38 {
39    // Add secs to class member seconds and calculate new time.
40    time24 temp ;
41    temp.seconds = seconds + secs ;
42    temp.minutes = minutes + temp.seconds / 60 ;
43    temp.seconds %= 60 ;
44    temp.hours = hours + temp.minutes / 60 ;
45    temp.minutes %= 60 ;
46    temp.hours %= 24 ;
47    return temp ;  // Return the new time.
48 }
49
50 void main()
51 {
52    int h, m, s ;
53    time24 t1( 23, 59, 57 ) ; // t1 represents 23:59:57
54    time24 t2 ;
55
56    t2 = t1 + 4 ;                // t2 should now be 0:0:1
57    t2.get_time ( h, m, s ) ;
58    cout << "Time t2 is " << h << ":" << m << ":" << s << endl ;
59 }
```

The output from this program is:

```
Time t2 is 0:0:1
```

The prototype for the overloaded + operator is on line 12. This line specifies that an integer is passed to the `operator+` function and the function returns a `time24` object. The const at the end of the declaration ensures that the object that called the function is not modified within the function.

Lines 37 to 48 define the overloaded + operator for adding an integer number of seconds to a
`time24` object and returning the result. Like any other function, `operator+()` has a return
type and a name: `operator+`. Since `operator+()` is like any other function, it can be
called like any other function; line 56 can also be written as

```
t2 = t1.operator+( 4 ) ;
```

The call to the operator + function on line 56 is obviously more intuitive, but the above form
is useful in understanding how the function is actually called and the type of arguments it
takes.

The way the + operator has been overloaded in this program restricts its use to adding an `int`
to a `time24` object. An expression such as `t3 = t1 + t2` is not valid, because this
expression is equivalent to `t3 = t1.operator+( t2 )`. The problem here is that the
parameter of the member function `operator+` is an integer and `t2` is a `time24` object.
The solution to this problem is to write another `operator+` member function that has a
`time24` object as a parameter. This is done in the next program.

```
1   // Program example P10B
2   // Demonstration of an overloaded + operator: version 2.
3   #include <iostream>
4   using namespace std ;
5
6   class time24      // A simple 24-hour time class.
7   {
8   public:
9     time24( int h = 0, int m = 0, int s = 0 ) ;
10    void set_time( int  h, int  m, int  s ) ;
11    void get_time( int& h, int& m, int& s ) const ;
12    time24 operator+( int secs ) const ;
13    time24 operator+( const time24& t ) const ;
14  private:
15    int hours ;   // 0 to 23
16    int minutes ; // 0 to 59
17    int seconds ; // 0 to 59
18  } ;
19
20  // Constructor.
21  time24::time24( int h, int m, int s ) :
22          hours( h ), minutes( m ), seconds( s )
23  {}
24
25  // Mutator function.
26  void time24::set_time( int  h, int m, int  s )
27  {
28    hours = h ; minutes = m ; seconds = s ;
29  }
30
31  // Inspector function.
32  void time24::get_time( int& h, int& m, int& s ) const
33  {
34    h = hours ; m = minutes ;  s = seconds ;
35  }
36
```

```
37 // Overloaded + operator.
38 time24 time24::operator+( int secs ) const
39 {
40    // Add secs to class member seconds and calculate new time.
41    time24 temp ;
42    temp.seconds = seconds + secs ;
43    temp.minutes = minutes + temp.seconds / 60 ;
44    temp.seconds %= 60 ;
45    temp.hours = hours + temp.minutes / 60 ;
46    temp.minutes %= 60 ;
47    temp.hours %= 24 ;
48    return temp ;   // Return the new time.
49 }
50
51 time24 time24::operator+( const time24& t ) const
52 {
53    // Add total seconds in t to seconds and calculate new time.
54    time24 temp ;
55    long int secs = t.hours * 3600 + t.minutes * 60 + t.seconds ;
56    temp.seconds = seconds + secs ;
57    temp.minutes = minutes + temp.seconds / 60 ;
58    temp.seconds %= 60 ;
59    temp.hours = hours + temp.minutes / 60 ;
60    temp.minutes %= 60 ;
61    temp.hours %= 24 ;
62    return temp ;   // Return the new time.
63 }
64
65 void main()
66 {
67    int h, m, s ;
68    time24 start_time( 23, 0, 0 ) ;
69    time24 elapsed_time( 1, 2, 3 ) ;
70    time24 finish_time ;
71
72    finish_time = start_time + elapsed_time ;
73    finish_time.get_time( h, m, s ) ;
74    cout << "Finish Time is "
75         << h << ":" << m << ":" << s << endl ;
76 }
```

The output from this program is:

```
Finish Time is 0:2:3
```

There are now two member functions called operator+. The second operator+ member function is tested on line 72. This line is equivalent to

```
finish_time = start_time.operator+( elapsed_time ) ;
```

This means that the member function operator+() is called for the object start_time using elapsed_time as an argument. Since the argument is a time24 object, the operator+() function that takes a time24 rather than an int argument is called, i.e. the operator+() function on lines 51 to 63.

Note that the parameter on line 51 is a reference to a const time24 object. By using a reference, the address of the object, rather than a copy of the entire object, is passed, and using const guarantees that the passed object (elapsed_time) is not changed in the function. The const at the end of line 51 guarantees that the calling object (start_time) is not changed in the function.

One last problem still exists when using the overloaded operator+ functions. The class can handle assignments such as t2 = t1 + 4 and t3 = t2 + t1, but the assignment t2 = 4 + t1 will cause a compiler error.

To understand the problem, consider the equivalent statement to t2 = 4 + t1 ; which is

```
t2 = 4.operator+( t2 ) ;   // Invalid.
```

The data type of the object making the call to operator+() in this statement is an int, not a time24 object.

To preserve symmetry, t2 = 4 + t1 should be the same as t2 = t1 + 4. This cannot be done with a time24 member function, because 4 is not a time24 object. A standalone non-class function must be used. This is demonstrated in the next program.

```
1   // Program example P10C
2   // Demonstration of an overloaded + operator: version 3.
3   #include <iostream>
4   using namespace std ;
5
6   class time24      // A simple 24-hour time class.
7   {
8   public:
9     time24( int h = 0, int m = 0, int s = 0 ) ;
10    void set_time( int  h, int  m, int  s ) ;
11    void get_time( int& h, int& m, int& s ) const ;
12    time24 operator+( int secs ) const ;
13    time24 operator+( const time24& t ) const ;
14  private:
15    int hours ;    // 0 to 23
16    int minutes ; // 0 to 59
17    int seconds ; // 0 to 59
18  } ;
19
20  // Constructor.
21  time24::time24( int h, int m, int s ) :
22          hours( h ), minutes( m ), seconds( s )
23  {}
24
25  // Mutator function.
26  void time24::set_time( int  h, int m, int  s )
27  {
28    hours = h ; minutes = m ; seconds = s ;
29  }
30
31  // Inspector function.
32  void time24::get_time( int& h, int& m, int& s ) const
33  {
34    h = hours ; m = minutes ;  s = seconds ;
```

```
35 }
36
37 // Overloaded + operators.
38 time24 time24::operator+( int secs ) const
39 {
40    // Add secs to class member seconds and calculate new time.
41    time24 temp ;
42    temp.seconds = seconds + secs ;
43    temp.minutes = minutes + temp.seconds / 60 ;
44    temp.seconds %= 60 ;
45    temp.hours = hours + temp.minutes / 60 ;
46    temp.minutes %= 60 ;
47    temp.hours %= 24 ;
48    return temp ;   // Return the new time.
49 }
50
51 time24 time24::operator+( const time24& t ) const
52 {
53    // Add total seconds in t to seconds and calculate new time.
54    time24 temp ;
55    long int secs = t.hours * 3600 + t.minutes * 60 + t.seconds ;
56    temp.seconds = seconds + secs ;
57    temp.minutes = minutes + temp.seconds / 60 ;
58    temp.seconds %= 60 ;
59    temp.hours = hours + temp.minutes / 60 ;
60    temp.minutes %= 60 ;
61    temp.hours %= 24 ;
62    return temp ;   // Return the new time.
63 }
64
65 // Non-member overloaded + operator.
66 time24 operator+( int secs, const time24& t )
67 {
68    // Add secs to total seconds in t to calculate new time.
69    time24 temp ;
70    temp = t + secs ;   // Uses member function operator+( int ).
71    return temp ;       // Return the new time.
72 }
73
74 void main()
75 {
76    int h, m, s ;
77    time24 t1( 23, 59, 57 ) ;
78    time24 t2 ;
79
80    t2 = 4 + t1 ;
81    t2.get_time ( h, m, s ) ;
82    cout << "Time t2 is " << h << ":" << m << ":" << s << endl ;
83 }
```

The output from this program is:

```
Time t2 is 0:0:1
```

The program contains a non-class standalone function called `operator+()` on lines 66 to 72. This function is not a member of the `time24` class. Like any other function it can be called in the conventional way with a statement such as

```
t2 = operator+( 4, t1 ) ;
```

which is equivalent to the statement on line 80.

10.3 Rules of operator overloading

The following rules apply to operator overloading:

All the C++ operators in appendix B with the exception of the following five operators can be overloaded:

```
        .       .*       ::       ?:      sizeof
```

1. New operators cannot be invented. For example, it is not possible to overload `<>` to mean 'not equal to' or ** to mean 'to the power of'.

2. The overloaded operator must have the same number of operands as the corresponding predefined operator. For example, an overloaded equivalent operator `==` must have two operands and an overloaded `++` operator must have one operand.

3. The priority of an overloaded operator remains the same as its corresponding predefined operator. For example, regardless of whether `*` is overloaded or not, it will always have a higher precedence than `+` and `-`.

4. Overloaded operators cannot have default arguments.

5. The operators for the built-in data types, e.g. `int`, `float` and so on, cannot be redefined.

10.4 Overloading ++
The next program includes a class member function to overload the increment operator `++`.

```
1  // Program example P10D
2  // Program to demonstrate overloading the prefix ++ operator.
3  #include <iostream>
4  using namespace std ;
5
6  class time24     // A simple 24-hour time class.
7  {
8  public:
9    time24( int h = 0, int m = 0, int s = 0 ) ;
10   void set_time( int  h, int  m, int  s ) ;
11   void get_time( int& h, int& m, int& s ) const ;
12   time24 operator+( int secs ) const ;
13   time24 operator+( const time24& t ) const ;
14   time24 operator++() ;
15 private:
```

```
16   int hours ;    // 0 to 23
17   int minutes ; // 0 to 59
18   int seconds ; // 0 to 59
19 } ;
20
21 // Constructor.
22 time24::time24( int h, int m, int s ) :
23         hours( h ), minutes( m ), seconds( s )
24 {}
25
26 // Mutator function.
27 void time24::set_time( int   h, int m, int   s )
28 {
29   hours = h ; minutes = m ; seconds = s ;
30 }
31
32 // Inspector function.
33 void time24::get_time( int& h, int& m, int& s ) const
34 {
35   h = hours ; m = minutes ;  s = seconds ;
36 }
37
38 // Overloaded + operators.
39 time24 time24::operator+( int secs ) const
40 {
41   // Add secs to class member seconds and calculate new time.
42   time24 temp ;
43   temp.seconds = seconds + secs ;
44   temp.minutes = minutes + temp.seconds / 60 ;
45   temp.seconds %= 60 ;
46   temp.hours = hours + temp.minutes / 60 ;
47   temp.minutes %= 60 ;
48   temp.hours %= 24 ;
49   return temp ;  // Return the new time.
50 }
51
52 time24 time24::operator+( const time24& t ) const
53 {
54   // Add total seconds in t to seconds and calculate new time.
55   time24 temp ;
56   long int secs = t.hours * 3600 + t.minutes * 60 + t.seconds ;
57   temp.seconds = seconds + secs ;
58   temp.minutes = minutes + temp.seconds / 60 ;
59   temp.seconds %= 60 ;
60   temp.hours = hours + temp.minutes / 60 ;
61   temp.minutes %= 60 ;
62   temp.hours %= 24 ;
63   return temp ;  // Return the new time.
64 }
65
66 // Overloaded prefix ++ operator.
67 time24 time24::operator++()
68 {
69   // Add 1 second to the calling object's seconds.
70   *this = *this + 1 ;  // Uses member function operator+( int ).
71   return *this ;  // Return updated time of calling object.
```

```
72 }
73
74 // Non-member overloaded + operator.
75 time24 operator+( int secs, const time24& t )
76 {
77   // Add secs to total seconds in t to calculate new time.
78   time24 temp ;
79   temp = t + secs ;  // Uses member function operator+( int ).
80   return temp ;      // Return the new time.
81 }
82
83 void main()
84 {
85   int h, m, s ;
86   time24 t1( 23, 59, 57 ) ;
87
88   ++t1 ;
89   t1.get_time ( h, m, s ) ;
90   cout << "Time t1 is " << h << ":" << m << ":" << s << endl ;
91 }
```

The output from this program is:

```
Time t1 is 23:59:58
```

The prototype for the overloaded ++ operator is on line 14. No parameters are used and the function returns a time24 object.

The function definition of the ++ operator is on lines 67 to 72. The function makes use of the special built-in pointer this. The this pointer is available in all member functions of a class and is a pointer to the object that called the member function.

When operator++() is called on line 88, this contains the address of t1. Line 70 therefore adds 1 to t1. The member function operator+() on lines 39 to 50 (with the argument secs equal to 1) is called to do the addition.

10.4.1 Overloading prefix and postfix forms of ++
The increment operator ++ needs to be overloaded in both its prefix and postfix forms. For example, if t1 and t2 are time24 objects then the following two statements will produce different results

```
t2 = ++t1 ;  // Use of prefix ++.
t2 = t1++ ;  // Use of postfix ++.
```

The first statement increments t1 before assigning its value to t2. The second statement assigns t1 to t2 and then increments t1.

To distinguish between the two operator ++ functions, the postfix version uses a 'dummy' integer parameter.

The next program overloads both forms of the ++ operator.

```
1    // Program P10E
2    // Program to demonstrate overloading prefix and postfix ++.
3    #include <iostream>
4    using namespace std ;
5
6    class time24      // A simple 24-hour time class.
7    {
8    public:
9       time24( int h = 0, int m = 0, int s = 0 ) ;
10      void set_time( int  h, int  m, int  s ) ;
11      void get_time( int& h, int& m, int& s ) const ;
12      time24 operator+( int secs ) const ;
13      time24 operator+( const time24& t ) const ;
14      time24 operator++() ;          // prefix.
15      time24 operator++( int ) ;   // postfix.
16   private:
17      int hours ;    // 0 to 23
18      int minutes ; // 0 to 59
19      int seconds ; // 0 to 59
20   } ;
21
22   // Constructor.
23   time24::time24( int h, int m, int s ) :
24            hours( h ), minutes( m ), seconds( s )
25   {}
26
27   // Mutator function.
28   void time24::set_time( int  h, int m, int  s )
29   {
30      hours = h ; minutes = m ; seconds = s ;
31   }
32
33   // Inspector function.
34   void time24::get_time( int& h, int& m, int& s ) const
35   {
36      h = hours ; m = minutes ;  s = seconds ;
37   }
38
39   // Overloaded + operators.
40   time24 time24::operator+( int secs ) const
41   {
42      // Add secs to class member seconds and calculate new time.
43      time24 temp ;
44      temp.seconds = seconds + secs ;
45      temp.minutes = minutes + temp.seconds / 60 ;
46      temp.seconds %= 60 ;
47      temp.hours = hours + temp.minutes / 60 ;
48      temp.minutes %= 60 ;
49      temp.hours %= 24 ;
50      return temp ;  // Return the new time.
51   }
52
53   time24 time24::operator+( const time24& t ) const
54   {
55      // Add total seconds in t to seconds and calculate new time.
56      time24 temp ;
```

```
57   long int secs = t.hours * 3600 + t.minutes * 60 + t.seconds ;
58   temp.seconds = seconds + secs ;
59   temp.minutes = minutes + temp.seconds / 60 ;
60   temp.seconds %= 60 ;
61   temp.hours = hours + temp.minutes / 60 ;
62   temp.minutes %= 60 ;
63   temp.hours %= 24 ;
64   return temp ;  // Return the new time.
65 }
66
67 // Overloaded prefix ++ operator.
68 time24 time24::operator++()
69 {
70   // Add 1 second to the calling object's seconds.
71   *this = *this + 1 ;  // Uses member function operator+( int ).
72   return *this ;  // Return updated time of calling object.
73 }
74
75 // Overloaded postfix ++ operator.
76 time24 time24::operator++( int )    ◄──── Dummy integer parameter.
77 {
78   // Save calling object before incrementing seconds.
79   time24 temp ;
80   temp = *this ;
81   *this = *this + 1 ;  // Uses operator+( int ),
82                        // could also use ++(*this).
83   return temp ;  // Return the saved calling object.
84 }
85
86 // Non-member overloaded + operator.
87 time24 operator+( int secs, const time24& t )
88 {
89   // Add secs to total seconds in t to calculate new time.
90   time24 temp ;
91   temp = t + secs ;  // Uses member function operator+( int ).
92   return temp ;      // Return the new time.
93 }
94
95 void main()
96 {
97   int h, m, s ;
98   time24 t1( 23, 59, 57 ) ;
99   time24 t2 ;
100
101   t2 = t1++ ;   // Test postfix ++
102   t1.get_time ( h, m, s ) ;
103   cout << "Using postfix ++: " << "time t1 is: "
104        << h << ":" << m << ":" << s ;
105   t2.get_time( h, m, s ) ;
106   cout << ", time t2 is: "
107        << h << ":" << m << ":" << s << endl ;
108
109   t1.set_time (23, 59, 57 ) ;  // Reset the time.
110
111   t2 = ++t1 ;   // Test prefix ++
112   t1.get_time ( h, m, s ) ;
```

```
113    cout << "Using prefix  ++: " << "time t1 is: "
114         << h << ":" << m << ":" << s ;
115    t2.get_time ( h, m, s ) ;
116    cout << ", time t2 is: "
117         << h << ":" << m << ":" << s << endl ;
118 }
```

The output from this program is:

```
Using postfix ++: time t1 is: 23:59:58, time t2 is: 23:59:57
Using prefix  ++: time t1 is: 23:59:58, time t2 is: 23:59:58
```

Both versions of the ++ operator are tested in main().

Lines 101 to 107 test and display the result of using the postfix operator ++ and lines 111 to 117 test and display the result of using the prefix operator ++. The value of t1 is identical in both tests, but t2 is assigned two different values.

The postfix version of operator ++ is defined in lines 76 to 84. The original value of the time24 object that called the member function is stored in temp. Only after saving the original value of the time24 object is its value incremented. The original value of the time24 object (stored in temp) is then returned.

10.4.2 Improving the prefix ++ operator member function

The return statement on line 72 of program P10E returns a copy of the object. It would be more efficient (especially for large objects) to return a reference to the object instead. To do this requires only two small changes to the class. The operator++ function header on line 68 changes to

```
time24& time24::operator++()
```

and the function prototype on line 14 changes to

```
time24& operator++() ;
```

The same improvement cannot be made for the overloaded postfix version of ++. The reason for this is that the object returned on line 92 is the local object temp, which will be out of scope and therefore undefined when the function ends. Returning a reference to an undefined object will cause problems, so a copy of temp has to be returned.

The overloaded + operator on lines 40 to 51 also returns a copy of a local object temp. Attempting to return a reference to this object will also cause problems.

10.5 Overloading relational operators

An equality operator (==) for the time24 class can be defined to test two time24 objects for equality.

The next program uses an overloaded == operator to verify that t1 and t2 are equal after the statement

```
t1 = ++t2 ; // t1 and t2 should be equal.
```

```
1   // Program example P10F
2   // Program to demonstrate the overloading of the == operator.
3   #include <iostream>
4   using namespace std ;
5
6   class time24      // A simple 24-hour time class.
7   {
8   public:
9     time24( int h = 0, int m = 0, int s = 0 ) ;
10    void set_time( int  h, int  m, int  s ) ;
11    void get_time( int& h, int& m, int& s ) const ;
12    time24 operator+( int secs ) const ;
13    time24 operator+( const time24& t ) const ;
14    time24& operator++() ;        // prefix.
15    time24 operator++( int ) ;   // postfix.
16    bool operator == ( const time24& t ) const ;
17  private:
18    int hours ;    // 0 to 23
19    int minutes ; // 0 to 59
20    int seconds ; // 0 to 59
21  } ;
22
23  // Constructor.
24  time24::time24( int h, int m, int s ) :
25          hours( h ), minutes( m ), seconds( s )
26  {}
27
28  // Mutator function.
29  void time24::set_time( int  h, int m, int  s )
30  {
31    hours = h ; minutes = m ; seconds = s ;
32  }
33
34  // Inspector function.
35  void time24::get_time( int& h, int& m, int& s ) const
36  {
37    h = hours ; m = minutes ;  s = seconds ;
38  }
39
40  // Overloaded + operators.
41  time24 time24::operator+( int secs ) const
42  {
43    // Add secs to class member seconds and calculate new time.
44    time24 temp ;
45    temp.seconds = seconds + secs ;
46    temp.minutes = minutes + temp.seconds / 60 ;
47    temp.seconds %= 60 ;
48    temp.hours = hours + temp.minutes / 60 ;
49    temp.minutes %= 60 ;
50    temp.hours %= 24 ;
51    return temp ;  // Return the new time.
52  }
53
54  time24 time24::operator+( const time24& t ) const
55  {
56    // Add total seconds in t to seconds and calculate new time.
```

```
57     time24 temp ;
58     long int secs = t.hours * 3600 + t.minutes * 60 + t.seconds ;
59     temp.seconds = seconds + secs ;
60     temp.minutes = minutes + temp.seconds / 60 ;
61     temp.seconds %= 60 ;
62     temp.hours = hours + temp.minutes / 60 ;
63     temp.minutes %= 60 ;
64     temp.hours %= 24 ;
65     return temp ;   // Return the new time.
66   }
67
68   // Overloaded prefix ++ operator
69   time24& time24::operator++()
70   {
71     // Add 1 second to the calling object's seconds.
72     *this = *this + 1 ;   // Uses member function operator+( int ).
73     return *this ;   // Return updated time of calling object.
74   }
75
76   // Overloaded postfix ++ operator.
77   time24 time24::operator++( int )
78   {
79     // Save calling object before incrementing seconds.
80     time24 temp ;
81     temp = *this ;
82     *this = *this + 1 ;   // Uses operator+( int ),
83                           // could also use ++(*this).
84     return temp ;   // Return the saved calling object.
85   }
86
87   // Overloaded equality operator ==.
88   bool time24 ::operator == ( const time24& t ) const
89   {
90     if ( hours == t.hours &&
91          minutes == t.minutes &&
92          seconds == t.seconds )
93       return true ;
94     else
95       return false ;
96   }
97
98   // Non-member overloaded + operator.
99   time24 operator+( int secs, const time24& t )
100  {
101    // Add secs to total seconds in t to calculate new time.
102    time24 temp ;
103    temp = t + secs ;   // Uses member function operator+( int ).
104    return temp ;       // Return the new time.
105  }
106
107 void main()
108  {
109    int h, m, s ;
110    time24 t1( 23, 59, 57 ) ;
111    time24 t2 ;
112
```

```
113   t2 = ++t1 ;      // t1 and t2 should be equal.
114   t1.get_time ( h, m, s ) ;
115   cout << "t1 is "
116         << h << ":" << m << ":" << s ;
117   t2.get_time ( h, m, s ) ;
118   cout << ", t2 is "
119         << h << ":" << m << ":" << s << endl ;
120
121   if ( t1 == t2 )  // Test equality operator ==.
122     cout << "t1 and t2 are equal. Prefix ++ is working."
123           << endl ;
124   else
125     cout << "t1 and t2 are not equal. Prefix ++ is not working."
126           << endl ;
127 }
```

The output from this program is:

```
t1 is 23:59:58, t2 is 23:59:58
t1 and t2 are equal. Prefix ++ is working.
```

The overloaded operator == for the time24 class on lines 88 to 96 returns a bool value of true if the data members of the calling object (t1) and the argument (t2) are equal, otherwise false is returned.

10.6 Overloading << and >>

Just like any other operator, the insertion and extraction operators << and >> can be overloaded. This enables the time24 class to have its own insertion and extraction operators << and >>.

```
1    // Program example P10G
2    // Program to demonstrate the overloading of << and >>.
3    #include <iostream>
4    #include <iomanip>
5    using namespace std ;
6
7    class time24      // A simple 24-hour time class.
8    {
9    public:
10     time24( int h = 0, int m = 0, int s = 0 ) ;
11     void set_time( int  h, int  m, int  s ) ;
12     void get_time( int& h, int& m, int& s ) const ;
13     time24 operator+( int secs ) const ;
14     time24 operator+( const time24& t ) const ;
15     time24& operator++() ;        // prefix.
16     time24 operator++( int ) ;  // postfix.
17     bool operator == ( const time24& t ) const ;
18   private:
19     int hours ;    // 0 to 23
20     int minutes ; // 0 to 59
21     int seconds ; // 0 to 59
22   } ;
23
24   // Constructor.
```

```
25  time24::time24( int h, int m, int s ) :
26          hours( h ), minutes( m ), seconds( s )
27  {}
28
29  // Mutator function.
30  void time24::set_time( int  h, int m, int  s )
31  {
32    hours = h ; minutes = m ; seconds = s ;
33  }
34
35  // Inspector function.
36  void time24::get_time( int& h, int& m, int& s ) const
37  {
38    h = hours ; m = minutes ;  s = seconds ;
39  }
40
41  // Overloaded + operators.
42  time24 time24::operator+( int secs ) const
43  {
44    // Add secs to class member seconds and calculate new time.
45    time24 temp ;
46    temp.seconds = seconds + secs ;
47    temp.minutes = minutes + temp.seconds / 60 ;
48    temp.seconds %= 60 ;
49    temp.hours = hours + temp.minutes / 60 ;
50    temp.minutes %= 60 ;
51    temp.hours %= 24 ;
52    return temp ;  // Return the new time.
53  }
54
55  time24 time24::operator+( const time24& t ) const
56  {
57    // Add total seconds in t to seconds and calculate new time.
58    time24 temp ;
59    long int secs = t.hours * 3600 + t.minutes * 60 + t.seconds ;
60    temp.seconds = seconds + secs ;
61    temp.minutes = minutes + temp.seconds / 60 ;
62    temp.seconds %= 60 ;
63    temp.hours = hours + temp.minutes / 60 ;
64    temp.minutes %= 60 ;
65    temp.hours %= 24 ;
66    return temp ;  // Return the new time.
67  }
68
69  // Overloaded prefix ++ operator.
70  time24& time24::operator++()
71  {
72    // Add 1 second to the calling object's seconds.
73    *this = *this + 1 ;  // Uses member function operator+( int ).
74    return *this ;  // Return updated time of calling object.
75  }
76
77  // Overloaded postfix ++ operator.
78  time24 time24::operator++( int )
79  {
80    // Save calling object before incrementing seconds.
```

```
 81    time24 temp ;
 82    temp = *this ;
 83    *this = *this + 1 ;  // Uses operator+( int ),
 84                         // could also use ++(*this).
 85    return temp ;  // Return the saved calling object.
 86  }
 87
 88  // Overloaded equality operator ==.
 89  bool time24::operator == ( const time24& t ) const
 90  {
 91    if ( hours == t.hours &&
 92         minutes == t.minutes &&
 93         seconds == t.seconds )
 94      return true ;
 95    else
 96      return false ;
 97  }
 98
 99  // Non-member overloaded + operator.
100  time24 operator+( int secs, const time24& t )
101  {
102    // Add secs to total seconds in t to calculate new time.
103    time24 temp ;
104    temp = t + secs ;  // Uses member function operator+( int ).
105    return temp ;      // Return the new time.
106  }
107
108  // Non-member overloaded << operator.
109  ostream& operator<<( ostream& os, const time24& t )
110  {
111    // Format time24 object, precede single digits with a 0.
112    int h, m, s ;
113    t.get_time( h, m, s ) ;
114    os << setfill( '0' )
115       << setw( 2 ) << h << ":"
116       << setw( 2 ) << m << ":"
117       << setw( 2 )<< s << endl ;
118    return os ;
119  }
120
121  // Non-member overloaded >> operator.
122  istream& operator>>( istream& is, time24& t )
123  {
124    // Input a time24 object data in the format h:m:s.
125    int h, m, s ;
126    do
127      is >> h ;
128    while ( h < 0 || h > 23 ) ;
129    // Ignore the separator.
130    is.ignore( 1 ) ;
131    do
132      is >> m ;
133    while ( m < 0 || m > 60 ) ;
134    // Ignore the separator.
135    is.ignore( 1 ) ;
136    do
```

```
137     is >> s ;
138   while ( s < 0 || s > 60 ) ;
139   t.set_time ( h, m, s ) ;
140   return is ;
141 }
142
143 void main()
144 {
145   time24 t1( 1, 2, 3 ) ;
146   time24 t2 ( 10, 10, 10 ) ;
147
148   cout << t1 << t2 ;
149
150   time24 t3 ;
151   cin  >> t3 ;
152   cout << t3 ;
153 }
```

A sample run of this program is:

```
01:02:03
10:10:10
4:5:6          ◄──────── Input a time.
04:05:06
```

Both >> and << are implemented as non-member functions. The headers for these functions on lines 109 and 122 look complicated and require an explanation.

Firstly, cout is an object of type ostream and cin is an object of type istream. These objects and classes are defined in the header file iostream included in the program on line 3.

A statement such as

```
cout << "hello"
```

results in a change in the output stream object cout. Any function that uses an output stream will modify it, which means that the output stream must be passed by reference, rather than by value, to a function. This is why the first parameter on line 109 is a reference to an object of type ostream.

The second parameter t is declared as a reference to a const time24 object for the purpose of efficiency. By using a reference, the address of the object, rather than a copy of the object is passed to t. Using a const ensures that the time24 object that t refers to cannot be modified within the function.

The return type on line 109 is a reference to the output stream which is returned on line 118. To understand the reason for this, consider a statement such as cout << t1 << t2 ;
The first part of this statement (cout << t1) displays the value of t1 and also returns a reference to cout enabling the next part of the statement (<< t2) to also use cout.

If the multiple uses of `<<` in the same statement were not required, the return type on line 109 could be simply `void` and line 118 could be omitted.

There is a similar explanation for the function header for `>>` on line 122. The first parameter must be a reference to `istream` to enable `>>` to be used more than once in the same statement. The second parameter `t` must be a reference, since the object that `t` refers to will be modified by the function.
The function itself inputs values for the `private` data members of a `time24` class object, performing some elementary validation on the input values.

10.7 Conversion operators

A conversion operator function is used to convert from a class object to a built-in data type or to another class object. The conversion operator member function has the same name as the data type to which the class is to be converted. For example, to convert a `time24` object to a `long int` a conversion operator named `operator long` is required. This is demonstrated in the next program.

```
1    // Program example P10H
2    // Demonstration of a class conversion operator.
3    #include <iostream>
4    #include <iomanip>
5    using namespace std ;
6
7    class time24      // A simple 24-hour time class.
8    {
9    public:
10     time24( int h = 0, int m = 0, int s = 0 ) ;
11     void set_time( int  h, int  m, int  s ) ;
12     void get_time( int& h, int& m, int& s ) const ;
13     time24 operator+( int secs ) const ;
14     time24 operator+( const time24& t ) const ;
15     time24& operator++() ;          // prefix.
16     time24 operator++( int ) ;  // postfix.
17     bool operator == ( const time24& t ) const ;
18     operator long() ;
19   private:
20     int hours ;    // 0 to 23
21     int minutes ; // 0 to 59
22     int seconds ; // 0 to 59
23   } ;
24
25   // Constructor.
26   time24::time24( int h, int m, int s ) :
27           hours( h ), minutes( m ), seconds( s )
28   {}
29
30   // Mutator function.
31   void time24::set_time( int  h, int m, int  s )
32   {
33     hours = h ; minutes = m ; seconds = s ;
34   }
35
36   // Inspector function.
```

```
37  void time24::get_time( int& h, int& m, int& s ) const
38  {
39    h = hours ; m = minutes ;  s = seconds ;
40  }
41
42  // Overloaded + operators.
43  time24 time24::operator+( int secs ) const
44  {
45    // Add secs to class member seconds and calculate new time.
46    time24 temp ;
47    temp.seconds = seconds + secs ;
48    temp.minutes = minutes + temp.seconds / 60 ;
49    temp.seconds %= 60 ;
50    temp.hours = hours + temp.minutes / 60 ;
51    temp.minutes %= 60 ;
52    temp.hours %= 24 ;
53    return temp ;   // Return the new time.
54  }
55
56  time24 time24::operator+( const time24& t ) const
57  {
58    // Add total seconds in t to seconds and calculate new time.
59    time24 temp ;
60    long int secs = t.hours * 3600 + t.minutes * 60 + t.seconds ;
61    temp.seconds = seconds + secs ;
62    temp.minutes = minutes + temp.seconds / 60 ;
63    temp.seconds %= 60 ;
64    temp.hours = hours + temp.minutes / 60 ;
65    temp.minutes %= 60 ;
66    temp.hours %= 24 ;
67    return temp ;   // Return the new time.
68  }
69
70  // Overloaded prefix ++ operator
71  time24& time24::operator++()
72  {
73    // add 1 second to the calling object's seconds.
74    *this = *this + 1 ;  // Uses member function operator+( int ).
75    return *this ;   // Return updated time of calling object.
76  }
77
78  // Overloaded postfix ++ operator.
79  time24 time24::operator++( int )
80  {
81    // Save calling object before incrementing seconds.
82    time24 temp ;
83    temp = *this ;
84    *this = *this + 1 ;  // Uses operator+( int ),
85                        // could also use ++(*this).
86    return temp ;   // Return the saved calling object.
87  }
88
89  // Overloaded equality operator ==.
90  bool time24 ::operator == ( const time24& t ) const
91  {
92    if ( hours == t.hours &&
```

```
 93        minutes == t.minutes &&
 94        seconds == t.seconds )
 95      return true ;
 96    else
 97      return false ;
 98 }
 99
100 // Conversion operator from time24 to long.
101 time24::operator long()
102 {
103   long no_of_seconds ;
104   no_of_seconds = hours * 3600 + minutes * 60 + seconds ;
105   return no_of_seconds ;
106 }
107
108 // Non-member overloaded + operator.
109 time24 operator+( int secs, const time24& t )
110 {
111   // Add secs to total seconds in t to calculate new time.
112   time24 temp ;
113   temp = t + secs ;   // Uses member function operator+( int ).
114   return temp ;       // Return the new time.
115 }
116
117 // Non-member overloaded << operator.
118 ostream& operator<<( ostream& os, const time24& t )
119 {
120   // Format time24 object, precede single digits with a 0.
121   int h, m, s ;
122   t.get_time( h, m, s ) ;
123   os << setfill( '0' )
124      << setw( 2 ) << h << ":"
125      << setw( 2 ) << m << ":"
126      << setw( 2 )<< s << endl ;
127   return os ;
128 }
129
130 // Non-member overloaded >> operator.
131 istream& operator>>( istream& is, time24& t )
132 {
133   // Input a time24 object data in the format h:m:s.
134   int h, m, s ;
135   do
136     is >> h ;
137   while ( h < 0 || h > 23 ) ;
138   // Ignore the separator.
139   is.ignore( 1 ) ;
140   do
141     is >> m ;
142   while ( m < 0 || m > 60 ) ;
143   // Ignore the separator.
144   is.ignore( 1 ) ;
145   do
146     is >> s ;
147   while ( s < 0 || s > 60 ) ;
148   t.set_time ( h, m, s ) ;
```

```
149  return is ;
150 }
151
152 void main()
153 {
154   time24 t( 1, 2, 3 ) ;
155   long s ;
156
157   s = t ;  // Conversion from time24 to long.
158   cout << "Time = " << t
159       << "Equivalent number of seconds = " << s << endl ;
160 }
```

The output from this program is:

```
Time = 01:02:03
Equivalent number of seconds = 3723
```

The `time24` object `t` is converted to a `long int` value on line 157. This statement is equivalent to the statement `s = long( t )` and results in a call to the conversion operator `long()` on lines 101 to 106. This function must be a class member function that has no return type, even though it returns a value. The return type is implied by the name of the conversion operator.

10.8 Use of `friend` functions

The values of the `private` members `hours`, `minutes` and `seconds` of the `time24` class are accessed using the class member function `get_time()` and given values using the member function `set_time()`. To access the private data members of a class directly in a non-member function, the function must be declared to be a `friend` of the class.

To declare the non-member functions operator >> and operator << as friends of the `time24` class, the following declarations are inserted in the class.

```
friend ostream& operator<<( ostream& os, const time24& t ) ;
friend istream& operator>>( istream& is, time24& t ) ;
```

These declarations can be placed anywhere in the class, but they are usually placed in the `public` section.

The overhead involved in calling the member functions `get_time()` and `set_time()` can now be eliminated by direct reference to the `private` data members `hours`, `minutes` and `seconds`. The function `operator<<`, for example, can now be re-written as:

```
ostream& operator<<( ostream& os, const time24& t )
{
  // Format time24 object, precede single digits with a 0.
  os << setfill( '0' )
     << setw( 2 ) << t.hours << ":"
     << setw( 2 ) << t.minutes << ":"
     << setw( 2 ) << t.seconds << endl ;
  return os ;
}
```

Friend functions override a basic principle of object-oriented programming – that of data hiding. Friends of a class have access to all the private data of a class and their use should be minimised where possible.

10.9 Overloading the assignment operator =

10.9.1 A class with a pointer data member

Consider a class for recording the components required to assemble a product for sale. For example, a computer consists of a keyboard, a monitor, a CPU, memory and so on.

To simplify matters, the class will include in its `private` data members the number of components and the stock codes of each of the components in the product. Different products will have a different number of components, but the maximum number of components in a product is say, one hundred.

A first attempt at writing the class might be like this:

```
class product
{
public:
  product() ;            // Constructor.
  ...
private:
  int prod_code ;        // Product code.
  int num_components ;   // Number of components in the product.
  int comp_codes[100] ;  // Component codes.
} ;
```

Each `product` object has storage for one hundred component codes. If a product has only two or three components it would still be allocated storage for one hundred. This would be a very inefficient. It would be better to use dynamic memory allocation to allocate the exact storage required by each product for its component codes. This requires a class pointer data member as demonstrated in the next program.

```
1   // Program example P10I
2   // Demonstration of a class with a pointer data member.
3   #include <iostream>
4   using namespace std ;
5
6   class product   // A class containing a pointer data member.
7   {
8   public:
9     product( int product_code, int number_of_components,
10              const int component_codes[] ) ;
11    ~product() ;
12    void set_component( int component_index, int component_code ) ;
13    // Purpose   : change a component code.
14    // Parameters: component_index - component to change.
15    //             component_code - new component code.
16    void display() const ;
17    // Purpose   : display product and component codes.
18  private:
19    int prod_code ;        // Product code.
20    int num_components ;   // Number of components in the product.
21    int *comp_codes ;      // Pointer to component codes.
22  } ;
```

```
23
24  // Constructor.
25  product::product( int product_code, int number_of_components,
26                    const int component_codes[] )
27  {
28    prod_code = product_code ;
29    num_components = number_of_components ;
30    comp_codes = new int[number_of_components] ;
31    for ( int i = 0 ; i < number_of_components ; i++ )
32      comp_codes[i] = component_codes[i] ;
33  }
34
35  // Destructor.
36  product::~product()
37  {
38    delete[] comp_codes ;
39  }
40
41  void product::set_component( int component_index,
42                               int component_code )
43  {
44    if ( component_index >= 0 && component_index < num_components )
45      comp_codes[component_index] = component_code ;
46  }
47
48  void product::display() const
49  {
50    cout << "Product code:" << prod_code << " Component codes:" ;
51    for ( int i = 0 ; i < num_components ; i++ )
52      cout << comp_codes[i] << ' ' ;
53    cout << endl ;
54  }
55
56  void main()
57  {
58    int component_list1[] = { 18122, 35122, 14115, 19865, 23412 } ;
59    // Instance a product with 5 components and display it.
60    product product1( 123, 5, component_list1 ) ;
61    product1.display() ;
62  }
```

Allocation of memory for the component codes.

Line 60 creates a product object with a product code of 123 and five components. The exact storage required for the component codes is allocated using new in the constructor on line 30. Lines 36 to 39 is a special class function called a *destructor*.

A destructor always has the same name as the class itself, but is preceded with a tilde(~).

A destructor is generally used in a class that has a pointer data member that points to memory allocated by the class. In such a case, a destructor can be used to free the memory allocated by the class. In this example, line 38 deletes the memory allocated by the constructor on line 30.

Just as a class constructor is called automatically when a class object is created, a class destructor is called automatically just before the class object is destroyed. An object is destroyed, for example, when the program ends or a function in which the object is created ends.

A class can only have one destructor. A destructor has no parameters and no return type.

10.9.2 Assigning one object to another

When assigning one object to another object of the same type, member-wise assignment is performed by default. For example, if t1 and t2 are time24 objects then the statement

```
t1 = t2 ;
```

has the effect of copying each member one by one as in

```
t1.hours = t2.hours ;
t1.minutes = t2.minutes ;
t1.seconds = t2.seconds ;
```

Each data member of t2 is copied byte by byte to its corresponding data member in t1. The default assignment operator works well for most classes, but fails to work properly for classes that allocate memory for one or more of its data members.

```
1    // Program example P10J
2    // Program to demonstrate the default assignment operator problem
3    // for a class with a pointer data member.
4    #include <iostream>
5    using namespace std ;
6
7    class product    // A class containing a pointer data member.
8    {
9    public:
10     product( int product_code, int number_of_components,
11             const int component_codes[] ) ;
12     ~product() ;
13     void set_component( int component_index, int component_code ) ;
14     // Purpose    : change a component code.
15     // Parameters: component_index - component to change.
16     //             component_code - new component code.
17     void display() const ;
18     // Purpose    : display product and component codes.
19    private:
20     int prod_code ;        // Product code.
21     int num_components ;   // Number of components in the product.
22     int *comp_codes ;      // Pointer to component codes.
23    } ;
24
25    // Constructor.
26    product::product( int product_code, int number_of_components,
27                      const int component_codes[] )
28    {
29     prod_code = product_code ;
30     num_components = number_of_components ;
31     comp_codes = new int[number_of_components] ;
32     for ( int i = 0 ; i < number_of_components ; i++ )
33       comp_codes[i] = component_codes[i] ;
34    }
35
36    // Destructor.
37    product::~product()
38    {
39     delete[] comp_codes ;
```

```
40  }
41
42  void product::set_component( int component_index,
43                               int component_code )
44  {
45    if ( component_index >= 0 && component_index < num_components )
46      comp_codes[component_index] = component_code ;
47  }
48
49  void product::display() const
50  {
51    cout << "Product code:" << prod_code << " Component codes:" ;
52    for ( int i = 0 ; i< num_components ; i++ )
53      cout << comp_codes[i] << ' ' ;
54    cout << endl ;
55  }
56
57  void main()
58  {
59    int component_list1[] = { 1812, 3512, 1411, 1986, 2342 } ;
60    int component_list2[] = { 2452, 3115, 3161 } ;
61
62    product product1( 123, 5, component_list1 ) ;
63    product product2( 124, 3, component_list2 ) ;
64
65    cout << "Before assignment:" << endl ;
66    cout << "product1:" << endl ;
67    product1.display() ;
68    cout << "product2:" << endl ;
69    product2.display() ;
70
71    product2 = product1 ;
72
73    cout << endl << "After assignment:" << endl ;
74    cout << "product1: " << endl ;
75    product1.display() ;
76    cout << "product2: " << endl ;
77    product2.display() ;
78
79    // Change first component code of product1 to 999.
80    product1.set_component( 0, 9999 ) ;
81
82    cout << endl
83         << "After changing first component of product1 to 9999:"
84         << endl ;
85    cout << "product1: " << endl ;
86    product1.display() ;
87    cout << "product2: " << endl ;
88    product2.display() ;
89  }
```

The output from this program is:

```
Before assignment:
product1:
Product code:123 Component codes:1812 3512 1411 1986 2342
product2:
Product code:124 Component codes:2452 3115 3161

After assignment:
product1:
Product code:123 Component codes:1812 3512 1411 1986 2342
product2:
Product code:123 Component codes:1812 3512 1411 1986 2342

After changing first component of product1 to 9999:
product1:
Product code:123 Component codes:9999 3512 1411 1986 2342 ✓
product2:
Product code:123 Component codes:9999 3512 1411 1986 2342 ✗
```

After line 63, a sketch of memory might be as shown below. Fictitious memory addresses are to the left of each memory location.

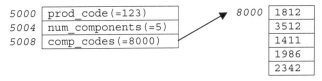

Object product1   *Allocated memory.*

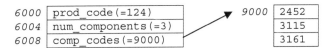

Object product2   *Allocated memory.*

On line 71, product1 is copied to product2. By default, a member-wise copy occurs. This means that the block of memory occupied by product1 is copied to the memory block occupied by product2, byte by byte.

This results in the following changes in memory:

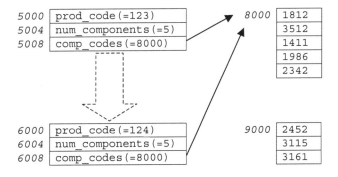

The contents of each data member of product1 has been copied to the corresponding fields in product2. Note that the contents of the pointers were copied and not the actual memory locations they point to. This type of copy is called a *shallow copy*.

As a result of the shallow copy, the comp_codes pointer in the two objects are pointing to the same memory block. A *deep copy* is required, in which the memory pointed to by a pointer, rather than just the pointer itself, is copied.

Line 80 changes the first component code of product1 to 9999. This results in the following changes to the memory:

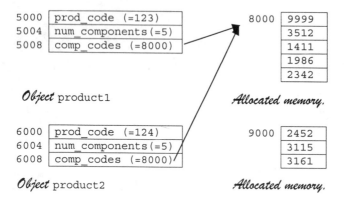

Lines 86 and 88 display the data stored in both objects. Despite having changed the first component code for product1 only on line 80, the first component code in product2 has also changed to 9999.

Further complications arise when the destructor on lines 37 to 40 is called for each object. At the end of the program, when the destructor de-allocates the memory pointed to by comp_codes for one of the objects, it also de-allocates the memory used by the other object. When the destructor is called again for the second object, it tries to de-allocate memory which has already been de-allocated!

The next program corrects theses errors by overloading the assignment operator =.

```
1    // Program example P10K
2    // Program to demonstrate the overloaded assignment operator =
3    // for a class with a pointer data member.
4    #include <iostream>
5    using namespace std ;
6
7    class product    // A class containing a pointer data member.
8    {
9    public:
10      product( int product_code, int number_of_components,
11              const int component_codes[] ) ;
12      ~product() ;
13      void set_component( int component_index, int component_code ) ;
14      // Purpose   : change a component code.
15      // Parameters: component_index - component to change.
```

```
16   //               component_code - new component code.
17   void display() const ;
18   // Purpose    : display product and component codes.
19   const product& operator=( const product& p ) ;
20   private:
21     int prod_code ;        // Product code.
22     int num_components ;   // Number of components in the product.
23     int *comp_codes ;      // Pointer to component codes.
24   } ;
25
26   // Constructor.
27   product::product( int product_code, int number_of_components,
28                      const int component_codes[] )
29   {
30     prod_code = product_code ;
31     num_components = number_of_components ;
32     comp_codes = new int[number_of_components] ;
33     for ( int i = 0 ; i < number_of_components ; i++ )
34       comp_codes[i] = component_codes[i] ;
35   }
36
37   // Destructor.
38   product::~product()
39   {
40     delete[] comp_codes ;
41   }
42
43   void product::set_component( int component_index,
44                                int component_code )
45   {
46     if ( component_index >= 0 && component_index < num_components )
47       comp_codes[component_index] = component_code ;
48   }
49
50   void product::display() const
51   {
52     cout << "Product code:" << prod_code << " Component codes:" ;
53     for ( int i = 0 ; i < num_components ; i++ )
54       cout << comp_codes[i] << ' ' ;
55     cout << endl ;
56   }
57
58   // Overloaded assignment operator.
59   const product& product::operator=( const product& p )
60   {
61     if ( this != &p) // Avoid self-assignment.
62     {  // Copy each member from p.
63       prod_code = p.prod_code ;
64       num_components = p.num_components ;
65       // Delete old memory and allocate memory for new components.
66       delete[] comp_codes ;
67       comp_codes = new int[num_components] ;
68       // Copy component codes from p.
69       for ( int i = 0 ; i < num_components ; i++ )
70         comp_codes[i] = p.comp_codes[i] ;
71     }
```

```
72    return *this ;
73  }
74
75  void main()
76  {
77    int component_list1[] = { 1812, 3512, 1411, 1986, 2342 } ;
78    int component_list2[] = { 2452, 3115, 3161 } ;
79
80    product product1( 123, 5, component_list1 ) ;
81    product product2( 124, 3, component_list2 ) ;
82
83    cout << "Before assignment:" << endl ;
84    cout << "product1:" << endl ;
85    product1.display() ;
86    cout << "product2:" << endl ;
87    product2.display() ;
88
89    product2 = product1 ;        ◄──────  Assignment operator called.
90
91    cout << endl << "After assignment:" << endl ;
92    cout << "product1: " << endl ;
93    product1.display() ;
94    cout << "product2: " << endl ;
95    product2.display() ;
96
97    // Change first component code of product1 to 999.
98    product1.set_component( 0, 9999 ) ;
99
100   cout << endl
101       << "After changing first component of product1 to 9999:"
102       << endl ;
103   cout << "product1: " << endl ;
104   product1.display() ;
105   cout << "product2: " << endl ;
106   product2.display() ;
107 }
```

The output from this program is:
```
Before assignment:
product1:
Product code:123 Component codes:1812 3512 1411 1986 2342
product2:
Product code:124 Component codes:2452 3115 3161

After assignment:
product1:
Product code:123 Component codes:1812 3512 1411 1986 2342
product2:
Product code:123 Component codes:1812 3512 1411 1986 2342

After changing first component of product1 to 9999:
product1:
Product code:123 Component codes:9999 3512 1411 1986 2342 ✓
product2:
Product code:123 Component codes:1812 3512 1411 1986 2342 ✓
```

The overloaded assignment operator is called on line 89 and is equivalent to the statement

```
product2.operator=( product ) ;
```

For efficiency purposes, line 59 declares the parameter p as a reference to a product object. By declaring p as a reference, the address of the object, rather than a copy of the object, is passed to p. Using const ensures that the object that p is a reference to is not changed in the function.

Line 61 checks that the calling object and the passed object are not one and the same. This is to avoid a statement such as product1 = product1 causing a problem. Without this check the allocated memory for the component codes of both the left hand side (product1) and the right hand side objects (also product1) would be simultaneously released in line 66.

Unlike the default assignment operator, the overloaded assignment operator doesn't simply copy the comp_codes pointer value. Firstly, the memory pointed by comp_codes is released on line 66. New memory of the correct size is then allocated and the component codes are copied one by one in the loop in lines 69 and 70.

After line 83 a sketch of memory will look like this:

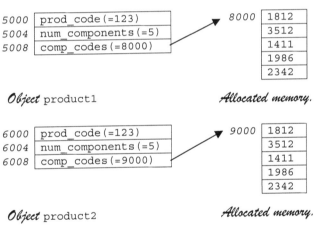

5000	prod_code(=123)
5004	num_components(=5)
5008	comp_codes(=8000)

8000
| 1812 |
| 3512 |
| 1411 |
| 1986 |
| 2342 |

Object product1   *Allocated memory.*

6000	prod_code(=123)
6004	num_components(=5)
6008	comp_codes(=9000)

9000
| 1812 |
| 3512 |
| 1411 |
| 1986 |
| 2342 |

Object product2   *Allocated memory.*

The updated object is returned on line 72 to allow multiple assignments to be chained. For example, if p1, p2 and p3 are product objects, the assignment operator is chained in the expression p1 = p2 = p3. This expression is equivalent to the expression p1.operator=(p2.operator=(p3)). In evaluating this expression, p2.operator= (p3) is evaluated first and the result is returned in a temporary variable t, say. The returned value is then used as an argument in p1.operator=(t).

10.10 The copy constructor

A copy constructor is a special constructor that is called automatically whenever any of the following occur:

(i) a new object is created and initialised. For example,

```
int component_list1[] = { 1812, 3512, 1411, 1986, 2342 } ;
product product1( 123, 5, component_list1 ) ;
product product2 = product1 ; // product2 is created and
                              // initialised with product1 values.
```

Initialisation is not the same as assignment. The statement `product1 = product2` on line 89 of program P10K is an example of an assignment.

(ii) when an object is passed by value to a function. For example,

```
void main()
{
  void any_function( product p ) ;
  product product1 ;
  any_function ( product1 ) ; // product1 is passed by value to
                              // the function product1
                              // i.e. a copy of is passed to p.
  ...
}

void any_function( product p )
{
  // p receives a copy of product1
  ...
}
```

(iii) when an object is returned by value from a function

```
void main()
{
  product another_function() ;
  product product1, product2 ;
  product2 = another_function() ;  // A copy of p is passed
                                   // back to product2.
  ...
}

product another_function()
{
  product p ;
  ...
  return p ; // p is returned by value.
}
```

Each class has a default copy constructor, which, like the default assignment operator, performs a member-wise copy. For most classes the default copy constructor and the default assignment operator are adequate and work as expected. However, for classes that allocate and de-allocate memory, the default copy constructor exhibits the same problems as the default assignment operator. In general, a class that defines its own assignment operator will also have to define its own copy constructor.

The next program extends program P10K by defining a copy constructor for the product class.

```
1    // Program example P10L
2    // Program to demonstrate the use of the copy constructor for
3    // a class with a pointer data member.
4    #include <iostream>
5    using namespace std ;
6
7    class product    // A class containing a pointer data member.
8    {
9    public:
10     product( int product_code, int number_of_components,
11             const int component_codes[] ) ;
12     product( const product& p ) ;
13     ~product() ;
14     void set_component( int component_index, int component_code ) ;
15     // Purpose   : change a component code.
16     // Parameters: component_index - component to change.
17     //             component_code - new component code.
18     void display() const ;
19     // Purpose   : display product and component codes.
20     const product& operator=( const product& p ) ;
21   private:
22     int prod_code ;      // Product code.
23     int num_components ; // Number of components in the product.
24     int *comp_codes ;    // Pointer to component codes.
25   } ;
26
27   // Constructor.
28   product::product( int product_code, int number_of_components,
29                     const int component_codes[] )
30   {
31     prod_code = product_code ;
32     num_components = number_of_components ;
33     comp_codes = new int[number_of_components] ;
34     for ( int i = 0 ; i < number_of_components ; i++ )
35       comp_codes[i] = component_codes[i] ;
36   }
37
38   // Copy constructor.
39   product::product( const product& p )
40   {
41     prod_code = p.prod_code ;
42     num_components = p.num_components ;
43     comp_codes = new int[num_components] ;
44     for ( int i = 0 ; i < num_components ; i++ )
45       comp_codes[i] = p.comp_codes[i] ;
46   }
47
48   // Destructor.
49   product::~product()
```

```
50  {
51    delete[] comp_codes ;
52  }
53
54  void product::set_component( int component_index,
55                               int component_code )
56  {
57    if ( component_index >= 0 && component_index < num_components )
58      comp_codes[component_index] = component_code ;
59  }
60
61  void product::display() const
62  {
63    cout << "Product code:" << prod_code << " Component codes:" ;
64    for ( int i = 0 ; i< num_components ; i++ )
65      cout << comp_codes[i] << ' ' ;
66    cout << endl ;
67  }
68
69  // Overloaded assignment operator.
70  const product& product::operator=( const product& p )
71  {
72    if ( this != &p ) // Avoid self-assignment.
73    {  // Copy each member from p.
74      prod_code = p.prod_code ;
75      num_components = p.num_components ;
76      // Delete old memory and allocate memory for new components.
77      delete[] comp_codes ;
78      comp_codes = new int[num_components] ;
79      // Copy component codes from p.
80      for ( int i = 0 ; i < num_components ; i++ )
81        comp_codes[i] = p.comp_codes[i] ;
82    }
83    return *this ;
84  }
85
86  void main()
87  {
88    int component_list1[] = { 1812, 3512, 1411, 1986, 2342 } ;
89
90    product product1( 123, 5, component_list1 ) ;
91    product product2 = product1 ;        ◄──────── Copy constructor called here.
92
93    cout << "product1:" << endl ;
94    product1.display() ;
95    cout << "product2:" << endl ;
96    product2.display() ;
97  }
```

The output from this program is:
```
product1:
Product code:123 Component codes:1812 3512 1411 1986 2342
product2:
Product code:123 Component codes:1812 3512 1411 1986 2342
```

The copy constructor for the product class is defined on lines 39 to 46. Like other constructors, the copy constructor has no return type, not even `void`.

A copy constructor has only one parameter which is a reference to an object of the same class. The parameter is a `const` reference so that the copy constructor cannot change the object passed to it by reference.

When the copy constructor is called on line 91, the parameter p on line 39 becomes a reference to `product1`. The non-pointer data members `prod_code` and `num_components` are assigned a value by copying the corresponding members of p. Memory is allocated for the component codes and the new memory address is stored in the pointer data member `comp_codes`. After memory has been allocated, the component codes are copied from p to `product2`.

10.11 Overloading the index operator [ ]

It is a common error to define an array with, for example, 10 elements and then attempt to access an element with an index value outside the range 0 to 9.

The next program includes a class for handling an array of integers that detects this type of error. The class contains an overloaded index operator [] for automatically checking for out-of-bounds values in the index.

```
1    // Program example P10M
2    // Program to demonstrate the overloading of index operator [] .
3    #include <iostream>
4    using namespace std ;
5
6    class int_array
7    {
8    public:
9      int_array( int number_of_elements = 10 ) ;
10     int_array( int_array const &array ) ;
11     ~int_array() ;
12     int_array const& operator=( int_array const &array ) ;
13     int &operator[]( int index ) ;
14   private:
15     int number_of_elements ;
16     int* data ;
17     void check_index( int index ) const;
18     void copy_array( int_array const &array ) ;
19   } ;
20
21   // Constructor.
22   int_array::int_array( int n )
23   {
24     if ( n < 1 )
25     {
26       cerr << "number of elements cannot be " << n
27            << ", must be >= 1" << endl;
28       return ;
29     }
30     number_of_elements = n ;
31     data = new int [number_of_elements] ;
32     for ( int i = 0 ; i < number_of_elements ; i++ )
33       data[i] = 0 ;
34   }
```

```
35
36   // Copy constructor.
37   int_array::int_array( int_array const &array )
38   {
39     copy_array( array ) ;
40   }
41
42   // Destructor.
43   int_array::~int_array()
44   {
45     delete[] data ;
46   }
47
48   // Assignment operator.
49   int_array const& int_array::operator=( int_array const &array )
50   {
51     if ( this != &array )   // Avoid self assignment.
52     {
53       delete[] data ;
54       copy_array( array ) ;
55     }
56     return  *this ;
57   }
58
59   // Index operator.
60   int& int_array::operator[]( int index )
61   {
62     check_index( index ) ;
63     return data[ index ] ;
64   }
65
66   // Non-member functions.
67   void int_array::copy_array( int_array const &array )
68   {
69     number_of_elements = array.number_of_elements;
70     data = new int [number_of_elements] ;
71     for ( int i = 0 ; i < number_of_elements ; i++ )
72       data[i] =  array.data[i] ;
73   }
74
75   void int_array::check_index( int index ) const
76   {
77     if ( index < 0 || index >= number_of_elements )
78     {
79       cerr << "invalid index " << index
80            << ", range is 0 to " << number_of_elements - 1 << endl ;
81       exit( 1 ) ;
82     }
83   }
84
85   void main()
86   {
87     int_array a( 15 ) ;   // An array of 15 integers.
88     int i ;
89
90     // Display the contents of the array.
```

```
91    for ( i = 0 ; i < 15 ; i++ )
92      cout << a[i] << ' ' ;
93    cout << endl ;
94
95    // Assign some values to elements of the array.
96    for ( i = 0 ; i < 15 ; i++ )
97      a[i] = i * 10   ;
98
99    // Display the new contents of the array.
100   for ( i = 0 ; i < 15 ; i++ )
101     cout << a[i] << ' ' ;
102   cout << endl ;
103 }
```

The output from this program is:

```
0 0 0 0 0 0 0 0 0 0 0 0 0 0 0
0 10 20 30 40 50 60 70 80 90 100 110 120 130 140
```

The class uses a pointer to allocate the exact memory for the size of the array specified in the constructor.

The overloaded index operator [] simply checks the value of the index before returning the array element. If the value of the index is invalid, an error message is displayed and the program is terminated. Line 81 calls exit() to terminate the program and return to the operating system with a status code of 1. The status code is usually set to 0 to indicate a normal exit and to some other value to indicate an error.

The class also contains a copy constructor, an overloaded assignment operator and a destructor. These functions are standard for any class that manages its own memory.

Programming pitfalls

1. Overloading arithmetic operators such as + or − do not overload the corresponding compound operators += and −=. Each operator must be overloaded separately.

2. Using a class such as the time24 class, the following will work as expected:

```
time24 t( 1, 2, 3 ) ;
++( ++t ) ;        // t is 1:02:05
```

The last statement is equivalent to

```
( t.operator++() ).operator++() ;
```

The expression t.operator++() increments t and returns a reference to t that is used in the second call. The result is that t gets incremented twice.

Consider the equivalent test using the overloaded postfix operator ++.

```
time24 t( 1, 2, 3 ) ;
( t++ )++ ;        // t is 1:02:04
```

The last statement is equivalent to

```
( t.operator++(0) ).operator++( 0 )  ;// 0 = dummy int argument
```

In this case, `t.operator++(0)` increments `t` and returns a copy of a temporary object (not `t`) that is used in the second call. The result is that `t` gets incremented once and the copy of the temporary object also gets incremented once.

There is no way around this problem, other than to break the expression into two separate statements `t++ ; t++ ;`

3. If a class has pointer data members that allocate storage dynamically, it will require an overloaded assignment operator, a destructor and a copy constructor. In general, if a class requires one of these then it will require all three.

Quick syntax reference

	Syntax	Examples

Operator overloading	`<return type>`
	`operator <operator symbol>`
	`( operand parameter₁,`
	`    ...`
	`  operand parameterₙ )`
	`{`
	`  ...`
	`}`
		`const product& operator=`
		`          ( const product& b )`
		`{`
		`  ...`
		`}`

Copy constructor	`class name`
	`( const class name & )`
	`{`
	`  ...`
	`}`
		`product( const product &b )`
		`{`
		`  ...`
		`}`

Summary of overloaded operator member function prototypes:

operator	parameter	return	const function?	class member?
arithmetic (+, -, *, /)	`const reference`	by value	yes	no
assignment (=,+=,-=)	`const reference`	by reference	no	yes
relational (==,!=,>,<)	`const reference`	by value	yes	no
prefix ++ and --	none	by reference	no	yes
postfix ++ and --	none	by value	no	yes
unary (-,+)	none	by value	yes	yes
Index ([])	value	by reference	no	yes

If an operator changes the value of the calling object then return a reference to the object, otherwise create a temporary object to hold the results of the operation and return the temporary object by value.

Exercises

1. Modify the `time24` class to include a constructor to initialise a `time24` object with a time in the 12-hour format. For example,

   ```
   time24 t( 1, 0, 0, "pm" ) ;
   ```

   is equivalent to

   ```
   time24 t( 13,  0,  0 ) ;
   ```

   The prototype of the new constructor is

   ```
   time24( int h, int m, int s, const string& am_pm ) ;
   ```

2. Modify the `time24` class to include an overloaded relational operators for less than <, greater than > and not equal to !=. See program P10F.

3. Modify the `time24` class to include an overloaded operator -=. The prototype for the new member function is:

   ```
   const time24& operator-=( const time24& t ) ;
   ```

4. A complex number k is written as k = a+bi, where a is the real part and b is the imaginary part. A class to represent complex numbers will have two `private` data members.

   ```
   class complex
   {
   public:
   ...
   private:
     int real ;
     int imaginary ;
   } ;
   ```

   (a) define arithmetic operators + and − for complex numbers
   (b) define relational operators ==, !=, < and > for the complex numbers
   (c) define input and output operators >> and << for complex numbers
   (d) test the class with the following statements in `main()`:

   ```
   complex c1, c2, c3, c4, c5 ;
   cin >> c1 >> c2 ;
   c3 = c1 + c2 ;
   c4 = c1 - c2 ;
   if ( c3 != c4 )
   {
     if (c3 < c4)
     {
       cout << "c3 is less than c4" ;
       c5 = c4 - c3 ;
     }
     if ( c3 > c4 )
     {
   ```

```
        cout << "c3 is greater than c4" ;
        c5 = c3 - c4 ;
      }
    }
    if ( c3 == c4 )
    {
      cout << "c3 and c4 are equal";
      c5 = c4 ;
    }
    cout << c5 ;
```

5. Write a class `cal_date` to represent a calendar date. The class should include the following:
   (a) three `private` data members representing the day, the month and the year of a date
   (b) a default constructor that initialises a date to the start of the Gregorian calendar 14/9/1752
   (c) a constructor that takes three integer arguments to set a `cal_date` object to a specific date
   (d) a `public` inspector member function for each of the private data members of the class
   (e) a `public` mutator member function to assign a `cal_date` object to a specific date
   (f) an overloaded – operator to subtract an integer from a `cal_date` object
   (g) an overloaded – operator to subtract two `cal_date` objects, resulting in the number of days between the two dates
   (h) overloaded ++ and -- operator functions
   (i) overloaded relational operators <, >, == and !=
   (j) an input operator >> and an output operator <<.

   Write statements in `main()` to test each of the above functions.

6. Modify the `int_array` class of program P10M to overload the function call operator () to have the same meaning as the index operator []. This means that a[i] and a(i) will both access the same element of the integer array a.

CHAPTER ELEVEN

Inheritance

11.1 What is inheritance?

Inheritance is one of the fundamental concepts of object-oriented programming. Inheritance allows a new class to be constructed using an existing class as a basis. The new class incorporates or *inherits* the data members and member functions of the existing class. Additional data members and member functions can be added to the new class, thereby extending the existing class. The existing class is known as the *base* class and the new class is known as the *derived* or *inherited* class..

Data Members	Member Functions
int d1 ; float d2 ;	f1 () ; f2 () ; f3 () ;

An existing class with various data members d1 *and* d2, *say. It also has member functions* f1 (), f2 () *and* f3 ().
This is called the base class.

The arrow means 'inherits from'

Data Members	Member Functions
int d3 ;	f4 () ; f5 () ;

A new class with an additional data member d3 *and two additional member functions* f4 () *and* f5 ().
This class has now 3 data members and 5 member functions.
This is called the derived or inherited

Note that the base class is not modified in any way and is simply used as a basis for writing the derived class. This is called *reusability* (the base class is being reused) and is a major goal of object-oriented programming. Reusing an existing class that is known to be working has obvious advantages with respect to the time taken to develop and debug a new program.

The derived class can, in turn, be used as a base class from which other classes may be derived, thus creating a *class hierarchy*. For example, a factory, a college and a hospital are all specific examples of a more general concept known as a building. Every building has a basic set of properties – the floor area, the number of windows, the number of doors, etc. A college building, for example, has some additional properties such as a number of lecture theatres and computer laboratories. A hospital has operating theatres, wards, etc. These properties are unique to these buildings and do not, in general, exist in all buildings. A factory will have yet another set of additional properties that are unique to factories.
These types of buildings can be further sub-divided into different types of factories, colleges and hospitals.

Using buildings as an example, a simple class hierarchy would look like this:

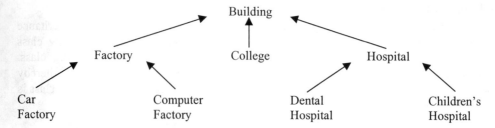

Moving down the hierarchy from the top to the bottom, the classes go from a general base class to more specialised classes that have been extended from the base class.

This type of relationship between classes is known as "*a-kind-of*" relationship. For example, a car factory is a kind of factory and a factory is a kind of building.

There are plenty of other examples of inheritance in common objects that we see or use in everyday life. Mountain bikes and racing bikes are specialisations of bicycles, personal computers and mainframe computers are specialisations of computers, books on object-oriented programming are specialisations of books on programming which are a specialisation of books.

11.2 Inheritance syntax

In its simplest form, inheritance is used by first defining the base class:

```
class base
{
// class data members and
// class member functions.
} ;
```

This is the same as defining any class.
Next the derived classes are defined:

Note the keyword `public`.

```
class inherited public : base
{
// additional class data members for this class and
// additional class member functions for this class
} ;
```

The next program implements part of the buildings class hierarchy, by defining a base class for a building and deriving a college class from this base class.

```
1  // Program example P11A
2  // Simple demonstration of inheritance.
3  #include<iostream>
4  using namespace std ;
5
6  class building      // This is the base class.
7  {
8  public:
```

```
9    building() ;
10   float get_floor_area() ;
11   int get_number_of_windows() ;
12 private:
13   float floor_area ; // Some simple properties of a building.
14   int number_of_windows;
15 } ;
16
17 // Base class member functions.
18 building::building()
19 {
20   cout << "Enter floor area: " ;
21   cin >> floor_area ;
22   cout << "Enter number of windows: " ;
23   cin >> number_of_windows ;
24 }
25
26 float building::get_floor_area()
27 {
28   return floor_area ;
29 }
30
31 int building::get_number_of_windows()
32 {
33   return number_of_windows ;
34 }
35
36 class college : public building  // This is the derived class.
37 {
38 public:
39   college() ;
40   int get_number_of_lecture_theatres() ;
41   int get_number_of_laboratories() ;
42 private:
43   int number_of_lecture_theatres; // Some simple properties.
44   int number_of_laboratories ;
45 } ;
46
47 // Derived class member functions.
48 college::college()
49 {
50   cout << "Enter number of lecture theatres: " ;
51   cin >> number_of_lecture_theatres ;
52   cout << "Enter number of laboratories: " ;
53   cin >> number_of_laboratories ;
54 }
55
56 int college::get_number_of_lecture_theatres()
57 {
58   return number_of_lecture_theatres ;
59 }
60
61 int college::get_number_of_laboratories()
62 {
63   return number_of_laboratories ;
64 }
```

```
65
66 void main()
67 {
68    college my_college ;
69
70    // Display the properties derived from the building class.
71    cout << endl << "Floor area = " ;
72    cout << my_college.get_floor_area() << endl ;
73    cout << "Number of windows = " ;
74    cout << my_college.get_number_of_windows() << endl ;
75
76    // Display the properties specific to the college class.
77    cout << "Number of lecture theatres = " ;
78    cout << my_college.get_number_of_lecture_theatres() << endl;
79    cout << "Number of laboratories = " ;
80    cout << my_college.get_number_of_laboratories() << endl ;
81 }
```

A sample run of this program is:

```
Enter floor area: 1000
Enter number of windows: 2
Enter number of lecture theatres: 1
Enter number of laboratories: 4

Floor area = 1000
Number of windows = 2
Number of lecture theatres = 1
Number of laboratories = 4
```

Lines 6 to 34 declare the base class building. This is declared just like any other C++ class. Lines 36 to 64 declare the inherited class college.

When the object my_college is defined on line 68, the constructor for the base class (lines 18 to 24) is called first, followed by the constructor for the derived class (lines 48 to 54). The constructor for the base class is always called before the constructor of a derived class. The opposite applies in the case of destructors; the destructor of the base class is always called after the destructor of the derived class.

Lines 71 to 80 display the data members of my_college, which include the data members inherited from the base class. The member functions of the base class are also inherited as demonstrated on line 72. The function get_floor_area() is a member of the base class building, but is used by the college object my_college to display its floor area.

To further demonstrate inheritance, the next example uses a simplified class hierarchy to represent current and past employees of an organisation.

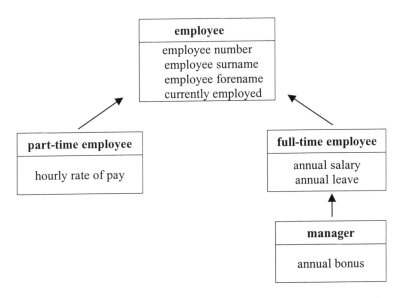

Employees in the company are either part-time or full-time. The employee number and name are common to both types of employee. Whether the person is currently employed or is a past employee is also common to both types of employees.

Part-time employees are paid an hourly rate while full-time employees are on a salary and are allowed an annual paid leave. Managers are also full-time employees, who in addition to their annual salary and paid leave are also paid an annual bonus.

```
1    // Program example P11B
2    // Demonstration of inheritance.
3    #include<iostream>
4    #include<string>
5    using namespace std ;
6
7    class employee     // Base class.
8    {
9    public:
10     employee() ;
11     void display_data() ;
12     void left() ;
13   private:
14     unsigned long int employee_number ;
15     string surname ;
16     string forename ;
17     bool currently_employed ;
18   } ;
19
20   // employee member functions.
21   employee::employee()
22   {
23     cout << endl << "Enter Employee Number: " ;
24     cin >> employee_number ;
25     cout << "Enter Employee Name: " ;
26     cin >> surname >> forename ;
27     currently_employed = true ;
```

```
28  }
29
30  void employee::left()
31  {
32    currently_employed = false ;
33  }
34
35  void employee::display_data()
36  {
37    if (currently_employed)
38      cout << "Currently Employed" ;
39    else
40      cout << "Not Currently Employed" ;
41    cout << endl << "Employee Number: " << employee_number << endl
42        << "Name: " << surname << ' ' << forename << endl ;
43  }
44
45  class part_time : public employee
46  { // part_time is a kind of employee
47  public:
48    part_time() ;
49    void display_data() ;
50  private:
51    double hourly_rate ;
52  } ;
53
54  // part_time member functions.
55  part_time::part_time()
56  {
57    cout << "Enter Hourly Rate: " ;
58    cin >> hourly_rate ;
59  }
60
61  void part_time::display_data()
62  {
63    employee::display_data() ;
64    cout << "Hourly Rate: " << hourly_rate << endl ;
65  }
66
67  class full_time : public employee
68  { // full_time is a kind of employee
69  public:
70    full_time() ;
71    void display_data() ;
72  private:
73    double annual_salary ;
74    int annual_leave ;
75  } ;
76
77  // full_time member functions.
78  full_time::full_time()
79  {
80    cout << "Enter Salary: " ;
81    cin >> annual_salary ;
82    cout << "Enter Annual Leave (in days): " ;
83    cin >> annual_leave ;
```

```
84  }
85
86  void full_time::display_data()
87  {
88    employee::display_data() ;
89    cout << "Salary: " << annual_salary << endl ;
90    cout << "Annual Leave: " << annual_leave << endl ;
91  }
92
93  class manager : public full_time
94  {  // manager is a kind of full_time employee
95  public:
96    manager() ;
97    void display_data() ;
98  private:
99    double bonus ;
100 } ;
101
102 // manager member functions.
103 manager::manager()
104 {
105   cout << "Enter Bonus: " ;
106   cin >> bonus ;
107 }
108
109 void manager::display_data()
110 {
111   full_time::display_data() ;
112   cout << "Bonus: " << bonus << endl ;
113 }
114
115 void main()
116 {
117   part_time pt ;
118   full_time ft ;
119   manager man ;
120
121   // Display employee data.
122   cout << endl << "Part-time Employee Data:" << endl ;
123   pt.display_data() ;
124   cout << endl<< "Full-time Employee Data:" << endl ;
125   ft.display_data() ;
126   man.left() ;
127   cout << endl << "Manager Employee Data:" << endl ;
128   man.display_data() ;
129 }
```

A sample run of this program follows:

```
Enter Employee Number: 123
Enter Employee Name: Smith John
Enter Hourly Rate: 5.12

Enter Employee Number: 124
Enter Employee Name: Jones Mary
```

```
Enter Salary: 21500
Enter Annual Leave (in days): 21

Enter Employee Number: 124
Enter Employee Name: Other A.N.
Enter Salary: 32000
Enter Annual Leave (in days): 30
Enter Bonus: 9500

Part-time Employee Data:
Currently Employed
Employee Number: 123
Name: Smith John
Hourly Rate: 5.12

Full-time Employee Data:
Currently Employed
Employee Number: 124
Name: Jones Mary
Salary: 21500
Annual Leave: 21

Manager Employee Data:
Not Currently Employed
Employee Number: 124
Name: Other A.N.
Salary: 32000
Annual Leave: 30
Bonus: 9500
```

The derived classes `part_time` and `full_time` inherit the data members `employee_number`, surname, forename and `currently_employed` from the base class employee. The manager class also derives `annual_salary` and `annual_leave` from its base class `full_time`, which in turn is derived from the `employee` class. The class manager is said to be *indirectly derived* from the class `employee` and *directly derived* from the class `full_time`.

The member functions of `employee` are also inherited as is illustrated by the use of the base class member function `left()` by the manager object man on line 126.

A derived class can have a data member or member function with the same name as one in its base class. For example, each of the derived classes has a member function `display_data()`. In this case, the base class member function `display_data()` is *overridden* by the inherited class member function of the same name. However, the base class member function `display_data()` can still be called to display the base class data members by the statement

```
employee::display_data() ;
```

This is shown on lines 63 and 88.

The manager class has its own `display_data()` member function which calls (line 111) the `display_data()` member function of the `full_time` class, which in turn calls (line 88) the `display_data()` member function of the `employee` class. Note the use of the

scope resolution operator (::) to remove any ambiguity as to which display_data()
function to call.

11.3 Passing arguments to a base class constructor

Program P11B used constructors to initialise the data members from keyboard input. To
allow for initialisation of an object when it is created, a constructor with a parameter list is
required.

When a derived object is created, it should take care of the construction of the base object by
calling the constructor for the base class. As seen in the previous program, the base class
default constructor is automatically called from the derived class. When an object has initial
values, the initialisation of the base class object is done by the use of an initialisation list in
the derived class constructor.

The next program illustrates the technique.

```
1    // Program example P11C
2    // Demonstration of inheritance.
3    #include<iostream>
4    #include<string>
5    using namespace std ;
6
7    class employee     // Base class.
8    {
9    public:
10     employee() ;
11   employee::employee( unsigned long int number,
12                       string sname, string fname ) ;
13     void display_data() ;
14     void left() ;
15   private:
16     unsigned long int employee_number ;
17     string surname ;
18     string forename ;
19     bool currently_employed ;
20   } ;
21
22   // employee member functions.
23   employee::employee()
24   {
25     cout << endl << "Enter Employee Number: " ;
26     cin >> employee_number ;
27     cout << "Enter Employee Name: " ;
28     cin >> surname >> forename ;
29     currently_employed = true ;
30   }
31
32   employee::employee( unsigned long int number,
33                       string sname, string fname )
34   {
35     employee_number = number ;
36     currently_employed = true ;
37     surname = sname ;
38     forename = fname ;
39   }
40
```

```
41  void employee::left()
42  {
43    currently_employed = false ;
44  }
45
46  void employee::display_data()
47  {
48    if (currently_employed)
49       cout << "Currently Employed" ;
50    else
51       cout << "Not Currently Employed" ;
52    cout << endl << "Employee Number: " << employee_number << endl
53         << "Name: " << surname << ' ' << forename << endl ;
54  }
55
56  class part_time : public employee
57  {  // part_time is a kind of employee
58  public:
59    part_time() ;
60    part_time( unsigned long int number,
61                        string sname, string fname,
62                        double rate ) ;
63    void display_data() ;
64  private:
65    double hourly_rate ;
66  } ;
67
68  // part_time member functions.
69  part_time::part_time()
70  {
71    cout << "Enter Hourly Rate: " ;
72    cin >> hourly_rate ;
73  }
74
75  part_time::part_time( unsigned long int number,
76                        string sname, string fname,
77                        double rate )
78              : employee( number, sname, fname ), hourly_rate( rate )
79  {}
80
81  void part_time::display_data()
82  {
83    employee::display_data() ;
84    cout << "Hourly Rate: " << hourly_rate << endl ;
85  }
86
87  class full_time : public employee
88  {  // full_time is a kind of employee
89  public:
90    full_time() ;
91    full_time( unsigned long int number,
92                        string sname, string fname,
93                        double salary, int leave ) ;
94    void display_data() ;
95  private:
96    double annual_salary ;
```

```
97   int annual_leave ;
98  } ;
99
100 // full_time member functions.
101 full_time::full_time()
102 {
103   cout << "Enter Salary: " ;
104   cin >> annual_salary ;
105   cout << "Enter Annual Leave (in days): " ;
106   cin >> annual_leave ;
107 }
108
109 full_time::full_time( unsigned long int number,
110                       string sname, string fname,
111                       double salary, int leave )
112             : employee( number, sname, fname ),
113               annual_salary( salary ), annual_leave( leave )
114 {}
115
116 void full_time::display_data()
117 {
118   employee::display_data() ;
119   cout << "Salary: " << annual_salary << endl ;
120   cout << "Annual Leave: " << annual_leave << endl ;
121 }
122
123 class manager : public full_time
124 {  // manager is a kind of full_time employee
125 public:
126   manager() ;
127   manager( unsigned long int number,
128                    string sname, string fname,
129                    double salary, int leave, double bonus ) ;
130   void display_data() ;
131 private:
132   double bonus ;
133 } ;
134
135 // manager member functions.
136 manager::manager()
137 {
138   cout << "Enter Bonus: " ;
139   cin >> bonus ;
140 }
141
142 manager::manager( unsigned long int number,
143                   string sname, string fname,
144                   double salary, int leave, double annual_bonus )
145         : full_time( number, sname, fname, salary, leave ),
146           bonus( annual_bonus )
147 {}
148
149 void manager::display_data()
150 {
151   full_time::display_data() ;
152   cout << "Bonus: " << bonus << endl ;
```

```
153 }
154
155 void main()
156 {
157    part_time pt( 123, "Smith", "John", 5.12 ) ;
158    full_time ft( 124, "Jones", "Mary", 21500, 21 ) ;
159    manager man( 125, "Other", "A.N.", 32000, 30, 9500 ) ;
160
161    // Display employee data.
162    cout << endl << "Part-time Employee Data:" << endl ;
163    pt.display_data() ;
164    cout << endl << "Full-time Employee Data:" << endl ;
165    ft.display_data() ;
166    man.left() ;
167    cout << endl << "Manager Employee Data:" << endl ;
168    man.display_data() ;
169 }
```

Line 157 now initialises the object pt with the values in the parentheses. The constructor on lines 75 to 79 is called. The expression employee(number, sname, fname) in the initialisation list on line 78 is an explicit call to the base class constructor on lines 32 to 39.

The base class constructor is always called to initialise the base class data members before the data members of the derived class are initialised. The actual order of the items in the initialisation list is not important. The constructor on lines 75 to 79 can therefore be also written as:

```
    part_time::part_time( unsigned long int number,
                          string sname, string fname,
                          double rate )
                : hourly_rate( rate ), employee( number, sname, fname )
    {}
```

11.4 Protected class members

The keywords private and public are used to control access to both the data members and the member functions of a class. A private data member or member function of a base class cannot be accessed from a member function of a derived class, thus ensuring that the principle of data hiding is upheld.

In practice it can be convenient to share data between a base class and a derived class. There are two ways of doing this. One possibility is to change the access level of the relevant private members to public, thus allowing the derived class the required access to these members. However, this violates the principle of data hiding by making the data members available for uncontrolled modification from any part of the program. To get over this problem, C++ has a third level of access known as protected access. This level of access allows derived classes (and only derived classes) to have access to specified base class members.

The next program demonstrates the use of protected class data members.

```
1  // Program example P11D
2  // Demonstration of protected class data members.
3  #include<iostream>
4  using namespace std ;
5
6  class rectangle
7  {
8  public:
9     rectangle( int w, int h ) ;
10    int calc_area() ;
11    void display_dimensions() ;
12    void display_area() ;
13 protected:       // Available to derived classes.
14    int width, height ;
15 };
16
17 // rectangle member functions.
18 rectangle::rectangle( int w, int h ):width( w ), height( h )
19 {}
20
21 int rectangle::calc_area()
22 {
23   return( width * height ) ;
24 }
25
26 void rectangle::display_dimensions()
27 {
28   cout << "Dimensions of rectangle: " << width
29        << " X " << height   << endl ;
30 }
31
32 void rectangle::display_area()
33 {
34   cout << "Area of rectangle: " << calc_area() << endl ;
35 }
36
37 class square : public rectangle
38 {
39 public:
40   square( int size ) ;
41   void display_dimension() ;
42   void display_area() ;
43 } ;
44
45 // square member functions.
46 square::square( int size ):rectangle( size, size )
47 {}
48
49 void square::display_dimension()
50 {
51   cout << "Dimension of square: " << width << endl ;
52 }
53
54 void  square::display_area()
55 {
56   cout << "Area of square: " << calc_area() << endl ;
```

```
57 }
58
59 void main()
60 {
61    rectangle r( 1, 2 ) ;
62    square s( 3 ) ;
63
64    r.display_dimensions() ;
65    s.display_dimension() ;
66    r.display_area() ;
67    s.display_area() ;
68 }
```

The output from this program is:

```
Dimensions of rectangle: 1 X 2
Dimension of square: 3
Area of rectangle: 2
Area of square: 9
```

In this example, the class square (lines 37 to 57) is derived from a rectangle class (lines 6 to 35).

In main(), line 61 defines a rectangle object r with sides of width 1 and height 2.

Line 62 defines a square object s with sides of size 3.

Line 64 displays the dimensions of the rectangle and line 65 displays the dimension of the square. In order to display the dimension of the square, line 51 requires access to the base class data member width. This is achieved by making width a protected data member by placing it in the protected section of the class.

It could be argued that width should be a private data member and an inspector member function should be included in the base class to return its value. However, accessing data members through inspector functions is less efficient than accessing them directly. Where efficiency is critical, protected base class members provide an alternative to the overheads involved in calling inspector functions.

In summary, if a base class member is declared as private, then this member is not accessible outside the base class, not even from a derived class. Protected members are accessible from within a base class and from within any of its derived classes. Public members (usually member functions) are accessible from any part of the program.

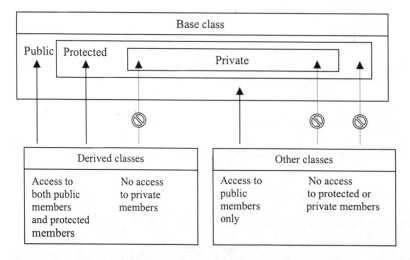

11.5 Types of inheritance: `public`, `protected` and `private`

Declaring a base class member as `public`, `protected` or `private` is not the only way of setting the access rights of a base class member within a derived class. The access rights of a base class member within a derived class can also be specified when the derived class is declared.

In the previous examples, `public` inheritance was used. For example line 37 of P11D defines the inherited class `square` with

```
class square : public rectangle
```

The keyword `public` defines the type of inheritance to be applied to the derived class. Public inheritance specifies that the access rights of the inherited members will be the same as they were in the base class.

Replacing the keyword `public` with the keyword `protected` makes all `public` and `private` members in the base class become `protected` members in the derived class. Protected members in the base class become `private` members in the derived class.

Private inheritance is specified by using the keyword `private`. With `private` inheritance, all the members of the base class become `private` in the inherited class.

The three types of inheritance are summarised in the following table:

Type of inheritance	Base class member access	Derived class member access
public	public	public
	protected	protected
	private	inaccessible
protected	public	protected
	protected	protected
	private	inaccessible
private	public	private
	protected	private
	private	inaccessible

Public inheritance is almost always used in practice because it models *"a-kind-of"* relationship found in inheritance.

Private inheritance is used much less frequently than `public` inheritance; it can be used when none of the members of the base class is used in the derived class or by objects created from the derived class.

Protected inheritance is used when the members of the base class are used in the derived class but are not required by objects created from the derived class.

As an example of how to use `protected` inheritance, consider program P11D. What would happen if a `square` object such as `s` used the `rectangle` member function `display_dimensions()`? A statement such as

```
s.display_dimensions()
```

would display:

```
Dimensions of rectangle: 3 X 3
```

The base class member function display_dimensions ()is not applicable to objects of the derived class square. One way to stop a square object from using the base class member function display_dimensions() is to write a 'dummy' member function display_dimensions() in the derived class, which will simply display an error message. This will override the base class function of the same name.

A preferred approach is to make the base class function unavailable to objects of the derived class by changing the inheritance type from public to protected. The statement s.display_dimensions()will now generate a compiler error.

11.6 Composition

Inheritance depicts "a-kind-of" relationship between classes. The other type of relationship that may exist between classes is the "*has-a*" relationship, also known as *composition*. In C++ this means that objects of one class are composed of objects of another class.

The next program uses a simple class point used to represent the row and column position of a point on a screen. From this class a line class is constructed using composition.

```
1   // Program example P11E
2   // Demonstration of composition in C++.
3   #include <iostream>
4   using namespace std ;
5
6   class point     // A simple point class.
7   {
8   public:
9     point() ;
10    point( int row, int col ) ;
11    int get_x() ;
12    int get_y() ;
13  private:
14    int x, y ;   // x and y coordinates of a point.
15  } ;
16
17  // point member functions.
18  point::point()
19  {
20    x = 0 ; y = 0 ;
21  }
22
23  point::point( int row, int col ) : x( row ), y( col )
24  {}
25
26  int point::get_x()
27  {
28    return x ;
29  }
30
31  int point::get_y()
32  {
33    return y ;
34  }
35
```

```
36 class line
37 {
38 public:
39   line( point start, point end ) ;
40   float slope() ;                    A line is composed of two joined points.
41 private:
42   point start, end ;    // Starting and ending points of a line.
43 } ;
44
45 // line member functions.
46 line::line( point start_point, point end_point )
47        : start( start_point ), end( end_point )
48 {}
49
50 float line::slope() // Calculates the slope of a line.
51 {
52   int x1, y1, x2, y2 ;
53   float slope ;
54
55   x1 = start.get_x() ;
56   y1 = start.get_y() ;
57   x2 = end.get_x() ;
58   y2 = end.get_y() ;
59   slope = static_cast<float>(y2 - y1) /  (x2 - x1) ;
60   return slope ;
61 }
62
63 void main()
64 {
65   point start( 10, 20 ), end( 30, 70 ) ;
66
67   line L( start, end ) ;
68   cout << "Slope of line L is " << L.slope() << endl ;
69 }
```

A line is composed of two point objects. When a line object is created, the constructor for the point object members is called before the constructor for the line object is called.

Whereas inheritance defines a relationship between classes, composition defines a relationship between objects.

11.7 Multiple inheritance

C++ allows inheritance from more than just one base class. This allows the construction of a hierarchy to express a relationship such as, class c is "a-kind-of" class a and is also "a-kind-of" class b.

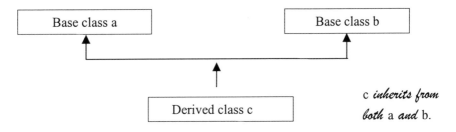

c inherits from both a and b.

Some example of multiple inheritance are:
- A clock radio is a kind of clock and is also a kind of radio.
- A fax-modem is a kind of fax and is also a kind of modem.
- A seaplane is a kind of plane and is also a kind of boat.

The next program uses multiple inheritance to derive a class `date_time` from existing date and time classes. The date class is called `calendar` and it is declared in the file `calendar.h`:

```cpp
// Header for a very simple date class.
#if !defined calendar_H
#define calendar_H

class calendar
{
public:
  calendar( int d = 1, int m = 1, int y = 1970 ) ;
  void set_date( int  d, int  m, int  y ) ;
  void get_date( int& d, int& m, int& y ) const ;
protected:
  int day ;
  int month ;
  int year ;
} ;

#endif
```

The `calendar` class member functions are contained in the file `calendar.cpp`.

```cpp
#include <iostream>
#include <iomanip>
#include "calendar.h"
using namespace std ;

// Constructor.
calendar::calendar( int d, int m, int y ) :
        day( d ), month( m ), year( y )
{}

// Mutator function.
void calendar::set_date( int  d, int m, int  y )
{
  day = d ; month = m ; year = y ;
}

// Inspector function.
void calendar::get_date( int& d, int& m, int& y ) const
{
  d = day ; m = month ;  y = year ;
}
```

The time class is the `time24` class from program P10H on page 193. The class header is in the file `time24.h` and contains lines 7 to 23 of program P10H. The `private` data members have been changed to `protected` so that they can be used by inherited classes. The `time24` class member functions are in the file `time24.cpp`.

```
1   // Program example P11F
2   // Demonstration of multiple inheritance.
3   #include <iostream>
4   #include "time24.h"
5   #include "time24.cpp"
6   #include "calendar.h"
7   #include "calendar.cpp"
8   using namespace std ;
9
10  class date_time : public calendar, public time24
11  {
12  public:
13    date_time( int d = 1, int mon = 1, int y = 1970,
14                int h = 0, int min = 0, int s = 0 ) ;
15  } ;
16
17  date_time::date_time( int d, int mon, int y,
18                        int h, int min, int s )
19            :calendar( d, mon, y ), time24( h, min, s )
20  {}
21
22  void main()
23  {
24    date_time dt( 25, 12, 1999, 0, 0, 0 ) ;
25    int day, month, year, hours, mins, secs ;
26
27    dt.get_date( day, month, year ) ;
28    dt.get_time( hours, mins, secs ) ;
29
30    cout << "Date and time is:" << endl ;
31    cout << day << "/" << month << "/" << year << endl ;
32    cout << hours << ":" << mins << ":" << secs << endl ;
33
34    dt.set_date( 1, 1, 2000 ) ;
35    dt.set_time( 1, 2, 3 ) ;
36
37    dt.get_date( day, month, year ) ;
38    dt.get_time( hours, mins, secs ) ;
39
40    cout << "Date and time is now:" << endl ;
41    cout << day << "/" << month << "/" << year << endl ;
42    cout << hours << ":" << mins << ":" << secs << endl ;
43  }
```

Lines 10 to 20 define a date_time class, derived from the two base classes calendar and time24. The date_time object dt defined on line 24 has six data members: day, month, year, hours, minutes and seconds inherited from the two base classes.

Lines 27 and 28 get the time and date values of dt using the member functions get_date() and get_time(), inherited from the calendar and time24 base classes.
Similarly, the date and time values of dt are assigned values on lines 34 and 35 using the member functions set_date() and set_time(), inherited from the calendar and time24 base classes.

11.8 Virtual base classes

Consider the following class hierarchy:

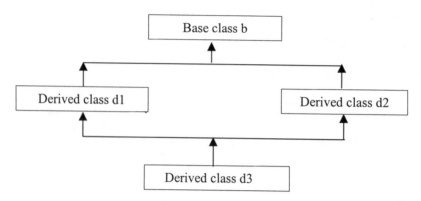

Class b is the base class of both d1 and d2, which are the base classes of d3. The protected and public members of b will be inherited by d1 and d2 from their immediate base class b. Since d3 is derived from both d1 and d2, it inherits the protected and public members of b from both d1 and d2. Two copies of the protected and public members of b now exist in d3. This is undesirable, as the next simple program shows.

```
1   // Program example P11G
2   // Demonstration of repeated inheritance.
3   #include <iostream>
4   using namespace std ;
5
6   class b
7   {
8   protected:
9     int b_data ;
10  public:
11    b()
12    {
13      cout << "Input a value for b_data " ;
14          cin >> b_data ;
15    }
16  } ;
17
18  class d1 : public b
19  {
20  protected:
21    int d1_data ;
22  public:
23    d1():d1_data( 0 )
24    {}
25  } ;
26
27  class d2 : public b
28  {
29  protected:
30    int d2_data ;
31  public:
```

```
32    d2():d2_data( 0 )
33    {}
34  } ;
35
36  class d3 : public d1, public d2
37  {
38  protected:
39    int d3_data ;
40  public:
41    d3():d3_data( 0 )
42    {}
43    void display_data() ;
44  } ;
45
46  void d3::display_data()
47  {
48    cout << "The two values of b_data are "
49            << d1::b_data << " and "
50            << d2::b_data << endl ;
51  }
52
53  void main()
54  {
55    d3 d3_obj ;
56    d3_obj.display_data() ;
57  }
```

A sample run of this program is:

```
Input a value for b_data 1
Input a value for b_data 2
The two values of b_data are 1 and 2
```

Although artificial, the program illustrates in a simple way the problem of *repeated inheritance*. When d3_obj is created on line 55, the base class constructor is called twice: once for class d2 and once for class d3. The data member b_data from the base class b is inherited twice in the derived class d3: once from d1 and once from d2. Lines 49 and 50 display the value of b_data as inherited from d1 (d1::b_data) and the value of b_data as inherited from d2 (d2::b_data).

To avoid duplication of inherited members, the classes d1 and d2 must specify their base classes as a *virtual base class*. This is done in lines 18 and 27 by using the keyword virtual.

```
18 class d1 : virtual public b
```

```
27 class d2 : virtual public b
```

Only one set of protected and public members is now inherited in d3 from the base class b and the base class constructor is called only once for d3_obj.

Include the keyword virtual in lines 18 and 27 and re-run the program to see the result of using virtual base classes.

Programming pitfalls

1. By default, the inheritance type is `private`, which is not the type that is usually required. So make sure to include the type of inheritance that is required, which is usually `public`.

2. A derived class automatically inherits all the `protected` and `public` data members of its base class, but not all of the member functions are automatically inherited. The following member functions are not inherited: constructors, destructors, overloaded operators and friends. The reason for this is that the code in constructors, destructors and overloaded operator functions are specific to a class and are unlikely to be of use in a derived class. Friends are not inherited because the friend of a base class need not necessarily be a friend of a derived class.

3. If a base class has no default constructor but has a constructor with a parameter list, then a derived class constructor must explicitly call the base class constructor in its initialisation list.

4. The keyword `virtual` must be used to avoid repeated inheritance of `protected` and `public` data members in inherited classes.

Quick syntax reference

	Syntax	Examples

Single Inheritance	`class derived : ` *access_level* ` base`
	`{`
	`// data and functions`
	`} ;`
	
	(*access_level* is either public, protected or private)
		`class b`
		`{`
		`  public:`
		`    ...`
		`  protected:`
		`    ...`
		`  private:`
		`    ...`
		`} ;`
		
		`class d : public b`
		`{`
		`  public:`
		`    ...`
		`  protected:`
		`    ...`
		`  private:`
		`    ...`
		`} ;`

Multiple Inheritance	`class derived : ` *access_level* ` base1,`
	`                 ` *access_level* ` base2,`
	`                   ...`
	`{`
	`// data and functions`
	`} ;`	

Exercises

1. A class hierarchy
    (a) shows seniority, like an organisation chart
    (b) shows "has-a" relationships
    (c) shows "a-kind-of" relationships.

2. In the code segment below, how many data members has the object d_obj?

```
class b
{
protected:
   int x ;
   int y ;
} ;
class d : public b
protected:
   float z ;
} ;
void main()
{
   d d_obj ;
}
```

3. Explain the error in the following code segment:

```
class b
{
   float x ;
} ;
class d : b
{
   int  y ;
   void f()
   {
      y = x ;
   }
} ;
```

4. Find the errors in the following code segment:

```
class b
{
protected:
   float x, y ;
public:
   int z ;
}
class d : b
{
public:
   void zero_x()
   {
      x = 0 ;
```

```
     }
   } ;

   void main()
   {
     d d_obj ;
     d_obj.x = y ;
     d_obj.zero_x() ;
   }
```

5. What is wrong with this program segment?

```
   class b
   {
     int x ;
   public:
     b( int v )
     {
       x = v ;
     }
   } ;
   class d : public b
   {
     int y ;
   public:
     d( int v ) : y( v )
     {}
   } ;
   void main()
   {
     d d_obj( 1 ) ;
   }
```

6. What is the output from the following program segment?

```
   class b
   {
   public:
     b()
     {
       cout << "default constructor for b called" << endl ;
     }
   } ;
   class d1 : public b
   {
   public:
     d1()
     {
       cout << "default constructor for d1 called" << endl ;
     }
     d1( int v )
     {
       cout << "int parameter constructor for d1 called" << endl ;
     }
   } ;
```

```
class d2 : public d1
{
public:
  d2()
  {
  cout << "default constructor for d2 called" << endl ;
  }
  d2( int v )
  {
  cout << "int parameter constructor for d2 called" << endl ;
  }
} ;

void main()
{
  b b_obj ;
  d1 d1_obj( 2 ) ;
  d1 d1_objs[ 2 ] ;
  d2 d2_obj( 3 ) ;
}
```

7. How many copies of the data member m, n and o does an object of class d inherit?

```
class a
{
private:
  int m ;
protected:
  int n ;
public:
  int o ;
  a()
  {
    cout << "default constructor for a called" << endl ;
  }
} ;
class b : public a
{
private:
  int p ;
} ;
class c : public a
{
private:
  int q ;
} ;
class d : public b, public c
{
private:
  int r ;
} ;
```

How many times is the constructor in the base class a called?

8. Modify the code in the exercise 7 so that the output is the single line

```
default constructor for a called
```

9. Place the following two classes into a class hierarchy so that they inherit from a common base class:

```
class book                      class magazine
{                               {
public:                         public:
  book() ;                        magazine() ;
private:                        private:
  string ISBN ;                   char frequency ;
  string title ;                  string title ;
  string author ;                 string publisher ;
  string publisher ;             string editor ;
  double price ;                  double price ;
} ;                             } ;
```

Write the base class with its constructor.

10. From the book class of exercise 9, use inheritance to derive a `library_book` class. This class will contain details of when the book was borrowed and by whom. For identification purposes, each library user has a six-digit library number.

11. Write a class, `postal_class`, to represent a postal address. The data members of this class are:

```
string addressline_1 ;
string addressline_2 ;
string town ;
string county ;
```

From this class derive an international postal address `inter_postal_address`. An international postal address has an extra line in the address, i.e. the country name. Write a default constructor for both the `postal_address` and `inter_postal_address`, which will initialise all the address lines to the empty string `""`.

Write a constructor for both classes to initialise the data members of the class with specified values. For example,

```
postal_address address1( "40 Mill Lane", "SeaRock Estate",
"Seatown", "Big County" ) ;
inter_postal_address address2( "1 Main Road", "Main Place",
"Main Town", "Main County", "Far-Away-Country" ) ;
```

CHAPTER TWELVE

Polymorphism

12.1 What is polymorphism?

The word *polymorphism* is derived from a Greek word meaning "many forms".

Polymorphism is one of the most important features in object-oriented programming and refers to the ability of different objects to respond differently to the same command (or 'message' in object-oriented programming terminology).

Polymorphism is used widely in our everyday language. For example, the command 'open' means different things when applied to different objects. Opening a bank account is very different from opening a window, which is different from opening a window on a computer screen. The command ('open') is the same, but depending on what it is applied to (the object) the resultant actions are different.

A very simple example of polymorphism is demonstrated in the next program.

```
1   // Program example P12A
2   // Simple demonstration of polymorphism.
3   #include <iostream>
4   using namespace std ;
5
6   class advanced_computer
7   {
8   public:
9   void hello()
10  {
11    cout << " Dave... My mind is going" << endl ;
12  }
13  } ;
14
15  class simple_computer
16  {
17  public:
18  void hello()
19  {
20    cout << "General Protection Fault" << endl ;
21  }
22  } ;
23
24  void main()
25  {
26    advanced_computer HAL ;
27    simple_computer PC ;
28    HAL.hello() ;  ◄─────────
29    PC.hello() ;   ◄─────────
30  }
```

Polymorphism:
The same command to different objects invokes different actions.

The output from this program is:

```
My mind is going Dave
General Protection Fault
```

It can be seen from the output that the objects HAL and PC have responded differently to the same hello() command sent to them on lines 28 and 29.

Polymorphism can be divided into two broad categories: *static* (or compile-time) and *dynamic* (or run-time) *polymorphism*. Static polymorphism occurs when the program is being compiled, dynamic polymorphism when the program is actually running.
C++ has three static polymorphism mechanisms: function overloading (chapter 7), operator overloading (chapter 10), and templates (chapter 13).

The use of the member function hello() in program P12A is an example of function overloading. In lines 28 and 29 the compiler inserts a function argument to identify the type of the calling object. The function headers on lines 9 and 18 are actually void hello(advanced_computer *this) and void hello(simple_computer *this), where this is a pointer to the object calling the function. Functions with the same names and different parameter lists mean function overloading.

When an operator is overloaded, a specific meaning is given to that operator. That meaning is dependent on the type of object that the operator is applied to. As seen in chapter 10, the meaning of the + operator, for example, can vary according to the type of object that it is applied to.

Before moving on to dynamic or run-time polymorphism the next program shows an example of static polymorphism involving inheritance.

```
1   // Program example P12B
2   // Demonstration of static polymorphism with inheritance.
3   #include <iostream>
4   using namespace std ;
5
6   const double pi = 3.14 ;
7
8   class circle
9   {
10  public:
11    circle( double r ) ;
12    double area() ;
13  protected:
14    double radius ;
15  } ;
16  // circle member functions.
17  circle::circle( double r ) : radius( r )
18  {}
19
20  double circle::area()
21  {
22    return pi * radius * radius ;
23  }
24
25  // class cylinder derived from circle.
26  class cylinder : public circle
27  {
28  public:
29    cylinder( double r, double l ) ;
```

```
30   double area() ;
31 private:
32   double length ;
33 } ;
34 // cylinder member functions.
35 cylinder::cylinder( double r, double l ) : circle( r ), length( l )
36 {}
37
38 double cylinder::area()
39 {
40   return  2 * pi * radius * ( radius + length ) ;
41 }
42
43 // class sphere derived from circle.
44 class sphere : public circle
45 {
46 public:
47   sphere( double r ) ;
48   double area() ;
49 } ;
50 // sphere member functions.
51 sphere::sphere( double r ) : circle( r )
52 {}
53
54 double sphere::area()
55 {
56   return  4 * pi * radius * radius ;
57 }
58
59 void main()
60 {
61   circle circle_1( 1 ) ;
62   cylinder cylinder_1( 2, 3 ) ;
63   sphere sphere_1( 4 ) ;
64
65   cout << "Area of the circle: " << circle_1.area() << endl ;
66   cout << "Area of the cylinder: " << cylinder_1.area() << endl ;
67   cout << "Area of the sphere: " << sphere_1.area() << endl ;
68 }
```

This program uses a simple class hierarchy in which a cylinder class and a sphere class are derived from a circle class. Each class has its own specific area() member function. Lines 65 to 67 illustrate polymorphism because the same command (area()) has been applied to the three different objects resulting in three different actions.

The output from this program is:

```
Area of the circle: 3.14
Area of the cylinder: 62.8
Area of the sphere: 200.96
```

12.2 Virtual functions

As demonstrated in the next program, polymorphism doesn't always work as intended.

As an example, let's modify the `circle` class of program P12B to include a new member function `area_message()` to display a message along with the value of the area.

```
1   // Program example P12C
2   // Demonstration of polymorphism 'going wrong'.
3   #include <iostream>
4   #include <string>
5   using namespace std ;
6
7   const double pi = 3.14 ;
8
9   class circle
10  {
11  public:
12    circle( double r ) ;
13    double area() ;
14    void area_message( string message ) ;
15  protected:
16    double radius ;
17  } ;
18  // circle member functions.
19  circle::circle( double r ) : radius( r )
20  {}
21
22  double circle::area()
23  {
24    return pi * radius * radius ;
25  }
26
27  void circle::area_message( string message )
28  {
29    cout << message <<  area() << endl ;      Which area() is called?
30  }
31
32  // class cylinder derived from circle.
33  class cylinder : public circle
34  {
35  public:
36    cylinder( double r, double l ) ;
37    double area() ;
38  private:
39    double length ;
40  } ;
41  // cylinder member functions.
42  cylinder::cylinder( double r, double l ) : circle( r ), length( l )
43  {}
44
45  double cylinder::area()
46  {
47    return  2 * pi * radius * ( radius + length ) ;
48  }
49
50  // class sphere derived from circle.
```

```
51 class sphere : public circle
52 {
53 public:
54    sphere( double r ) ;
55    double area() ;
56 } ;
57 // sphere member functions.
58 sphere::sphere( double r ) : circle( r )
59 {}
60
61 double sphere::area()
62 {
63    return  4 * pi * radius * radius ;
64 }
65
66 void main()
67 {
68    circle circle_1( 1 ) ;
69    cylinder cylinder_1( 2, 3 ) ;
70    sphere sphere_1( 4 ) ;
71
72    circle_1.area_message( "The area of the circle is: " ) ;
73    cylinder_1.area_message( "The area of the cylinder is: " ) ;
74    sphere_1.area_message( "The area of the sphere is: " ) ;
75 }
```

The output from this program is:

```
The area of the circle is: 3.14      ✓
The area of the cylinder is: 12.56   ✗
The area of the sphere is: 50.24     ✗
```

The output from the program is not as expected and illustrates the type of problem that can happen when using polymorphism.

What has happened is that the base class member function area() (lines 22 to 25) has been called (in line 29) for all objects, regardless of their type. The derived class versions of area() (lines 45 to 48 and lines 61 to 64) should have been called for the derived objects cylinder_1 and sphere_1.

Normally, which function a call refers to is made at compile time. The compiler knows which function to call based on the object that calls it. This is called *static* or *early binding*.

Since the member function area_message() is in the base class, the compiler assumes that the call to area() on line 29 is a call to the base class version of area() - a reasonable assumption.

In *dynamic* or *late binding*, it is left until run-time to determine which function should be called. This decision is based on the object making the call.

C++ uses virtual functions to implement dynamic binding. Virtual functions allow polymorphism to work in all situations.

The base class member function area() is made virtual by adding the keyword virtual to the function prototype on line 13.

```
virtual double area() ;
```

Since the base class member function `area()` is virtual, the derived class versions of `area()` are also virtual. The keyword `virtual` is optional in the derived classes, although it is probably a good idea to include it for the sake of clarity.

Running the amended program, the output is now:

```
The area of the circle is: 3.14      ✓
The area of the cylinder is: 37.68   ✓
The area of the sphere is: 200.96    ✓
```

To further demonstrate dynamic binding, the next program asks the user to specify which shape to construct when the program is running. The compiler cannot know in advance which shape is going to be chosen. The program dynamically creates the shape during run-time and displays its area.

This example clearly shows that the virtual function `area()` and the object calling it are not bound together until run-time.

```
1  // Program example P12D
2  // Demonstration of dynamic polymorphism.
3  #include <iostream>
4  #include <string>
5  using namespace std ;
6
7  const double pi = 3.14 ;
8
9  class circle
10 {
11 public:
12   circle( double r ) ;
13   virtual double area() ;
14   void area_message( string message ) ;
15 protected:
16   double radius ;
17 } ;
18 // circle member functions.
19 circle::circle( double r ) : radius( r )
20 {}
21
22 double circle::area()
23 {
24   return pi * radius * radius ;
25 }
26
27 void circle::area_message( string message )
28 {
29   cout << message <<  area() << endl ;
30 }
31
32 // class cylinder derived from circle.
33 class cylinder : public circle
34 {
35 public:
```

```
36   cylinder( double r, double l ) ;
37   virtual double area() ;
38 private:
39   double length ;
40 } ;
41 // cylinder member functions.
42 cylinder::cylinder( double r, double l ) : circle( r ), length( l )
43 {}
44
45 double cylinder::area()
46 {
47   return  2 * pi * radius * ( radius + length ) ;
48 }
49
50 // class sphere derived from circle.
51 class sphere : public circle
52 {
53 public:
54   sphere( double r ) ;
55   virtual double area() ;
56 } ;
57 // sphere member functions.
58 sphere::sphere( double r ) : circle( r )
59 {}
60
61 double sphere::area()
62 {
63   return  4 * pi * radius * radius ;
64 }
65
66 void main()
67 {
68   char shape ;
69   double radius, height ;
70   circle* ptr ;
71
72   cout << "Enter a shape (1=circle, 2=cylinder 3=sphere) " ;
73   cin >> shape ;
74
75   if ( shape > '0' && shape < '4' )
76   {
77     cout << "Enter Radius " ;
78     cin >> radius ;
79
80     if ( shape == '1' )
81     {
82       ptr = new circle( radius ) ;
83     }
84     else if ( shape == '2' )
85     {
86       cout << "Enter Height " ;
87       cin >> height ;
88       ptr = new cylinder( radius, height ) ;
89     }
90     else if ( shape == '3' )
91     {
```

```
92          ptr = new sphere( radius ) ;
93        }
94      ptr -> area_message( "The area is: " ) ;
95    }
96    else
97      cout << "Invalid input" << endl ;
98  }
```

Line 70 defines ptr to be a pointer to the base class circle. Normally, a pointer to one type of data cannot be used to point to data of another type, e.g. a pointer to an int data type cannot point to a float data type. However, a pointer to a base class can be used also as a pointer to an object of a class derived from the base class. This is why ptr can be used in lines 82, 88 and 92 as a pointer to any of the newly created objects. Line 94 uses ptr (which can be pointing to any of the objects) to call the member function message_area().

12.2.1 When to use virtual functions
There are memory and execution time overheads associated with virtual functions, so be judicious in the choice of whether a base class function is virtual or not. In general, declare a base class member function as virtual if it may be overridden in a derived class.

12.2.2 Overriding and overloading
Both the terms *overriding* and *overloading* are used in object-oriented programming.
Overloading is a compiler technique that distinguishes between functions with the same name but with different parameter lists. Which function to call is decided on by the compiler. Function overloading is covered in chapter 7.

Overriding occurs in inheritance when a member function of a derived class has the same name and the same parameters as a member function of its base class. Unlike overloading, which member function to call is not decided until run-time.

12. 3 Abstract base classes
The next example program derives a deposit account class and a current account class using a bank account class as a base. The bank account class is similar to the one used in program P8G, but some changes have been made for the purposes of this example.

```
1   // Program example P12E
2   // Demonstration of an abstract base class.
3   #include<iostream>
4   using namespace std ;
5
6   class bank_ac
7   {
8   public:
9     bank_ac() ;
10    void deposit( int amount ) ;
11    void withdraw( int amount ) ;
12
13  protected:
14    unsigned long int ac_no ;
15    double balance;
16  } ;
17  // bank_ac member functions.
```

```
18  bank_ac::bank_ac()
19  {
20    cout << "Enter account number: " ;
21    cin >> ac_no ;
22    balance = 0 ;
23  }
24
25  void bank_ac::deposit( int amount )
26  {
27      balance += amount ;
28  }
29
30  void bank_ac::withdraw( int amount )
31  {
32    balance -= amount ;
33  }
34
35  // deposit_ac class.
36  class deposit_ac : public bank_ac
37  {
38  public:
39    deposit_ac() ;
40    virtual void display_details() ;
41  private:
42    double interest_rate ;
43  } ;
44  // deposit_ac member functions.
45  deposit_ac::deposit_ac()
46  {
47    cout << "Enter Interest Rate: " ;
48    cin >> interest_rate ;
49  }
50
51  void deposit_ac::display_details()
52  {
53    cout << "Deposit Account Details" << endl
54         << "Deposit Account No: " << ac_no << endl
55         << "Balance: " << balance << endl
56         << "Interest Rate: " << interest_rate << endl ;
57  }
58
59  // current_ac class.
60  class current_ac : public bank_ac
61  {
62  public:
63    current_ac() ;
64    virtual void display_details() ;
65  private:
66    double overdraft_limit ;
67    double overdraft_rate ;
68    double standing_charges ;
69  } ;
70
71  // current_ac member functions.
72  current_ac::current_ac()
73  {
```

```
74     cout << "Enter Overdraft Limit: " ;
75     cin  >>  overdraft_limit ;
76     cout << "Enter Overdraft Rate: " ;
77     cin  >> overdraft_rate ;
78     cout << "Enter Standing Charges: " ;
79     cin  >> standing_charges ;
80  }
81
82  void current_ac::display_details()
83  {
84     cout << "Current Account Details" << endl
85          << "Current Account No: " << ac_no << endl
86          << "Balance: " << balance << endl
87          << "Overdraft Limit: " << overdraft_limit << endl
88          << "Overdraft Rate: " << overdraft_rate << endl
89          << "Standing Charges: " << standing_charges << endl ;
90  }
91
92  void main(void)
93  {
94     char menu() ;
95     char choice ;
96     bank_ac *ptr ;
97
98     choice = menu() ;          // Get the type of account to create.
99     if ( choice == 'c' )       // Create a current_ac object.
100      ptr = new current_ac ;
101    else
102      ptr = new deposit_ac ;   // Create a deposit_ac object.
103
104    ptr -> display_details() ; // Display new account details.
105 }
106
107 char menu()
108 // Purpose: Display a menu and return a choice.
109 {
110    char choice ;
111
112    cout << "New Account Set Up" << endl ;
113    do
114    {
115      cout << "Enter Account Type" << endl ;
116      cout << "C    Current A/C" << endl ;
117      cout << "D    Deposit A/C" << endl ;
118      cin >> choice ;
119      choice = tolower( choice ) ;
120    }
121    while( choice != 'd' && choice != 'c' ) ;
122
123    return( choice ) ;
124 }
```

A sample run of this program is:

```
New Account Set Up
Enter Account Type
C    Current A/C
D    Deposit A/C
D
Enter account number: 12345
Enter Interest Rate: 5
Deposit Account Details
Deposit Account No: 12345
Balance: 0
Interest Rate: 5
```

The program dynamically creates either a `current_ac` object on line 100 or a `deposit_ac` object on line 102. Note that although `ptr` is defined as a pointer to the base class object `bank_ac`, it is used as a pointer to objects of the derived classes `current_ac` and `deposit_ac`.

In line 104, `ptr` is used to display the details of the object it points to.
The compiler doesn't know anything about dynamic binding and insists that since `ptr` is a pointer to the base class, then the base class should contain a member function `display_details()`, which it doesn't. The solution is to insert a 'dummy' `display_details()` member function in the `public` section of the base class:

```
void virtual display_details() = 0 ;
```

The base class member function `display_details()` has no code and is assigned to 0. A class member function defined in this way is called a *pure virtual function*. A pure virtual function is required by the compiler but doesn't actually do anything. A pure virtual function is overridden in all the derived classes and hence there is no need to implement it.

A base class that contains a pure virtual function is called an *abstract base class*.
Abstract base classes (ABCs) are not used to create objects, but exist solely as a base for deriving other classes. It is not possible to define an object of an abstract base class, i.e. objects of an abstract base class cannot be instantiated.

Although a class hierarchy does not have to contain an abstract base class, typically one is defined during the first stage of developing a class hierarchy.
An abstract base class is usually the common denominator of more concrete derived classes (CDCs). The bank account class is a good example of an ABC. Go into a bank and ask to open a bank account and the first question asked will be "what type of account?". There is no such object as a bank account in the real world, but there are deposit and current account objects. A bank account is therefore an abstract concept. Other examples of ABCs are the building class and employee class used in chapter 8. Such classes are not useful on their own without the added details provided by their derived classes.

Programming pitfalls

1. It is easy to get confused between virtual member functions and virtual base classes. Although both are used in the context of inheritance, they are not in fact related. Perhaps a better name for virtual functions would be 'run-time-replaceable' functions?

2. An abstract base class must have at least one derived class. It is an error to attempt to define an object of an abstract base class.

3. A virtual member function in a base class can only be overridden in a derived class if the member function in the derived class has the same prototype as the base class member function.

4. Virtual functions in a base class can be overridden in one or more derived classes. A function must be declared as virtual in the base class; a derived class cannot make a function virtual. Unfortunately, this reduces the ability to reuse the base class without first modifying it.

5. The keyword `virtual` cannot be used outside the class declaration. It is a common error to include the keyword `virtual` when defining a non-inline member function.

```
class b
{
public:
  virtual void mf() ; // virtual is ok here.
} ;
virtual void b::mf()  // error: virtual is not valid here.
{
   ...
}
```

Quick syntax reference

	Syntax	Examples
Declaring a virtual function	```class base { virtual member function } ;```	```class circle { public: virtual double area() ... } ;```
Declaring an abstract base class	```class base { virtual member function = 0 ; } ;```	```class bank_ac { public: void virtual display_details() = 0 ; ... };```

Exercises

1. What is the relationship between an abstract base class and a pure virtual function?

2. Explain the difference between late and early binding.

3. An abstract base class is a class containing a virtual function. True or false?

4. How can a base class force a derived class to include certain member functions?

5. Explain the error in the following program segment:

```
class b
{
public:
  virtual int mf() ;
} ;
virtual b::mf()
{
  cout << "member function mf called" << endl ;
}
```

6. What is the output from (a), (b), (c) and (d)?
    (a)
```
#include<iostream>
using namespace std ;

class b
{
public:
  void mf( int p ) ;
} ;
void b::mf( int p )
{
  cout << "member function mf in b called, "
       << "value of parameter is " << p << endl ;
}

class d : public b
{
public:
  void mf( int p ) ;
} ;
void d::mf( int p )
{
  cout << "member function mf in d called, "
       << "value of parameter is " << p << endl ;
}

void main()
{
  b* ptr ;
  d d_obj ;
  ptr = new d ;
```

```
    ptr -> mf( 1 ) ;
    d_obj.mf( 1 ) ;
  }
```

(b)
```
  #include<iostream>
  using namespace std ;

  class b
  {
  public:
    virtual void mf( int p ) ;
  } ;
  void b::mf( int p )
  {
    cout << "member function mf in b called, "
         << "value of parameter is " << p << endl ;
  }

  class d : public b
  {
  public:
    void mf( int p ) ;
  } ;
  void d::mf( int p )
  {
    cout << "member function mf in d called, "
         << "value of parameter is " << p << endl ;
  }

  void main()
  {
    b* ptr ;
    d d_obj ;
    ptr = new d ;
    ptr -> mf( 1 ) ;
    d_obj.mf( 1 ) ;
  }
```

(c)
```
  #include<iostream>
  using namespace std ;

  class b
  {
  public:
  void mf( int p ) ;
  } ;
  void b::mf( int p )
  {
    cout << "member function mf in b called, "
         << "value of parameter is " << p << endl ;
  }
```

```
class d : public b
{
public:
  void mf( double p ) ;
} ;
void d::mf( double p )
{
  cout << "member function mf in d called, "
       << "value of parameter is " << p << endl ;
}

void main()
{
  b *ptr ;
  d d_obj ;
  ptr = new d ;
  ptr -> mf( 1 ) ;
  d_obj.mf( 1.1 ) ;
}
```

(d)
```
#include<iostream>
using namespace std ;

class b
{
public:
  virtual void mf( int p ) ;
} ;
void b::mf( int p )
{
  cout << "member function mf in b called, "
       << "value of parameter is " << p << endl ;
}

class d : public b
{
public:
  void mf( double p ) ;
} ;
void d::mf( double p )
{
  cout << "member function mf in d called, "
       << "value of parameter is " << p << endl ;
}

void main()
{
  b *ptr ;
  d d_obj ;
  ptr = new d ;
  ptr -> mf( 1 ) ;
  d_obj.mf( 1.1 ) ;
}
```

CHAPTER THIRTEEN

Templates

13.1 Introduction
A *template* is a framework for generating a class or a function. Instead of explicitly specifying the data types used in a class or a function, parameters are used. When actual data types are assigned to the parameters, the class or function is generated by the compiler.

13.2 Function templates
Consider the following function to find the maximum of two integer values.

```
int max( const int n1, const int n2 )
{
  if ( n1 > n2 )
    return n1 ;
  else
    return n2 ;
}
```

To find the maximum of two floating-point values, a nearly identical function is required.

```
float max( const float n1, const float n2 )
{
  if ( n1 > n2 )
    return n1 ;
  else
    return n2 ;
}
```

The reason two different functions are required is simply that the function header is different in the two functions. The first function has parameters of type int and returns an int, the second function has parameters of type float and returns a float. The if-else statement in both functions are identical.

Function templates allow both of these functions to be replaced by a single function in which the parameter types are replaced by a parameter T (for type) giving a generic or typeless function that can be used for all data types.

```
1   // Program example P13A
2   // Demonstration of a function template.
3   #include <iostream>
4   using namespace std ;
5
6   template <typename T>
7   T max( const T n1, const T n2 )
8   {
9     if ( n1 > n2 )
10      return n1 ;
11    else
12      return n2 ;
13 }
```

T *is called the type parameter.* T *is normally used, but any valid name can be used.*

256

```
14
15 void main()
16 {
17    char c1 = 'a', c2 = 'b' ;
18    int i1 = 1, i2 = 2 ;
19    float f1 = 2.5, f2 = 3.5 ;
20
21    cout << max( c1, c2 ) << endl ; // Instantiates max() for chars
22    cout << max( i1, i2 ) << endl ; // Instantiates max() for ints
23    cout << max( f1, f2 ) << endl ; // Instantiates max() for floats
24 }
```

Running this program gives:

```
b
2
3.5
```

Line 6 is an example of a function template declaration. A function template declaration consists of the keyword `template` and a list of one or more data type parameters. The data type parameter is preceded by either the keyword `class` or the more meaningful keyword `typename`. Type parameters are enclosed within angle brackets < and >. When multiple data type parameters are used, they are separated by commas.

Line 21 has the effect of replacing the type parameter T in line 6 with the data type of the arguments c1 and c2, i.e. char. As a result, the compiler generates a function with the prototype

```
    char max( const char n1, const char n2 ) ;
```

In line 22, the type parameter T is replaced by the data type of i1 and i2, i.e. int. This generates a function with the prototype

```
    char max( const int n1, const int n2 ) ;
```

Similarly in line 23, T is replaced by the data type of f1 and f2, i.e. float. This generates a function with the prototype

```
    float max( const double, const double ) ;
```

This process is called *instantiation* of the template and the result is a conventional function generated by the compiler.

Instead of using three separate functions in the program, a single function template is used. The program source file is smaller, but since the compiler generates three separate functions from the template, the executable file size remains the same.

Template definitions can be placed in a header file. Placing lines 6 to 13 of program P13A into a header file `max.h`, this file can be `#included` into a program file. This is done in the next program.

```
1   // Program example P13B
2   // Demonstration of including a function template in a program.
3   #include<iostream>
4   #include "max.h"
5   using namespace std ;
6
7   void main()
8   {
9     char c1 = 'a', c2 = 'b' ;
10    int i1 = 1, i2 = 2 ;
11    float f1 = 2.5, f2 = 3.5 ;
12
13    cout << max( c1, c2 ) << endl ;
14    cout << max( i1, i2 ) << endl ;
15    cout << max( f1, f2 ) << endl ;
16  }
```

Function templates are very useful when a program requires a function to sort the elements of an array. If the sorting algorithm is implemented as a function template, functions to sort all types of arrays can be automatically generated by the compiler.

The next program uses the bubble algorithm to sort and display arrays of different data types. The program uses three templates contained in the header files bubble.h, swap.h and show.h.

```
1   // Program example P13C
2   // Demonstration of three template functions to sort
3   // and display arrays of any data type.
4   #include <iostream>
5   #include "swap.h"
6   #include "bubble.h"      ◄──  Header files containing function
7   #include "show.h"              templates.
8   using namespace std ;
9
10  void main()
11  {
12    int int_array[] = { 23, 4, 12, -9, 55 } ;
13    float float_array[] = { 4.2, 7.8, 77.3, 1.2 } ;
14
15    bubble_sort( int_array, 5 ) ;
16    show_array( int_array, 5 ) ;        Use of function templates
17    bubble_sort( float_array, 4 ) ;  ◄──  with different data types.
18    show_array( float_array, 4 ) ;
19  }
```

Contents of bubble.h:

```
// Declaration of bubble template function.
#if !defined BUBBLE_T_H
#define BUBBLE_T_H

template <typename T>
void bubble_sort( T array[], int n )
// Purpose   : sorts an array using bubble sort algorithm.
// Parameters: the array to sort and
```

```
//                  the number of elements in the array.
{
bool swapping = true ;
while( swapping )
{
  swapping = false;
  for ( int i = 0 ; i < n-1 ; i++ )
  {
    if ( array[i] > array[i+1] )
    {
      swapping = true ;
      swap_values( array[i], array[i+1] ) ;
    }
  }
}
}

  #endif
```

Contents of swap.h:

```
// Declaration of swap template function.
#if !defined SWAP_T_H
#define SWAP_T_H

template <typename T>
void swap_values( T &x, T &y )
// Purpose    : swap two values.
// Parameters: two values of any data type.
{
  T temp = x ;
  x = y ;
  y = temp ;
}

  #endif
```

Contents of show.h:

```
// Declaration of show_array template function.
#if !defined SHOW_T_H
#define SHOW_T_H

template <typename T>
void show_array( T array[], int n )
// Purpose    : displays an array.
// Parameters: array[] - the array to display.
//                  n - the number of elements in the array.

{
  for ( int i = 0 ; i < n ; i++ )
    cout << array[i] << ' ' ;
}

  #endif
```

As with previous uses of header files, the preprocessor statements are used in each of these header files to prevent the header file from being inadvertently included more than once in a program.

13.3 Class templates

As well as generating functions, templates can be also used for generating entire C++ classes. Common data structures such as linked lists and stacks are independent of the data type they contain. Instead of having a class for a stack of integers and another class for a stack of floating-point values and yet another class for a stack of strings, templates allow one class to be written for all data types.

Class templates are also known as *parameterised types*. A parameterised type is a data type defined in terms of other data types, some of which are unspecified.

To demonstrate the use of class templates, the next example uses a class template for a stack data structure.

The operations that can be performed on a stack of plates, whereby plates are only added and removed from the top of the stack, are analogous to the operations that can be performed on a stack data structure.

A stack data structure is implemented with two principal operations:

push: adds an item to the top of the stack.
pop : retrieves the most recently pushed item from the stack.

For example,

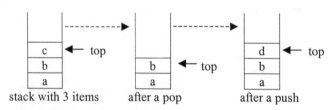

stack with 3 items   after a pop   after a push

A simple way to implement a stack is to use an array to hold the items and a variable to hold the index value of the 'top' of the array.

A stack can therefore be defined as a class template with a type parameter that specifies the data type of the items to be stored on the stack and an integer variable to indicate the current top of the stack.

The definition of a stack class template is stored in a header file stack.h and contains the following:

Contents of stack.h:

```
1   // Declaration of stack class template.
2   #if !defined STACK_T_H
3   #define STACK_T_H
4
5   template <typename T>
6   class stack
7   {
```

```
8   public:
9     stack( int n = 10 ) ;
10    // Purpose    : Class constructor.
11    // Parameters: n - size of stack.
12    ~stack() ;
13    // Purpose    : class destructor.
14    bool pop( T& data_item ) ;
15    // Purpose    : remove an item from the stack.
16    // Parameters: data_item - data item on top of the stack is
17    //                copied to this reference.
18    // Returns    : true - operation successful.
19    //               false - operation failed.
20    bool push( const T& data_item ) ;
21    // Purpose    : add an item to the stack.
22    // Parameters: data_item to be placed on top of the stack.
23    // Returns    : true - operation successful.
24    //               false - operation failed.
25     inline int number_stacked() ;
26    // Purpose    : inspector function.
27    // Returns    : number of items currently on the stack.
28     inline int stack_size() ;
29    // Purpose    : inspector function.
30    // Returns    : the size of the stack.
31  private:
32    int max_size ;
33    int top ;
34    T* data ;
35  } ;
36  // stack member functions.
37  template <typename T>
38  stack <T>::stack( int n )
39  {
40    max_size = n ;
41    top = -1 ;
42    data = new T[ n ] ;
43  }
44
45  template <typename T>
46  stack <T>::~stack()
47  {
48    delete [] data ;
49  }
50
51  template <typename T>
52  bool stack <T>::push( const T& data_item )
53  {
54    if ( top  <  max_size )
55    {
56      data[ ++top ] = data_item ;
57      return true ;
58    }
59    else
60      return false ;
61  }
62
63  template <typename T>
```

```
64 bool stack <T>::pop( T& data_item )
65 {
66   if ( top > -1 )
67   {
68     data_item = data [ top-- ] ;
69     return true ;
70   }
71   else
72     return false ;
73 }
74
75 template <typename T>
76 int stack <T>::number_stacked()
77 {
78   return top + 1 ;
79 }
80
81 template <typename T>
82 int stack <T>::stack_size()
83 {
84   return max_size ;
85 }
86
87 #endif
```

A reference to a class template must include its parameter list. This is why the definition of the member functions use stack <T> instead of just stack, which would be used if the class were not a template.

The next program demonstrates the use of the stack class template.

```
1   // Program example P13D
2   // Demonstration of a class template.
3   #include <iostream>
4   #include "stack.h"
5   using namespace std ;
6
7   void main()
8   {
9     stack <int> i_stack ;        // A stack to hold 10 integers.
10    stack <char> c_stack( 5 ) ; // A stack to hold 5 characters.
11    int i, n, int_data ;
12    char char_data ;
13    bool success ;
14
15    // Push some values onto c_stack.
16    c_stack.push( 'a' ) ;
17    c_stack.push( 'b' ) ;
18    c_stack.push( 'c' ) ;
19
20    // Use a for loop to fill i_stack.
21    n = i_stack.stack_size() ;
22    for ( i = 0 ; i < n ; i++ )
23      i_stack.push( i ) ;
24
25    // Display items on c_stack.
```

```
26   cout << "character stack data:" << endl ;
27   n = c_stack.number_stacked() ;
28   for ( i = 0 ; i < n ; i++ )
29   {
30     success = c_stack.pop( char_data ) ;
31     if ( success )
32       cout << char_data << endl ;
33   }
34
35   // Display items on i_stack.
36   cout << "integer stack data:" << endl ;
37   n = i_stack.number_stacked() ;
38   for ( i = 0 ; i < n ; i++ )
39   {
40     success = i_stack.pop( int_data ) ;
41     if ( success )
42       cout << int_data << endl ;
43   }
44 }
```

The data type of the stack data is specified between the angle brackets < and >.

Line 9 instantiates a stack to process up to ten integer data items (ten is the default value in the class constructor).

Line 10 instantiates a stack to process up to five character data items.

Lines 16 to 18 and lines 22 to 23 push some sample data onto each of the stack objects c_stack and i_stack. Lines 28 to 33 and lines 38 to 43 pop and display data from each of the stacks.

Compared with non-template functions and classes, function templates and class templates look daunting. To create templates, first write a non-template data type specific version of the function or class. When the data type specific version is working satisfactorily, replace the specific data types with template parameters. For example, the bubble sort function template was initially developed with an int data type. When the function was working for integer data, the data type int was replaced with the type parameter T, enabling it to work with any data type.

Programming pitfalls

1. Do not assume that all operators in a function prototype are defined for the data type passed to the template parameter. For example, using the function template max() in program P13A for objects of a point class,

```
point p( 1, 2 ), p2( 3, 4 ), p3( 0, 0 ) ;
p3 = max( p1, p2 ) ;
```

An error occurs if > is not overloaded in the definition of the point class.

2. The keyword typename must be included for each template parameter.

```
template <typename T1, T2> // Error - typename T2
```

3. Each specified type parameter must be used in the function.

```
template <typename T1, typename T2>
int my_function ( T1 var )  // Error - T2 is not used!
```

Quick syntax reference

	Syntax	Examples

Defining a function template	`template <typename T1,`
	`          typename T2, ...>`
	`// function definition.`
		`template <typename T>`
		`T min( const T n1,`
		`        const T n2 )`
		`{`
		`   ...`
		`}`

Defining a class template	`template <typename T1,`
	`          typename T2, ...>`
	`// class definition.`
		`template <typename T>`
		`class stack`
		`{`
		`   ...`
		`} ;`

Exercises

1. Write a function template `maximum()` that returns the largest value in an array. The array may contain elements of any type. The function has two parameters. The first parameter is the name of the array and the second parameter is the integer number of elements in the array. The return type of the function is the same type as its first parameter.

2. Write a function template `locate()` that finds and returns the first position of a value in an array. The array may contain elements of any type. The function has two parameters. The first parameter is the name of the array and the second parameter is a variable of the same type as the first parameter. If the value does not exist in the array, −1 is returned.

3. Write a function template `power()` that returns the value of its first parameter raised to the power of its second parameter. The first parameter may be of any type and the second parameter is an integer. The return type of the function is the same type as its first parameter.

4. Convert the following function into a function template.

```
void sort ( int& a, int &b )
{
  if ( a > b )
  {
    int t = a ;
    a = b ;
    b = a ;
  }
}
```

5. The binary search or binary chop algorithm is used to search an array, when the elements of the array are sorted. The algorithm is analogous to searching for a name in a telephone book or looking up the meaning of a word in a dictionary.
   The following function searches a sorted array a of n integer elements for an integer value held in `item`.

```
int bin_search( int a[], int n, int item )
{
  int mid ;
  int top = n - 1 ;
  int bottom = 0 ;

  while( top >= bottom )
  {
    mid = ( top + bottom ) / 2 ;

    if ( item == a[ mid ] )   // Is the key found?
      return mid ;            // Yes - return the index value.

    if ( item > a[mid] )      // No - the key is not found.
      bottom = mid + 1 ;      // Try the top half.
    else
      top = mid - 1 ;         // Try the bottom half.
  }
```

```
        return -1 ;                        // Not found.
    }
```

Convert the function to a function template so that it will work with any data type.
Test the function template by instantiating `bin_search()` with T bound to a built-in
type such as `double`. For example,

```
    float numbers[] = { 0.8, 1.1, 1.2, 3.9, 8.7, 15.92, 71.9, 80.31} ;
    cout  <<  bin_search( numbers, 8, 1.2 ) << endl ;
```

6. Add a new member function `is_full()` to the stack class template. This member function
    returns `true` or `false`, depending on whether the stack contains its maximum number of
    values or not.

7. The member function `push()` simply returns false if the stack is full. Modify `push()` so
    that the stack size is dynamically increased by 10 to allow for ten more data items. The
    values already on the stack should not be lost.

8. Write a class template for a Queue class. A Queue is like a stack, except that insertions
    are at the end and removals are from the front. It simulates an everyday waiting queue.
    Test the template with the following program:

```
    void main()
    {
        queue<char> q( 4 ) ;
        q.insert( 'A' ) ;       // Like push(), except at the end.
        q.insert( 'B' ) ;
        q.insert( 'C' ) ;
        cout << q.remove() ; // Same as pop(), except from the front.
        // Should display A.
        q.insert( 'D' ) ;
        cout << q.remove() ; // Should display B.
    }
```

CHAPTER FOURTEEN

Files and Streams

The input-output statements used so far were those that read data from the keyboard and displayed data on the screen. When a program reads data from the keyboard, it stores the data in the computer's memory. When the program terminates, the data is lost and must be re-entered every time the program is run. This chapter covers file stream input and output. Unlike data that is kept in the computer's memory, files use external storage devices, such as hard disks and floppy disks. These are permanent storage devices that allow data to be stored after the program terminates.

14.1 The C++ input/output class hierarchy

Unlike many programming languages, C++ has no built-in input/output (I/O) commands. In C++ the I/O commands are included in a class library. A simplified diagram of the I/O class hierarchy is shown below and a brief explanation of the hierarchy follows.

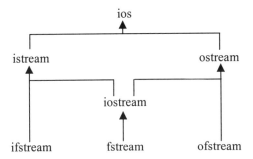

The base class `ios` contains data members to indicate conditions such as whether a stream object is opened for input or output and whether the end of the file has been reached.

The derived class `istream` extends the base class by adding member functions to input data from a stream. This class provides basic input processing by including overloaded operators `>>` for reading the built-in data types (`char`, `int`, `float` etc.) from a stream. As seen in program P10G, additional `>>` overloads can be written for user-defined classes. The stream `cin`, which is normally attached to the keyboard, is an object of this class.

The derived class `ostream` contains member functions to output data to a stream. This class provides basic output processing by including overloaded insertion operators (`<<`) for writing built-in data types to a stream. Additional overloaded insertion operators can be written for user-defined classes (see program P10G). The stream `cout` is an object of this class, which is normally attached to the screen.

The class `ifstream` is derived from `istream` and is used to create input file objects.

The class `ofstream` is derived from `ostream` and is used to create output file objects.

Finally, the class `fstream` is used to create file objects that can be used for both input and output.

The definition of the library classes is contained in the header files `iostream` and `fstream`, summarised below.

iostream	Includes the definition of • ios, istream, ostream, and iostream classes • stream objects cin, cout, clog and cerr • stream manipulators endl, ws, dec, hex and oct.
fstream	Includes the definition of the ifstream, ofstream, and fstream classes.

14.2 Opening a file

To open a file, first create an instance of the appropriate class, as shown in the following statements:

```
ifstrem in ;      // in is an input file object

ofstream out ;    // out is an output file object
```

After creating an instance of the appropriate class, the file object must be opened to associate it with a physical file stored on a hard disk or some other storage medium.

```
in.open( "in.dat" ) ;    // in is associated with in.dat

out.open( "out.dat" ) ;  // out is associated with out.dat
```

Creating an instance of a file object and opening a file can be combined into one statement by using the `ifstream` and `ofstream` class constructors.

```
ifstrem in( "in.dat" ) ;

ofstream out( "out.dat" ) ;
```

It is good practice to close a file after processing it.

```
in.close() ;   // Close input stream in, i.e. in.dat

out.close() ;  // Close output stream out, i.e. out.dat
```

The next program is a simple demonstration of writing data to a file and reading the same data back again. Both methods of opening a file are demonstrated.

```
1   // Program example P14A
2   // Demonstration of file output and file input.
3   #include <iostream>
4   #include <fstream>
5   #include <string>
6   using namespace std ;
7
8   void main()
9   {
10    char c = 'A' ;
```

```
11    int i = 1 ;
12    string s = "Hello" ;
13
14    ofstream out ;              // Create a file object out and
15    out.open( "file.txt" ) ;   // open file.txt
16
17    // Write some data to the file using <<
18    out << s << ' ' << c << ' ' << i << endl ;
19    out.close() ;   // Close the output file.
20
21    ifstream in( "file.txt" ) ;   // Use constructor to open file.
22    // Read data from the file using >>
23    in >> s >> c >> i ;
24    in.close() ;   // Close the input file
25
26    cout << "Data read from file:" ;
27    cout << s << ' ' << c << ' ' << i << endl ;
28 }
```

The output from this program is:

```
Data read from file:Hello A 1
```

Note that the header file fstream is included on line 4.

Line 14 creates an instance out of an output file object. Line 15 associates out with the external file file.txt and opens the file for processing. If the file does not exist, by default it will be created in the same folder (directory) as the program.

Line 18 outputs some data to the file stream using << in the same way that data would be sent to the stream cout.

The ifstream class constructor is used on line 21 to open file.txt for input processing. Line 23 is similar to the way data is input from the keyboard, except in is used instead of cin.

The contents of file.txt can be viewed using any text editor such as Windows Notepad, DOS Edit or Unix vi.

14.3 File error checking

It is good practice to check for errors when opening a file. Possible errors that can occur include errors due to no space being available on an output device or attempting to open a non-existent file for reading.

The ios class contains member functions that can be used to check for errors. Since ifstream and ofstream are inherited from ios, these functions are available for use with ifstream and ofstream objects. Some of the member functions and their return values are on the next page.

fail	Returns the Boolean value true if the operation failed, otherwise the Boolean value false is returned.
good	Returns the Boolean value true if the operation succeeded, otherwise the Boolean value false is returned. The opposite of fail.
operator!	Returns the same result as fail.
operator void *	This conversion operator returns a null pointer if fail returns true, otherwise a non-null value is returned.
eof	Returns the Boolean value true if the end of the file has been reached, otherwise the Boolean value false is returned.

The next program modifies program P14A by using the member functions fail and operator! to check for errors when opening a file.

```
1   // Program example P14B
2   // Program to demonstrate file open error checking.
3   #include <iostream>
4   #include <fstream>
5   #include <string>
6   using namespace std ;
7
8   void main()
9   {
10    char c = 'A' ;
11    int i = 1 ;
12    string s = "Hello" ;
13    ofstream out ;
14
15    out.open( "file.txt" ) ;
16    if ( out.fail() )   // Has the file failed to open?
17    {
18      cerr << "Failure to open file.txt for output" << endl ;
19      return ;
20    }
21    // Write some data to the file using <<
22    out << s << ' ' << c << ' ' << i << endl ;
23    out.close() ;
24
25    ifstream in( "file.txt" ) ;
26    if ( !in )   // Same as in.fail().
27    {
28      cerr << "Failure to open file.txt for input" << endl ;
29      return ;
30    }
31    // Read data from the file using >>
32    in >> s >> c >> i ;
33    in.close() ;   // Close the input file.
34    cout << "Data read from file:" ;
35    cout << s << ' ' << c << ' ' << i << endl ;
36  }
```

The additional program statements can be tested by adding a non-existent drive letter to the file path, e.g. instead of "file.txt" specify "xx:file.txt" on lines 15 and 25.

14.4 Single character I/O and detecting the end of a file

When reading data from an input file, it is necessary to be able to detect the end of the file so that processing on the file may stop. The end of a file may be detected using the `ios` member function `eof()` inherited by the `ifstream` class.

The next program demonstrates the use of `eof()` in making a copy of a text file. The `istream` member function `get()` is used to read a character from the input file and the `ofstream` member function `put()` is used to write the character to an output file.

```
1    // Program example P14C
2    // Program to demonstrate member functions eof, get and put.
3    #include <iostream>
4    #include <fstream>
5    using namespace std ;
6
7    void main()
8    {
9      char c ;
10     int count ;
11
12     ifstream in( "file.txt" ) ;  // Open input file.
13     if ( in.fail() )
14     {
15       cerr << "Open failure on file.txt" ;
16       return ;
17     }
18
19     ofstream out( "file.bak" ) ;  // Open output file.
20     if ( out.fail() )
21     {
22       cerr << "Open failure on file.bak" ;
23       return ;
24     }
25
26     in.get( c ) ; // Read first character in the file.
27     count = 1 ;
28     while( !in.eof() ) // Loop while not end of file.
29     {
30       out.put( c ) ;   // Write character.
31       in.get( c ) ;    // Read next character.
32       count++ ;
33     }
34
35     in.close() ;
36     out.close() ;
37
38     cout << "Copy completed. "
39          << count - 1 << " characters copied." << endl ;
40   }
```

After opening both files, the program reads the first character of the input file on line 26. The loop on lines 28 to 33 continues to write a character to the output file and read the next character from the input file until the end of the input file is detected.

A message displaying the number of characters copied is displayed on lines 38 and 39.

The program can be improved by looking at the prototypes for the `istream` member functions `get`.

```
istream& get( unsigned char& )
```

The prototype specifies that the function returns a reference to the input stream that called it. This means that lines 26 and 28 can be combined as

```
while ( ! ( in.get( c ) ).eof() )
```

Evaluates to in

An even easier version of this `while` statement is

```
while ( in.get( c ) )
```

Evaluates to `true` or `false`

The condition inside the parentheses of a `while` statement should evaluate to a `bool` `true` or `false` value, not a reference to a stream. So how does this work?

In this case, the returned stream reference is converted automatically to a pointer by the `ios` type conversion member function `operator void *`. This function returns a null pointer value if the last read was unsuccessful. A null value terminates the `while` loop.

The modification is made in the next program. Note that there is no special processing necessary for the first character as required in program P14C (line 26).

```
1   // Program example P14D
2   // Program to demonstrate get, put and end of file detection.
3   #include <iostream>
4   #include <fstream>
5   using namespace std ;
6
7   void main()
8   {
9     char c ;
10    int count = 0 ;
11
12    ifstream in( "file.txt" ) ;  // Open input file.
13    if ( in.fail() )
14    {
15      cerr << "Open failure on file.txt" ;
16      return ;
17    }
18
19    ofstream out( "file.bak" ) ;  // Open output file.
20    if ( out.fail() )
21    {
22      cerr << "Open failure on file.bak" ;
23      return ;
24    }
25
26    while( in.get( c ) ) // Loop while not end of file.
```

```
27   {
28     out.put( c ) ;   // Write character.
29     count++ ;
30   }
31
32   in.close() ;
33   out.close() ;
34   cout << "Copy completed. "
35        << count << " characters copied." << endl ;
36 }
```

The same technique for detecting the end of file can be applied to any member function that returns a reference to a stream. The next program demonstrates this by reading a file "word" by "word" using the extraction operator >>.

```
1  // Program example P14E
2  // Program to demonstrate end of file detection when using >>.
3  #include <iostream>
4  #include <fstream>
5  #include <iomanip>
6  #include <string>
7  using namespace std ;
8
9  void main()
10 {
11   string word ;
12   int word_count = 0 ;
13
14   ifstream in( "words.txt" ) ;
15   if ( in.fail() )
16   {
17     cerr << "Open failure on words.txt" ;
18     return ;
19 }
20
21   while ( in >> word ) // Loop while not end of file.
22   {
23     cout << word << endl ;
24     word_count++ ;
25   }
26
27   in.close() ;
28   cout << "No. of words in words.txt = " << word_count << endl ;
29 }
```

The program assumes that each "word" is delimited by one or more whitespace characters. Whitespace characters are ignored by >>.
The while loop from line 21 to line 25 continues to display each "word" in the file until the end of the file is detected.

14.5 Appending data to the end of a file

To add data to the end of a file, the file mode must be specified when opening the file. The file mode values are specified in the ios class. The possible file mode values are shown on the next page.

Mode	Meaning
ios::app	Opens a file for appending – additional data is written at the end of the file.
ios::ate	Start at the end of the file when a file is opened.
ios::binary	Opens a file in binary mode (default is text mode).
ios::in	Opens a file for input (default for ifstream).
ios::out	Opens a file for output (default for ofstream).
ios::trunc	Truncates (deletes) the file contents if the file already exists.
ios::nocreate	Do not create a new file. Open fails if the file does not already exist. For output files only.
ios::noreplace	Do not replace an existing file. Open fails if the file already exists. For output files only.

These values may be combined using the bitwise operator OR (|). For example, to open a file for input and output:

```
fstream in_out( "file.txt", ios::in | ios::out ) ;
```

In the previous programs the open mode of a file was not specified. This is because the default open mode for ifstream objects is is::in and is::out for ofstream objects.

The next program demonstrates appending data to the file file.txt, used in previous programs.

```
1   // Program example P14F
2   // Program to demonstrate adding data to the end of a file.
3   #include <iostream>
4   #include <fstream>
5   using namespace std ;
6
7   void main()
8   {
9     ofstream out( "file.txt", ios::app ) ;
10    if ( out.fail() )
11    {
12      cerr << "Open failure on file.txt" << endl ;
13      return ;
14    }
15    out << "This line is added to the end of the file" << endl ;
16  }
```

14.6 Reading lines from a file

The next program demonstrates how an entire line can be read from a file using the function
getline(). The program reads each line of a file and displays the line on the screen preceded
by a line number.

```
1   // Program example P14G
2   // Program to demonstrate reading a file line by line.
3   #include <iostream>
4   #include <fstream>
5   #include <string>
6   using namespace std ;
7
8   void main()
9   {
10    string line ;
11    int line_number = 0 ;
12
13    ifstream in( "p14g.cpp" ) ;
14    if ( in.fail() )
15    {
16      cerr << "Open failure on p14g.cpp" ;
17      return ;
18    }
19
20    while ( getline( in, line) )   // Read a line until eof.
21    {
22      cout << ++line_number << ":" << line << endl ;
23    }
24  }
```

14.7 Writing to a printer

DOS programs can write to a printer by opening the printer using its pre-defined name prn.
Writing to a printer requires the same statements required for writing to any file. For
example,

```
ofstream printer( "prn" ) ;
if ( printer.fail() )
{
    cerr << "Error on opening prn" << endl ;
    exit( 1 ) ;
}
printer << "this line will print on the printer" << endl ;
```

14.8 Random access

The previous programs all perform *serial file processing*. With serial file processing, data items
are read or written one after the other. For example, if you wanted to read the fifth data item in a
file, with serial processing you must read the previous four data items first. With *random* or
direct access you can move around in a file, reading and writing at any position in the file.
The position in a file is held in the file position marker (FPM).

The istream member function seekg (meaning 'seek get') is used to set the FPM for an input
file, from where the next input data is read. This function requires two arguments. The first

argument is an offset that tells the FPM how many bytes to skip. The second argument determines the point from where the offset is measured and has three possible values:

`ios::beg (=0)`	The offset is from the beginning of the stream.
`ios::cur (=1)`	The offset is from the current position in the stream.
`ios::end (=2)`	The offset is from the end of the stream.

Examples:
Open a file containing the characters A to J with

```
istream in( "letters.dat" ) ;.
```

When the file is opened the FPM is set to 0.

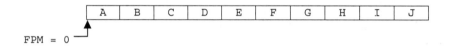

```
in.seekg( 4, ios::beg ) ;  // Move the FPM past the 4th. character
```
or
```
in.seekg( 4 ) ;            // ios::beg can be omitted.
```

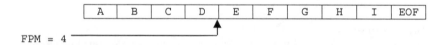

```
in.seekg( 1, ios::cur ) ;  // Move the FPM forward 1 character.
```

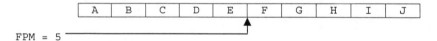

```
in.seekg( -3, ios::cur ) ; // Move the FPM back 3 characters.
```

```
in.seekg( 0, ios::beg ) ; // Move the FPM to the start of the file
```

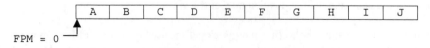

```
in.seekg( 0, ios::end ) ;   // Move the FPM to the end of the file.
```

A	B	C	D	E	F	G	H	I	J

FPM = 10

```
in.seekg( -2, ios::end ) ; // Move FPM to 2 characters before EOF.
```

A	B	C	D	E	F	G	H	I	J

FPM = 8

The equivalent function for setting the FPM for an output file is the seek put function, seekp().

There are also two other functions tellg() and tellp() that return the current value of the FPM for input and output streams respectively.

The next program is a simple demonstration of seekg() and tellg(). In this program the user enters a file position and the character at that position along with its ASCII value is displayed.

```
1    // Program example P14H
2    // Simple demonstration of random file access.
3    #include <iostream>
4    #include <fstream>
5    using namespace std ;
6
7    void main()
8    {
9      char c ;
10     long int file_pos, last_pos, offset ;
11
12     ifstream in( "letters.txt" ) ;
13     if ( in.fail() )
14     {
15       cerr << "Open failure on letters.txt" << endl ;
16       return ;
17     }
18
19     // Find the position of the last character in the file.
20     in.seekg( 0, ios::end ) ;
21     last_pos = in.tellg() ;
22
23     // Loop until user enters a 0.
24     do
25     {
26       cout << "Enter the file position (0 to end) " ;
27       cin >> file_pos ;
28       // Is this a valid position?
29       if ( file_pos > last_pos || file_pos < 0 )
30         cout << "Invalid position. Enter a value between 1 and "
31               << last_pos << endl ;
32       if ( file_pos > 0 && file_pos <= last_pos )
```

```
33      {
34        // The offset is 1 less than the position.
35        offset = file_pos - 1 ;
36        // Go directly to the character's offset.
37        in.seekg( offset, ios::beg ) ;
38        // Read the character and display.
39        in.get( c ) ;
40        cout << "Character at position " << file_pos
41             << ",offset " << offset
42             << " is "<< c << " ASCII "
43             << static_cast<int>( c ) << endl ;
44      }
45    }
46    while ( file_pos != 0 ) ;
47 }
```

The seekg() function on line 20 moves the FPM to the end of the file. The FPM is now positioned just after the last character in the file.

The tellg() function on line 21 reads the value of the FPM, which is also the number of characters in the file.

Line 27 inputs the required position in the file, which is converted to an offset on line 35.

The seekg() function on line 37 moves the FPM to just before the character to be read. The character is read on line 39 and displayed along with its ASCII value on lines 40 to 43.

Note the use of casting on line 43 to convert the value of c to its equivalent integer value.

14.9 Object I/O

In program P10G the >> and << operators were overloaded for keyboard input and screen output operations specific to the time24 class. No modifications to the time24 class are needed to use disk files instead of the keyboard and screen.

The next program opens a file and writes and reads time24 objects to and from this file.

```
1   // Program example P14I
2   // Demonstration of object I/O.
3   #include <iostream>
4   #include <fstream>
5   #include "time24.h"
6   #include "time24.cpp"
7   using namespace std ;
8
9   void main()
10  {
11    time24 t1( 1, 2, 3 ) ;              Both input and output.
12    time24 t2( 10, 10, 10 ) ;
13
14    fstream in_out( "times.dat", ios::in|ios::out ) ;
15    if ( in_out.fail() )
16    {
17      cerr << "error on opening times.dat" << endl ;
18      return ;
19    }
20
21    // Write objects to the file.
```

```
22    in_out <<  t1 << t2 ;
23
24    // Rewind the file to the start.
25    in_out.seekg( 0 ) ;
26
27    // Read objects back and display on the screen.
28    in_out  >> t1 >> t2 ;
29    cout << t1 << t2 ;
30 }
```

The output from this program is:

```
01:02:03
10:10:10
```

Line 5 includes the `time24` class declaration and line 6 includes the `time24` class member functions.
Line 14 opens the file `times.dat` as an `fstream` object for input and output.
Line 22 writes the `time24` objects `t1` and `t2` to the file.
Line 28 reads the objects back from the file and line 29 displays the objects.

14.10 Binary I/O

There are two types of files in C++: *text* (or *ASCII)* files and *binary* files. The difference between the two types of files is in the way they store numeric data types. In binary files, numeric data is stored in binary format, while in text files numeric data is stored as ASCII characters. For example, if you had

```
short int n  = 123 ;
```

The variable n occupies two bytes of memory.

Storing n in a text file requires three bytes of memory:

Character :	'1'	'2'	'3'
ASCII value in decimal:	49	50	51
ASCII value in binary:	00110001	00110010	00110011

Each digit of the number requires one byte of storage in an ASCII file.

In a binary file, the digits of a number do not occupy individual storage locations. Instead the number is stored in its entirety as a binary number. So the variable n, with a value of 123, will be stored as:

00000000	01111011

If, for example, you increase the value of n to 1234, the binary file will still require the same storage as it does for the number 123. However, an ASCII file would require one more byte to store the extra digit.

14.10.1 Serial writing of objects to a binary file

The two-argument istream member function write is used to write an object in binary format. The first argument is the address of the block of memory where the object is stored and the second argument is the size of the block in bytes.

It is important to note that the object must be stored in one contiguous block of memory. This means that the object cannot have a pointer data member to dynamically allocated memory. It also means that the class cannot have any string data members, since the string class uses a pointer data member.

The next program demonstrates write by writing stock objects to a file. The stock class uses a fixed length C-string to store the stock description.

```
1    // Program example P14J
2    // Demonstration of writing to a binary file.
3    #include <iostream>
4    #include "stock.h"
5    #include "stock.cpp"
6    using namespace std ;
7
8    void main()
9    {
10     // Initialise an array of stock objects.
11     class stock stationery[ 10 ] =
12     { stock( 1, "Pencil", 68 ),
13       stock( 2, "Pen", 30 ),
14       stock( 3, "Highlighter", 90 ),
15       stock( 4, "Eraser", 24 ),
16       stock( 5, "Pencil Sharpener", 5 ),
17       stock( 6, "Pocket Folder", 50 ),
18       stock( 7, "Paper Tie", 300 ),
19       stock( 8, "Glue Stick", 30 ),
20       stock( 9, "Box File", 35 ),
21       stock( 10, "Note Book", 97 ) } ;
22
23     int object_size = sizeof( stock ) ;
24
25     // Open stock file for binary output.
26     ofstream stock_file( "stock.dat", ios::binary ) ;
27     if ( stock_file.fail() )
28     {
29       cerr << "Open failure on stock.dat" << endl ;
30       return ;
31     }
32
33     // Write each object to output file.
34     for ( int i = 0 ; i < 10 ; i++ )
35     {
36       cout << "Writing Stock Code "
37            << stationery[ i ].get_code() << ' '
38            << stationery[ i ].get_description() << endl ;
39       stock_file.write( reinterpret_cast<char *>( &stationery[i] ),
40                         object_size ) ;
41     }
42 }
```

The file stock.h contains:

```
#if !defined STOCK_H
#define STOCK_H

// Header for a simple stock class.
#include <fstream>
using namespace std ;

class stock
{
public:
  stock() ;
  // Purpose   : default constructor.

  stock( int code, char desc[ ], int qty ) ;
  // Purpose    : constructor
  // Parameters: stock code, description and stock quantity.
  //           : Note that the description is a C string.

  void set_qty( int qty ) ;
  // Purpose   : assign a value to the stock quantity.
  // Parameter: qty - the quantity to be assigned.

  const int get_code() const ;
  // Purpose   : inspector function to return the stock code.

  const char* get_description() const ;
  // Purpose   : inspector function to return the stock description.
  //           : Note that the description is a C string.

  const int get_qty() const ;
  // Purpose   : inspector function to return the stock quantity.
private:
  int stock_code;
  char description[21] ;
  int qty_in_stock ;
} ;

#endif
```

The file stock.cpp contains:

```
// Member function definitions for stock class.
#include "stock.h"
#include <cstring>
stock::stock()
{
  stock_code = 0 ;
  qty_in_stock = 0 ;
  *description = '\0' ;
}

stock::stock( int code, char desc[ ], int qty )
{
```

```
      stock_code = code ;
      strcpy( description, desc ) ;
      qty_in_stock = qty ;
   }

   void stock::set_qty( int qty )
   {
      qty_in_stock = qty ;
   }

   const int stock::get_code() const
   {
      return stock_code ;
   }

   const char* stock::get_description() const
   {
      return description ;
   }

   const int stock::get_qty() const
   {
      return qty_in_stock ;
   }
```

The `write()` function on line 39 treats the stock object as a block of memory bytes or characters, which it copies from memory to a disk file without converting to ASCII.

Since the object is treated as a block of characters, the first argument in `write()` is a pointer to a character. This is why the address of the ith. stock object, `&stationery[i]`, is cast to a pointer to a character using

```
   reinterpret_cast<char*>( &stationery[i] )
```

This cast is used to get the C++ compiler to regard the address of the stock object (data type `stock*`) as an address to a character (data type `char*`), as required by `write()`.

The second argument is the number of bytes in the memory block, which is calculated on line 23.

14.10.2 Serial reading of objects from a binary file

The `istream` member function `read()` is used to read an object's data from a binary file into memory. This function uses the same arguments as `write()`, as demonstrated in the next program.

```
1    // Program example P14K
2    // Demonstration of serial reading of a binary file.
3    #include <iostream>
4    #include <iomanip>
5    #include "stock.h"
6    #include "stock.cpp"
7    using namespace std ;
8
9    void main()
10   {
```

```
11    stock stock_record ;
12
13    // Open stock file for binary input.
14    ifstream stock_file( "stock.dat", ios::binary ) ;
15    if ( stock_file.fail() )
16    {
17      cerr << "Open failure on stock.dat" << endl ;
18      return ;
19    }
20
21    int object_size = sizeof( stock ) ;
22
23    cout << "Code Description        Qty" << endl ;
24    cout << left ;  // Left justify data.
25    // Read and display stock records until eof.
26    while( stock_file.read
27            ( reinterpret_cast<char *>( &stock_record ),
28              object_size ) )
29    {
30      cout << setw(5) << stock_record.get_code()
31            << setw(20) << stock_record.get_description()
32            << stock_record.get_qty() << endl ;
33    } ;
34 }
```

The output from this program is:

```
Code Description        Qty
1    Pencil             68
2    Pen                30
...
10   Note Book          97
```

14.10.3 Binary I/O as class member functions
Binary I/O is made easier for the users of a class (the client programmers) if the details of the read and write functions are hidden in class member functions.
The member function to write to a binary file is:

```
void stock::binary_write( fstream& os )
{
  os.write( reinterpret_cast<char *>( this ), sizeof( *this ) ) ;
}
```

Using this member function in program P14J, line 39 becomes:

```
stationery[i].binary_write( stock_file ) ;
```

The output stream stock_file is passed to the parameter os of binary_write(). The built-in pointer this is a pointer to the object that invoked the member function, i.e. stationery[i]. The pointer this is therefore equivalent to &stationery[i] and sizeof(*this) is equivalent to sizeof(stationery[i]).

The member function to read from a binary file is:

```
bool stock::binary_read( fstream& is )
{
    is.read( reinterpret_cast<char *>( this ), sizeof( *this ) ) ;
    return !is.eof() ;
}
```

Using this member function in program P14K, lines 26 to 28 become

```
while ( stock_record.binary_read( stock_file ) )
```

In addition to reading an object from the input stream, `binary_read()` returns `false` if the end of file has been reached, otherwise it returns `true`. The while loop will therefore continue until the end of file is reached.

14.10.4 Binary file random access
The next program demonstrates the direct access of a stock object stored in a binary file. The layout of the file as created by program P14J is illustrated in the diagram below.

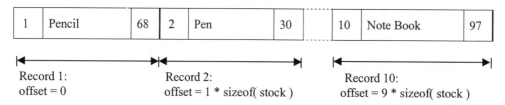

This type of file is called a *relative* file. In this file structure, the stock code is related to the position of the record in the file, i.e. stock code 1 is the first record, stock code 2 is the second record and stock code 3 is the third record and so on. The offset of a stock record in the file can be calculated by subtracting 1 from the stock code and multiplying the result by the size of the stock record.

The following program allows the user to enter a stock code and update the stock quantity. The user can update the records in any order. After the updates are complete, the program displays the contents of the file.

```
1   // Program example P14L
2   // Program to demonstrate serial reading of a binary file.
3   #include <iostream>
4   #include <iomanip>
5   #include "stock.h"
6   #include "stock.cpp"
7   using namespace std ;
8
9   // Non-class standalone functions.
10  int input_stock_code() ;
11  // Purpose: Function to input a stock code from the keyboard.
12  // Returns: The stock code entered.
13
14  void update_stock_record( int stock_code, fstream& stock_file ) ;
15  // Purpose  : Update the stock quantity.
```

```
16 // Parameters: stock code and output stream.
17
18 void main()
19 {
20    int stock_code, max_stock_code ;
21    stock stock_record ;
22
23    // Open stock file for binary input and output.
24    fstream stock_file( "c:/cppex/stock.dat",
25                           ios::binary | ios::in | ios::out) ;
26    if ( stock_file.fail() )
27    {
28      cerr << "Open failure on stock.dat" << endl ;
29      return ;
30    }
31
32    // Find the number of records in the file.
33    stock_file.seekg( 0, ios::end ) ;
34    max_stock_code = stock_file.tellg() / sizeof( stock ) ;
35
36    // Input a stock code and update stock qty, code 0 ends.
37    do
38    {
39      stock_code = input_stock_code() ;
40      if ( stock_code > 0 && stock_code <= max_stock_code)
41        update_stock_record( stock_code, stock_file ) ;
42    }
43    while ( stock_code != 0 ) ;
44
45    // Display the updated file.
46    cout << "Code Description         Qty" << endl ;
47    cout << left ;  // Left justify data.
48    // Read and display stock records until end of file.
49    stock_file.seekg(0) ;
50    while ( stock_record.binary_read( stock_file) )
51    {
52      cout << setw(5) << stock_record.get_code()
53             << setw(20)<< stock_record.get_description()
54             << stock_record.get_qty() << endl ;
55    }
56
57    stock_file.close() ;
58 }
59
60 int input_stock_code()
61 {
62    int code ;
63    cout << "Enter a stock code: " ;
64    cin >> code ;
65    return code ;
66 }
67
68 void update_stock_record( int stock_code, fstream& stock_file )
69 {
70    int qty ;
71    long int offset ;
```

```
72    stock stock_record ;
73
74    // Place the file position marker just before the record.
75    offset = ( stock_code -1 ) * sizeof( stock_record ) ;
76    stock_file.seekg( offset, ios::beg ) ;
77
78    // Read the record.
79    stock_record.binary_read( stock_file ) ;
80
81    // Get the new quantity.
82    cout << "Enter Stock Quantity for Stock Code : "
83         << stock_code << ", "
84         << stock_record.get_description() << ": ";
85    cin >> qty ;
86
87    // Update the record.
88    stock_record.set_qty( qty ) ;
89    stock_file.seekp( offset, ios::beg ) ;
90    stock_record.binary_write( stock_file ) ;
91  }
```

The program continually asks the user for a stock code and quantity until the user enters a stock code of 0.

The stock record corresponding to the entered stock code is retrieved by calculating the offset of the record in the file, moving the file position marker to the start of the record, and reading the record. This is done on lines 75 to 79.

After updating the stock quantity in memory with the member function set_qty(), it is necessary to write the updated record back to the file. This is done by first moving back to the start of the record (line 89) and then writing the updated record (line 90).

After the updating of the file is complete, the entire file is displayed on lines 49 to 55.

Programming pitfalls

1. File names frequently contain \, for example, `c:\newfile.dat`. To open such a file you have to use an extra \ as in:

   ```
   istream in( "c:\\newfile.dat" ) ;
   ```

   Without the extra \, the \n is interpreted as the newline escape sequence. UNIX uses / in file specifications, and so the problem does not arise.

2. In the `istream` member function `read()`, the first argument is a character pointer to a memory location. The memory location must be big enough to store the block of memory to be read.

3. The default open mode of an `ifstream` object is `is::in` and the default mode for an `ofstream` object is `in::out`. No default mode exists for an `fstream` object and must be specified, e.g.

   ```
   fstream in_out( "file.txt", is:in | is::out ) ;
   ```

4. The open mode values may be combined using the bitwise-OR operator |, not the logical-OR operator ‖.

Quick syntax reference

	Syntax	Examples

Open a file for input	`ifstream stream_name( filename, mode ) ;`	`ifstream in( "file" ) ;`
		`if ( in.fail() )`
		`{`
		`    cerr << "file error" ;`
		`    return ;`
		`}`

Open a file for output	`ofstream stream_name( filename, mode ) ;`	`ofstream out( "file" ) ;`
		`if ( out.fail() )`
		`{`
		`    cerr << "file error" ;`
		`    return ;`
		`}`

Open a file for input and output	`fstream stream_name( filename, mode ) ;`	`ofstream in_out( "file",`
		`           ios::in|ios::out ) ;`
		`if ( in_out.fail() )`
		`{`
		`    cerr << "file error" ;`
		`    return ;`
		`}`

Read a character from a file	`stream_name.get( variable ) ;`	`in.get( c ) ;`

Write a character to a file	`stream_name.put( variable ) ;`	`out.put( c ) ;`

Read a C++ string from a file	`getline( stream_name, variable );`
	
	or
	
	`>>`
		`getline ( in, line ) ;`
		
		`in >> word ;`

Read a C-string from a file	`stream_name.get (`
	`  c_string_variable,`
	`  max_number_of_characters,`
	`  delimiter ) ;`
	
	or
	
	`stream_name.read(`
	`   c_string_variable,`
	`   number_of_characters ) ;`
	
	or
	
	`>>`
		`in.get( str, 81,'\n' ) ;`
		
		`in.read( str, 80 ) ;`
		
		`in >> word ;`

Write a C-string from a file	`steam_name.write(`
	`   c_string,`
	`   number_of_characters ) ;`
		`out.write( "ABC", 3 ) ;`

Set the file position marker for an input file	`stream_name.seekg( offset,`
	`                   origin ) ;`
	`// offset = long integer value`
	`// origin = ios:beg,`
	`//          ios:cur or`
	`//          ios:end`
		`long int off = 0 ;`
		`in.seekg( off, ios:beg ) ;`

Set the file position marker for an output file	`stream_name.seekp( offset,` `                   origin ) ;`	`long int off = 0 ;` `in.seekp( off, ios:end ) ;`
Closing a file	`stream_name.close() ;`	`out.close() ;`

Binary file block input	`stream_name.read(`
	`       character_pointer,`
	`       number_of_characters ) ;`
		`in.read(`
		`reinterpret_cast<char *>`
		`( &stock_rec),`
		`  sizeof( stock_rec ) ) ;`

Binary file block output	`stream_name.write(`
	`       character_pointer,`
	`       number_of_characters ) ;`
		`out.write(`
		`reinterpret_cast<char *>`
		`( &stock_rec ),`
		`  sizeof( stock_rec ) ) ;`

Exercises

1. Write C++ statements to open the following files:

File name	Mode	File type
supp.dat	input	binary
cust.dat	input and output	binary
temp.txt	output	text
file.txt	append	text

2. Which mode would you use for the following?
   (a) updating existing data in a file
   (b) appending new data to the end of a file
   (c) deleting the contents of an existing file before writing new data to it.

3. Write a program to count the number of characters and the number of words in a text file.

4. Write a program to remove blank or zero length lines from a text file. An input file and an output file are required.

5. Write a program to compare two text files and display any differences between the files.

6. What does the file alpha.txt contain after this program is run?

```cpp
#include <iostream>
#include <fstream>
using namespace std ;

void main()
{
  char c ;
  fstream alpha_file( "alpha.txt", ios::in|ios::out ) ;
  if ( alpha_file.fail() )
  {
    cerr << "Unable to open alpha.txt" << endl ;
    return ;
  }
  for ( c = 'A' ; c <= 'Z' ; c++ )
  {
    alpha_file << c ;
  }
  alpha_file.seekg( 11, ios::beg) ;
  alpha_file >> c;
  alpha_file.seekp( -3, ios::cur ) ;
  alpha_file << c ;
  alpha_file.seekg( -1, ios::end ) ;
  alpha_file >> c ;
  alpha_file.seekp( 0 ) ;
  alpha_file << c ;
}
```

7. The Caesar cypher is a simple method for encrypting text. The cypher works by replacing each letter in the text with the letter that occurs a certain distance from it in the alphabet. Non-alphabetic characters are not encrypted. For example, ABcD is encrypted to BCdE when the distance is 1; xYZ1 is encrypted to zAB1 when the distance is 2. Write a program to encrypt a text file with a distance specified by the user. An input file and an output file are required.

8. Write a program to merge two text files containing names into a single text file.
    Each line of the files contains a surname, followed by a space and a first name.
    Assume the files are sorted in ascending order of surnames.

9. Modify program P14L to allow for batch updates of the stock quantity.
    Each line of a text file `trans.txt` contains a stock code and a stock quantity. Read each line of `trans.txt` and update the appropriate record in `stock.dat`.

10. Overload the insertion operator `<<` for the stock class in program P14L. The overloaded operator will display a stock record in the same format as lines 52 to 54 of P14L.

11. Modify program P14L to display a stock record, to delete a stock record and to add a new record.
    The program will require a menu:

    1. Update Stock Quantity
    2. Display a Stock Record
    3. Delete a Stock Record
    4. Add a Stock Record
    5. Delete all Records
    6. Display all Records
    0. Quit

    Enter option 0 to 6 :

    Options 1 to 4 require the user to enter a stock code in the range 1 to 10.

    The C++ code for options 1 and 6 already exist in the program.

    Option 3 "deletes" a record from the file. A record is signalled as deleted by writing a 0 in the stock code field of the record in the file. A "deleted" record should not be displayed by options 2 or 6 or updated by option 1.

    Option 4 "adds" a new record to the file. To add a new record, use the stock code to calculate the file offset and read the record at this offset. If the stock code of the record from the file is 0, overwrite the file record with the new record. If the stock code of the file record is not 0, display an error message "stock code already exists".

Appendix A

List of C++ Keywords

asm	auto	bad_cast	bad_typeid
bool	break	case	catch
char	class	const	const_cast
continue	default	delete	do
double	dynamic_cast	else	enum
except	explicit	extern	false
finally	float	for	friend
goto	if	inline	int
long	mutable	namespace	new
operator	private	protected	public
register	reinterpret_cast	return	short
signed	sizeof	static	static_cast
struct	switch	template	this
throw	true	try	type_info
typedef	typeid	typename	union
unsigned	using	virtual	void
volatile	while		

In addition to this list, consider all names beginning with an underscore (_) to be reserved for system use.

Appendix B

Precedence and Associativity of C++ Operators

Operator	Name
::	Scope access
::	Global
( )	Function call
[ ]	Subscripts
.	Member selection with an object
->	Member selection with a pointer
++	Postfix increment
--	Postfix decrement
const_cast	Const cast
dynamic_cast	Dynamic cast (checked at run-time)
reinterpret_cast	Reinterpret cast (unchecked)
static_cast	Static cast (checked at compile-time)
typeid	Type identification
-	Unary minus
+	Unary plus
~	Ones complement
!	Logical NOT
*	Indirection or dereference
&	Address
++	Prefix increment
--	Prefix decrement
new	Dynamically allocates storage
delete	Dynamically deallocates storage
sizeof	Size of object
sizeof(type)	Size of type
(type)	Cast
.*	Dereference
->*	Dereference

*	Multiply
/	Divide
%	Modulus
+	Add
-	Subtract
<<	Left shift
>>	Right shift
<	Less than
>	Greater than
<=	Less than or equal to
>=	Greater than or equal to
==	Equal to
!=	Not equal to
&	Bitwise inclusive AND
^	Bitwise exclusive OR
|	Bitwise inclusive OR
&&	Logical AND
||	Logical OR
=	Assignment
*=	Multiply and assign
/=	Divide and assign
%=	Modulus and assign
+=	Add and assign
-=	Subtract and assign
<<=	Left shift and assign
>>=	Right shift and assign
&=	Bitwise AND and assign
|=	Bitwise OR and assign
^=	Bitwise exclusive OR and assign
? :	Conditional
throw	Throw an exception
,	Comma (sequence)

Notes:

1. Operators are listed in descending order of precedence. Where several operators appear in the same box, they have equal precedence.

2. Expressions within parentheses have a higher precedence than expressions without parentheses.

3. When an expression contains several operators with equal precedence, evaluation proceeds according to the associativity of the operator, either from right to left or from left to right. Unary operators and assignment operators associate from right to left; all other operators associate from left to right. A unary operator has only one operand.

Appendix C

ASCII Character Codes

A character code is a numerical value used to represent a character in the computer's memory. The ASCII (American Standard Code for Information Interchange) character set is defined as a table of seven-bit codes that represent control characters and printable characters. For example, the letter 'A' is represented by ASCII code 65, and '1' is represented by ASCII code 49.

The circumflex symbol ^ is used in the following table to indicate that the control key Ctrl is pressed simultaneously with another key.

Decimal code	Hexadecimal code	Key	Decimal code	Hexadecimal code	Key
0	00	^@	33	21	!
1	01	^A	34	22	"
2	02	^B	35	23	#
3	03	^C	36	24	$
4	04	^D	37	25	%
5	05	^E	38	26	&
6	06	^F	39	27	'
7	07 BEL	^G	40	28	(
8	08 BS	^H	41	29	)
9	09 TAB	^I	42	2A	*
10	0A LF	^J	43	2B	+
11	0B VT	^K	44	2C	,
12	0C FF	^L	45	2D	–
13	0D CR	^M	46	2E	.
14	0E	^N	47	2F	/
15	0F	^O	48	30	0
16	10	^P	49	31	1
17	11	^Q	50	32	2
18	12	^R	51	33	3
19	13		52	34	4
20	14	^T	53	35	5
21	15		54	36	6
22	16		55	37	7
23	17	^W	56	38	8
24	18	^X	57	39	9
25	19	^Y	58	3A	:
26	1A	^Z	59	3B	;
27	1B ESC	^[	60	3C	<
28	1C	^\	61	3D	=
29	1D	^]	62	3E	>
30	1E	^^	63	3F	?
31	1F	^_	64	40	@
32	20	space			

Decimal code	Hexadecimal code	Key	Decimal code	Hexadecimal code	Key
65	41	A	97	61	a
66	42	B	98	62	b
67	43	C	99	63	c
68	44	D	100	64	d
69	45	E	101	65	e
70	46	F	102	66	f
71	47	G	103	67	g
72	48	H	104	68	h
73	49	I	105	69	I
74	4A	J	106	6A	j
75	4B	K	107	6B	k
76	4C	L	108	6C	l
77	4D	M	109	6D	m
78	4E	N	110	6E	n
79	4F	O	111	6F	o
80	50	P	112	70	p
81	51	Q	113	71	q
82	52	R	114	72	r
83	53	S	115	73	s
84	54	T	116	74	t
85	55	U	117	75	u
86	56	V	118	76	v
87	57	W	119	77	w
88	58	X	120	78	x
89	59	Y	121	79	y
90	5A	Z	122	7A	z
91	5B	[	123	7B	{
92	5C	\	124	7C	|
93	5D	]	125	7D	}
94	5E	^	126	7E	~
95	5F	_	127	7F	Del
96	60	'			

Appendix D

Fundamental C++ Built-in Data Types

Boolean	Character	Integer	Floating-point
bool	char	short int	float
	signed char	signed short int	double
	unsigned char	unsigned short int	long double
		int	
		signed int	
		unsigned int	
		long int	
		signed long int	
		unsigned long int	

Data Type[1]	Size[1]	Range[1]
char and signed char	8 bits	-128 to 127
unsigned char	8 bits	0 to 255
short int and signed short int	16 bits	-32,768 to 32,767
unsigned short int	16 bits	0 to 65,535
unsigned int	32 bits	0 to 4,294,967,295
int and signed int	32 bits	-2,147,483,648 to 2,147,483,647
unsigned long int	32 bits	0 to 4,294,967,295
long int and signed long int	32 bits	-2,147,483,648 to 2,147,483,647
float	32 bits	3.4×10^{-38} to $3.4 \times 10^{+38}$
double	64 bits	1.7×10^{-308} to $1.7 \times 10^{+308}$
long double	80 bits	1.2×10^{-4932} to $1.2 \times 10^{+4932}$

---

[1] compiler dependent.

Appendix E

Common `iomanip` Manipulators

Manipulator	Input/Output	Description
`endl`	Output	Write a newline character and flush the output stream.
`setw( w )`	Input/Output	Set the field width to w. Effects the next item only.
`setfill( c )`	Output	Sets the fill character to c. The default fill character is a space.
`setprecision( p )`	Output	Sets the number of places of accuracy to p. The default accuracy is 6.
`fixed`	Output	Display floating-point values in decimal fixed-point notation.
`scientific`	Output	Display floating-point values in scientific notation.
`skipws`	Input	Ignore whitespace characters in input stream. This is the default setting.
`noskipws`	Input	Read whitespace characters in input stream.
`showpos`	Output	Precede positive numbers with +.
`noshowpos`	Output	Do not precede positive numbers with +.
`flush`	Output	Flushes the output stream. Forces all the data in the output stream to be physically written to the output device.
`left`	Output	Align left.
`right`	Output	Align right (the default).
`showpoint`	Output	A decimal point is displayed for a floating-point number.
`noshowpoint`	Output	A decimal point is displayed for a floating-point number only if the decimal portion is non-zero.
`setbase( b )`	Input/Output	Set the conversion base to b (8, 10 or 16).
`showbase`	Output	If the base is set to 8 (octal), a zero precedes the number. If the base is set to 16, 0x precedes the number.
`noshowbase`	Output	The number base is not shown.

`#include <iomanip>` is required for any manipulator that uses an argument.
`#include <iostream>` is sufficient for other manipulators.

Appendix F

Escape Sequences

Character	Meaning
\a	alert (bell)
\n	newline
\t	tab
\b	backspace
\r	carriage return
\f	form feed
\\	backslash
\"	double quotation mark
\'	single quotation mark
\0	null
\ddd	up to three-digit octal value
\xddd	up to three-digit hexadecimal value

Note: When an escape sequence appears in a string it counts as a single character.

Appendix G

The C++ Preprocessor

The preprocessor, as its name implies, processes a C++ program before it is read by the compiler. A C++ program is read by the preprocessor and modified by *preprocessor directives*.

C++ program → preprocessor → modified C++ program → C++ compiler.

Preprocessor statements are placed in a C++ program and tell the preprocessor how to modify the program.

A preprocessor statement starts with a hash (#) and is followed by a preprocessor directive.

G.1 #Including files

The include directive includes a specified file in the source file at the point at which the directive appears. The general format of #include is:

```
#include <file_name>
```

or

```
#include "file_name"
```

The angle brackets < and > in the first format instructs the preprocessor to search for the specified files in the standard include directory (folder) only. The standard include directory is where the standard include files such as iostream are stored.

The double quotation marks in the second format instruct the preprocessor to search for the file in the current directory and, if it is not found there, to search in the standard include directory. However, if a directory is specified within the double quotation marks then this directory only is searched.

By convention, header files written by a programmer have a file name with an extension of .h. System header files do not include a file name extension.

Here are some examples of #include directives:

```
#include <iostream> // Include iostream from standard include
                    // directory.
#include "my.h"     // Include my.h from the current directory
                    // and if not there look for the file in
                    // the standard include directory.
#include "\myinclude\my.h" // Windows and MS-DOS uses a single
                    // backslash \.
#include "/myinclude/my.h" // UNIX uses a forward slash /
                    // Include my.h from the directory
                    //  myinclude. Only the specified
                    // directory myinclude is searched.
```

G.2 #define

Symbolic constants, such as the number of elements in an array (see line 9 of program P5B), have been defined in previous programs using const. It is also possible to define a symbolic constant using the #define preprocessor directive. The format of #define is:

```
#define NAME replacement
```

where NAME is the symbolic constant. By convention, NAME is usually in uppercase characters. The preprocessor replaces all occurrences of NAME within the source file by replacement before the program is compiled. NAME must conform to the rules for constructing valid C++ identifiers.

Examples:

```
#define SIZE 10
#define DAYS_IN_WEEK 7
#define PI 3.141592653
#define END_OF_SENTENCE '.'
#define DIGITS "0123456789"
#define FIVE_SPACES "     "
#define END_OF_STRING '\0'
#define NEWLINE '\n'
#define BACKSPACE '\b'
```

Once a symbolic constant has been defined, it cannot be assigned to a different value without first removing the original definition. This can be done with the #undef directive. For example:

```
#define SIZE 10    // SIZE is 10.
#undef  SIZE       // SIZE is no longer defined.
#define SIZE 20    // SIZE is now 20.
```

C++ programs generally use const rather than #define to define symbolic constants.

G.3 Conditional directives

The preprocessor conditional directives #if, #else, #elif and #endif can be used to include or omit blocks of C++ code. For example, suppose when debugging a program a programmer wants to check the values of three integer variables a, b and c at a certain point in the program. To do this, the following statements are placed in the program at the point where the variables are to be checked:

```
#if defined DEBUG
   cout << "a, b and c at this point are: " << a << b << c ;
#endif
```

If DEBUG has previously been defined (usually at the top of the program) with

```
#define DEBUG
```

the cout statement will be included in the program. If you leave out this #define or have DEBUG undefined with

```
#undef DEBUG
```

the cout statement will not be placed in the program. Debugging statements can be included or excluded in your program simply by defining or undefining DEBUG.

Symbolic constants can also be tested using the relational operators ==, !=, >, <, <= and >=.

```
#define DEBUG 'y'
...
#if DEBUG == 'y'
  cout << "a, b and c at this point are: " << a << b << c ;
#endif
```

The logical operators !, || and && can also be used.

The conditional directives are commonly used to prevent multiple inclusions of a header file in a program. Class declarations are often defined in header files, and commonly contain preprocessor directives to prevent their multiple inclusions into a program.
In the following, a class called my_class is declared in a header file myclass.h. The file myclass.h typically contains the following:

```
#if !defined MY_CLASS_H
#define MY_CLASS__H

class my_class
{
  ...
} ;

#endif
```

The above preprocessor statements check to see if the symbolic constant MY_CLASS_H is defined. If it is, then the class has already been included in the program and is not included again. If not already defined, MY_CLASS_H is defined and the class is included in the program.

Appendix H

Glossary of Terms

abstraction
a software model of a real world object or concept

abstract base class
a class that has at least one pure virtual member function; it can only be used as a base class for other classes; no objects can be created from this class

abstract data type
user-defined data type, including data and operations; used only as a base class to derive other classes; see *abstract base class*

accessor
a class member function that returns the value of a class data member

address
a number that identifies a particular memory location

algorithm
sequence of instructions that leads to a solution of a problem

allocate
to give memory space to an object

ampersand &
an operator used to find the address of a variable

ANSI/ISO
American National Standards Institute/International Standards Organisation; bodies responsible for defining the C++ programming language standard

argument
refers to the identifiers and values used in calling a function or a function-like macro or in the instantiation of a template; also called an actual parameter; see *parameter*

arithmetic conversion
conversion on integer and floating-point data

array
a set of built-in or user-defined elements of the same type

ASCII
American Standard Code for Information Interchange; a set of codes used to represent letters, digits, special characters, and other symbols

associativity
an attribute of an operator that determines whether it evaluates left to right or right to left in an expression

auto storage class
storage class for variables and objects that are local to the block where they are declared

base class
class from which other classes inherit data members and member functions; the most generalised class in a class hierarchy; see *inheritance*

binary
a number system that uses the base 2; it uses only two digits: 0 and 1

binary file
a file containing data in binary format

binary operator
an operator that has two operands

block
a collection of statements and declarations enclosed within braces ({ and })

bug
an error in a program

built-in data type
a data type defined in the language itself, e.g. char, int, float etc.

byte
the smallest unit of memory that can be addressed; it consists of eight binary digits (= 8 bits)

call
to transfer control of a program to a function

case-sensitive
distinguishing between lowercase and uppercase characters

cast
to convert from one data type to another

class
a user-defined data type consisting of data elements and functions that operate on the data

class hierarchy
an ordering of classes in which no derived class has more than one base class; see *single inheritance*

class network
an ordering of classes in which a derived class may have more than one base class; see *multiple inheritance*

class template
that from which a new class may be created by supplying a data type for each template parameter ; see *template class*

class interface
the public section of a class; shows how the public member functions of a class can be used

class library
set of related classes

compiler
a program that translates a program written in a high-level language such as C++ to machine or object code. A 16-bit or 32-bit compiler refers to the word size of the CPU. See *word size*

composite object
object that includes (*has-a*) other objects

concrete class
a class that can be instantiated

constant
numeric or string value that does not change

constant member function
a class member function that cannot modify class data members

constructor
a class member function used to initialise an object

copy constructor
a constructor used to initialise an object with another object

CPU
central processing unit

C-string
an array of characters, terminated by the null character (`'\0'`)

data type
an attribute of a data item, for example `char`, `int`, `float`, and `long int`

debugging
finding and removing logical errors or bugs from a program

deallocate
to free memory space previously used by an object; see *allocate*

declaration
a statement that binds an identifier with a constant, variable, function, or user-defined data type

decrement
the reduction of a value by 1

deep copy
a copy of a pointer and the memory that the pointer points to; see *shallow copy*

default argument
optional argument, the value of which is specified in the function declaration

default class constructor
a class constructor that has no parameters

definition
a statement that allocates storage for a variable, function, or user-defined data type

dereference
to access a value at a particular storage location through the use of a pointer

derived class
a class that inherits some or all data members and member functions from a *base class*; see *inheritance*

destructor
a class member function that is automatically called when an object of that class goes out of scope; usually used to free memory allocated to an object

dynamic binding
identification at run-time of which class member function to call

early binding
identification at compile-time of which class member function to call

element
an individual data item in an array

enumeration type
a user-defined data type; list of items that are names for integer values

encapsulation
defining data members and member functions together in a class

escape sequence
a combination of characters consisting of a backslash (\) followed by a letter or combination of digits

extraction operator
The input stream operator >>

expression
a combination of operands and operators

file
a named section of storage on a disk or other storage device

file pointer marker
a pointer that indicates the current position in a file

friend
used by a class to give other classes or functions access to its class members

function
a collection of declarations and statements that may return a value and can be called by name

function body
statements that are executed when the function is called

function header
first line of a function giving the return type of the function, the function name and a list of its parameters

function interface
function prototype and documentation on how to use the function

function template
from which a new function may be created by supplying a data type for each template parameter; see *template function*

fundamental data types
a set of basic C++ data types; it includes character, integer, floating-point and enumeration types

global
that which is accessible from any part of a program

header file
a text file that usually contains C++ preprocessor statements, class and function declarations; it is merged into a program using the #include preprocessor directive

hexadecimal or **hex**
a number system based on the number 16; it uses 0 to 9 and A to F as numerals

include file
see *header file*

increment
the increase of a value by 1

information hiding
separating a class interface from the details of its implementation

index
a variable or number used to access the elements of an array

inheritance
when one class, the *derived class,* shares the data members and member functions of another class, the *base class* ; the derived class will usually extend or modify those data members and member functions; defines *a-kind-of* relationship between classes

inline function
a request (that may not be granted) to the compiler to replace each function call by the body of a function

insertion operator
The output stream operator < <

inspector
see *accessor*

instance
an object created from a class

instantiation
creating an instance of a class

initialise
to give a starting value to a variable

initialisation list
a list in a class constructor that specifies the initial values for the data members of the class

integer
a positive or negative whole number or 0

keyword
a word with a special meaning for a compiler

late binding
see *dynamic binding*

library
a file of compiled object modules; the linker program combines modules from the library with a program object module to create an executable program file

linker
a program that links object modules to form an executable file

literal
data rather than a reference to data

local
accessible only from within the block in which it is defined

loop
a set of statements that is executed repeatedly

macro
an identifier defined in a #define preprocessor directive; used to define a substitution in a C++ program

manipulator
a value used to control input and output stream formatting

member
an element of a structure or a class

member function
an element of a class that operates on objects of that class; used to implement object behavior

memory leak
occurs when there is no longer a pointer containing the address of a dynamically allocated memory block; the program is unable to deallocate the memory block

message
a call to a class member function

method
see *member function*

multi-dimensional array
an array with more than one dimension: an array of arrays

multiple inheritance
when a class has more than one base class; supported by C++ but not by all object-oriented programming languages

mutator
a class member function that modifies a data member of a class

nested block
a block of code included within a larger block of code

name
an identifier for an object, a function, a class, a template and so on

namespace
a collection of names

newline character \n
a character used to mark the end of a line in a text file or when the Enter key is pressed on the keyboard; represented by the escape sequence \n. The Enter key generates a combination of carriage-return and line-feed (CR-LF) when pressed; C++ translates CR-LF into a single line-feed (LF) character on input and translates a line-feed character into the CR-LF characters on output

null character
the ASCII character having the value 0; the escape sequence '\0'

null character string
two consecutive double quotation marks that define a character string containing no characters

null pointer
a pointer to nothing

null statement
a statement that contains only a semicolon

null-terminated string
a character string ending with the null character ('\0')

object
an instance of a class; an object has an identity, a state and a behaviour

object code
program in the form of binary numbers; produced by a compiler from source code

object file
a file containing object (machine) code

object module
see *object file*

offset
the distance from some starting point or origin

OOA
Object-Oriented Analysis; answers the question "what is to be done"

OOD
Object-Oriented Design answers the question "how is it to be done"

OOP
Object-Oriented Programming; use of software modules called objects to encapsulate data and functions that process the data; an OOP language supports classes, objects, inheritance and polymorphism

operand
a constant or variable that is manipulated in an expression by an operator

operator
the 'verb' of the C++ language; it defines actions to be performed on the operand or operands of an expression

operator overloading
to redefine an operator to use class objects as operands

overloaded function name
a name used for two or more functions or class member functions having different parameter lists

overloaded operator
see *operator overloading*

overridden member function
a member function in a base class that is subsequently redefined in a derived class

parameter
refers to the identifiers enclosed in parentheses of a function header or a function prototype or a template; also called a formal parameter; see *argument*

pass by reference
an argument-passing method in which the address of a variable is passed to a function

pass by value
an argument-passing method in which a copy of the value of an argument is passed to a function

persistent objects
objects that have member functions that save and restore the values of their data members

pointer
a variable that contains the address of another variable

polymorphism
the ability to call the appropriate member function for a given class object

postfix
refers to an operator that appears after an operand; see *prefix*

prefix
refers to an operator that appears before an operand; see *postfix*

precedence
the order in which operators are executed

preprocessor
the first phase of a compiler in which a C++ source file is changed according to preprocessor directives

preprocessor directive
an instruction to the preprocessor, for example `#define`

private class member
class data member or member function which is accessible only to the member functions or friends of the class

private inheritance
type of inheritance in which public and protected members of a base class become private members of an inherited class

promotion
an expansion of the size of a data item, for example `int` to `long int`

protected class member
class data member or member function which is accessible within member functions of derived classes

protected inheritance
type of inheritance in which public and protected members of a base class become protected members of an inherited class

prototype
specifies the return type of a function and the type of each of the function's parameters

public class member
class data member or member function which is accessible everywhere within the scope of the class object

public inheritance
type of inheritance in which public members of a base class become public members of an inherited class, and protected members of a base class become protected members of an inherited class

pure virtual function
a class member function of a base class for which there is no definition and is overridden in derived classes

qualify
to prefix a name with the name of a class or a structure

random access
an access method by which data can be read, written or deleted in any order; compare with *serial access*

reference
an alias for an existing variable

run time
the time during which a program is running or executing

scope
parts of a program in which an identifier can be accessed

sentinel
a value that signifies the end of a list of values

serial access
an access method in which data is read, written or deleted in order from start to finish; compare with *random access*

shallow copy
a copy of a pointer; not the memory that the pointer points to; see *deep copy*

side effect
an inadvertent change in the value of a variable that occurs as a result of an expression evaluation

single inheritance
when a class is derived from a single *base class*

source code
program statements; a compiler converts the source code to object code

source file
a text file containing program statements

static binding
see *early binding*

static class member
a class member shared by all objects of that class

stream object
object used to represent an input or output device; the predefined object cout represents the standard output stream, cin represents the standard input stream, and cerr represents the standard error stream.

string literal
a list of characters and escape sequences enclosed in double quotation marks

structure
a user-defined type in which all the class members are by default public

structure tag
a name that identifies a structure

subscript
see *index*

symbolic constant
an identifier defined as `const` or in a `#define` preprocessor directive

syntax
the grammatical rules for the construction of a program statement

tag
the name of a structure, union, or enumeration

text editor
a program used in constructing or modifying a data or program file

template class
actual class generated by the compiler from a class template; see *class template*

template function
actual function generated by the compiler from a function template; see *function template*

this
a pointer to the object for which a member function is currently being executed

unary operator
an operator that takes a single operand; unary operators in C++ are the complement operators (- ~ !), the indirection operator (*), increment (++) and decrement (--), address-of (&), and `sizeof`

union
a set of data items of different types that occupy the same storage

user-defined data type
a data type defined by a programmer using, for example, a `class` or a `struct`

variable
a name used to represent a built-in or user-defined item whose value can change in a program

virtual function
a member function in a base class which can be overridden in a derived class; declared with the keyword `virtual`

visibility
see *scope*

whitespace character
any of the characters space, tab, line-feed, carriage return, form-feed, vertical-tab, and newline characters; together with the space character, they are seen as blank spaces on the screen

Bibliography

Ammeraal L., *C++ for Programmers*, 3rd Edition, Chichester, John Wiley & Sons, Inc., 2000.

Cline M.P., Lomov G.A., *C++ FAQs: frequently asked questions,* Reading MA, Addison-Wesley Publishing Company, 1994.

Dale N., Weems C., Headington M.R., *Programming and Problem Solving with C++*, 2nd Edition, Sandbury MA, Jones and Bartlett Publishers, 2000.

Friedman F.L., Koffman E.B., *Problem Solving, Abstraction, and Design Using C++*, 3rd Edition, Reading MA, Addison-Wesley Publishing Company, 2000.

Horstman C., *Mastering Object-Oriented Design in C++*, New York NY, John Wiley & Sons, Inc., 1995.

Horstman C., *Computing Concepts with C++ Essentials,* 2nd Edition, New York NY, John Wiley & Sons, Inc., 1999.

Kalev D., *ANSI/ISO C++ Professional Programmer's Handbook,* Indianapolis IN, QUE, 1999.

Kelly, P., *A Guide to C Programming*, 3rd Edition, Dublin, Gill & Macmillan, 1999.

Lippman S.B., Lajoie J., *C++ Primer*, 3rd Edition, Reading MA, Addison-Wesley Publishing Company, 1998.

Stroustrup B., *The C++ Programming Language*, 3rd edition, Reading MA, Addison-Wesley Publishing Company, 1997.

Index